AROUND

T42022

641.

591

FAA

4

16-7-03

MACMILLAN

First published 2003 by Macmillan
an imprint of Pan Macmillan Ltd
Pan Macmillan, 20 New Wharf Road, London N1 9RR
Basingstoke and Oxford
Associated companies throughout the world
www.panmacmillan.com

ISBN 0 333 90466 4

A CIP catalogue record for this book is available from
the British Library.

Typeset by SX Composing DTP, Rayleigh, Essex
Printed and bound in Great Britain by
Mackays of Chatham plc, Chatham, Kent

For Patroeska Engel

The publishers offer these recipes for historical interest,
but there is no guarantee they will suit the modern palate.

Contents

Foreword

This book is neither a history book nor a cookery book; it is a bit of both. The first part contains more history than it does recipes; the second part is the other way round. This is no historical treatise. It makes no claim to treat one subject exhaustively. Ancient religions, table manners, social history and medical theories are all described, but none of these sidelines is discussed in its entirety. Together they shed some light on the obscure history of ancient Roman cuisine.

It is not a practical cookery book, because few of the recipes are easy to prepare. They all come from another culture, now buried under more than a thousand years of rubble. None the less it may be tempting to take a fresh look at them, and perhaps try some. Nowadays cooking styles fall in and out of fashion in the blink of an eye, and we are much more accustomed to sampling foreign flavours than our grandfathers were. This book is designed to explode some myths that have developed about ancient Roman cuisine. Decadent flavours, exotic delicacies, excessive feasting and pagan orgies sometimes seem a little less absurd when seen from a broader perspective.

INTRODUCTION

Lost Flavours

The proof of the pudding is in the eating. This makes it hard to appreciate ancient Roman cuisine, because we cannot taste the dishes made by cooks who lived two thousand years ago. We can admire Roman architecture, because some of it still stands. Amazing works of glass, metal, stone and clay have been excavated. The achievements of Roman artists have remained a constant inspiration to others down the generations. Roman and Greek aesthetics have influenced countless fashions. But what we know of Roman cooking is often referred to with horror. In *Vita Romana* (1950), a book about daily life in ancient Rome, the Italian author U. E. Paoli had this to say of Roman cooking:

> It is highly likely that if any one of us had had to take part in a feast like those given by the Romans, we would have come away with a terribly spoiled stomach. The complicated recipes, prepared by cooks who were bought at a very high price, and who put all their knowledge of cookery into the management of the costliest spices and ingredients, would appear utterly impossible for us to enjoy.

Some people still hold that opinion. The modern Ristorante Internazionale stands in the middle of the excavations at Pompeii. On special occasions the cooks there make Roman dishes and are gradually becoming experts at it. But they wouldn't dream of eating the food themselves. Roman food contains cumin, coriander and lovage, which many modern Italians don't like. Italians can be conservative in their eating habits, too conservative in this case to appreciate their heritage.

Tradition has been broken, and tastes have been lost. Taste follows from experience: how can you acquire a taste for something if you can't experience it? Cumin, coriander and lovage are hard to find in Italy. And so is ancient Roman cuisine.

However, most modern folk have a yearning for new flavours, as did the ancient Romans. These days, cumin, coriander and lovage can be bought anywhere outside Italy and it may be time to re-evaluate that long-forgotten Roman cuisine. Perhaps it wasn't so bad. Could it inspire our own cooking, as Virgil inspired generations of poets, as the Roman monuments inspired architects? If we take the Romans at their word, their culinary artistry was sophisticated:

> *Syrus:* Everyone's already said so much about the art of cooking. Tell me something the other experts can't, or leave me in peace.
> *Cook:* Listen, Syrus, take it from me, I'm the only person in the world who knows the real tricks of the art of cooking. I haven't learned it by putting on an apron every now and again. I've devoted my whole life to the study and practice of every aspect of this art form – all the vegetables in existence, all the fish, every recipe for lentil soup. Yes, the tricks I have up my sleeve: whenever I have the opportunity to cook for a funeral, I whip the lid off the pot the minute the black-clad guests return, and thus I make the mourners laugh again . . . Any passer-by will inevitably stop at the front door, and stay there as though nailed to the wall, speechless and open-mouthed. Until someone else comes to his aid, blocks his nostrils and takes him away.
> *Syrus:* You're truly a great artist.   (Ath. Deipn. VII-290c)

It may be a little over-ambitious to attempt to revive Roman cookery to such high standards: it isn't easy to equal great art. Try painting a fresco like the ones found in Pompeii, or writing a poem in Latin in the style of Virgil. If you think that's hard, imagine trying to imitate an art form in which you can't experience the original.

Not all of Roman cuisine has been forgotten, of course. Its impact on Europe was enormous. We owe many common vegetables and fruit to Roman gardeners. Certain wild delicacies that the Romans craved, such as truffles, are still prized. And who can deny the importance of wine? We may recognize many aspects of ancient Roman cuisine as our own, but there are also major differences.

Difference in Time

The greatest difference that separates our cooking from that of the Romans is that in order to cook Roman we have to travel back in time. Obviously the Romans didn't have microwave ovens or electric mixers, but the gastronomic advantages of an aromatic wood stove should be self-evident.

Ancient cooking methods are cumbersome for anyone without an army of kitchen slaves – as slave labour was practically free, Romans were not into labour-saving devices. In addition, many laborious methods of preparation and production had religious significance. Plants were sown and harvested in harmony with nature, the gods and the constellations. Agriculture, cattle breeding, harvesting and slaughtering were performed according to holy rituals. Herbs and spices were pounded in a mortar, and grapes were crushed by bare feet. All of this affected the taste of food. It's easy enough to grind spices in a mortar, but making wine by dancing barefoot on macrobiotic grapes is a different matter. It's just a question of how far you want to go.

To the modern cook who might want to revive Roman cuisine, a greater restriction than the lack of a microwave is that in Roman times Europe was still pre-Columbian: America had yet to be discovered. Foods from the New World, such as potatoes, tomatoes, red peppers, brown beans, avocadoes, pineapple, papaya, cassava, paprika, maize, vanilla, cocoa, peanuts and turkeys were unknown, likewise aubergines, kiwis and kangaroo meat from other parts of the globe.

The lack of these products makes a substantial difference. Think of Italian cuisine without tomatoes, or Spanish without red peppers. On the other hand the Romans were familiar with many products from Africa and Asia, and frugality was not a characteristic of ancient Roman gastronomy. The Romans feasted on many kinds of meat that many of us wouldn't touch, such as pig's ears, fish eyes, wombs, udders and intestines. They ate all the birds, fish and mammals that were known at the time, prepared with a much more extensive arsenal of herbs and spices than many Europeans would use today.

Complexity

The Roman cook didn't believe that lamb had to taste of lamb. As far as he was concerned, a piece of meat was like an artist's blank canvas, to which he could apply colour and shape. Sauces were far from subtle: in Apicius' cookery book most consist of ground herbs and spices, sometimes diluted with a little vinegar, brine or wine. They were powerful spice mixtures, not unlike those used in Indian curries. Many resemble modern barbecue sauces, which is understandable: the Roman stove is much like a barbecue.

Unfortunately we have hardly any descriptions of the quantities of sauce that would have been poured over a dish. A tablespoon of a spice mixture would strike us as enough to flavour a chicken, but were the Romans equally moderate? Roman recipes rarely mention precise proportions or quantities. One strange exception is the following recipe for a single chicken:

Pullum Oxyzonium:	Oxyzonum Chicken:
olei acetabulum maius	oil, a good 6 ml
laseris satis modice	*asafoetida*, a little is enough
liquamenis acetabulum minus	*garum*, less than 6 ml
aceti acetabulum perquam minus	vinegar, much less than 6 ml
piperis scripulos sex	pepper, 7 mg
petroselini scripulum	parsley, 1 g
porri fasciculum	stalk of leek

(Ap. 241)

Try this recipe: boil a small leek, crush it finely with the other ingredients then serve it with a boiled or roast chicken. It would be delicious, except that it contains far too much pepper for our palates. You'll burn your mouth, and be amazed that the Romans managed to swallow it. Perhaps Roman pepper was milder than ours: it came from India on slow camel trains – but even if you make this dish with well-aged pepper it will still be pretty spicy.

Hot sauces possibly presented advantages in an age when transport was slower, fridges were non-existent and food went off quickly. Ingredients were expensive, too, so the Romans didn't like to throw things away when they'd 'developed a goaty whiff', to use Apicius' phrase. Apicius' cookbook contains a special sauce for rotten poultry, instructions for saving a fish sauce that has started to smell, and treating rancid honey so that it can still be sold. This is not to say that hot spices served only to mask the taste of rotten food. To some extent they may have acted as a preservative, but their most important function, as in contemporary Italy, was to 'improve digestion'.

One major difference from today's Italian cooking lies in the way in which spices were used. In Italy, for example, pork is often cooked with fennel seeds. Chops are sprinkled with salt, pepper and fennel then grilled with olive oil. Simple, but spiced none the less. Compare that with a sauce for pork from Apicius:

piper, careum, ligusticum,	pepper, caraway, lovage,
coriandri semen frictum,	roasted coriander seed,
anethi semen, apii semen,	dill seed, celery seed,
thymum, origanum, cepulam,	thyme, oregano, onion,
mel, acetum, sinape,	honey, vinegar, mustard,
liquamen, oleum	*garum* and oil

(Ap. 336)

All of these ingredients were ground finely and mixed together. It was hard to distinguish the individual flavours, but that wasn't the intention. The Roman cook was after a bouquet of flavours, not the monotheism of a single, recognizable spice.

Food Art

The third difference between the cookery of the Romans and our own is a matter of culinary ethics. These days, we prize honesty in cookery. The Romans, however, found cheating tremendously entertaining.

A: When King Nicomedes found himself twelve days' travel from the sea, he developed a craving for fresh anchovies, which my teacher Sosterides gave him, in the middle of winter.* Everyone gasped in amazement.

B: But how can that be?

A: You see, he had taken a fresh turnip and cut it into long, thin strips, the very shape of anchovies. Then he blanched the strips, put oil on them, salt to taste, and exactly forty black peppercorns. The king's craving was satisfied. When he tasted the turnip, he told his friends how delicious the anchovies were. In this way we can see the similarity between the cook and the poet. Art lies in imagination.   (Athn. Deipin. I-7e)

Food fakery wasn't seen as deception but as artistry. Art is artificial: art imitates nature, or illustrates an idea, but it is never what it seems. The Venus de Milo is a woman made of marble, not flesh and blood. Where is the art in preparing lamb to taste like lamb?

Some cooks took food disguise too far, even for Roman taste. Petronius describes a meal at the house of a rather vulgar man called Trimalchio:

There were prunes stuck full of thorns to make them like sea urchins. That would have been fine, if an even more curious recipe hadn't convinced us that we would rather die of starvation.

A bowl was served with, as we thought, a fat duck on it, surrounded by all kinds of fish and birds, but Trimalchio said: 'Friends, everything you see here on the table is made from the same ingredient.'

I was clever enough to know what it was, so I said to Agamemnon, 'I wouldn't be surprised if it's all made of other foods, or otherwise out of clay. I once saw something similar at the Saturnalia in Rome.'

I hadn't finished talking when Trimalchio said, 'As I hope to enlarge my fortune rather than my belly, my cook has prepared all of this out of pork. There is none more valuable than he. If you wish, he'll prepare you a fish out of pig's womb, a wood pigeon from bacon, a turtle-dove from ham, and a chicken from loin of pork . . .'   (Petr. Sat. Trim. 69)

* Little fishing was done in winter.

The above quotation comes from a satire and the detail should be taken with a pinch of salt, as it were. But such situations were not entirely invented. Trimalchio was a typical parvenu, and the Roman reader would probably have laughed in recognition at his excesses.

Martial wrote a mocking poem about a certain Caecilius, who served whole meals in which everything was made of courgette, from fish and mushrooms to black pudding and pastry.

It was not only humorists who described the Roman habit of food disguise. In the second century BC the very serious Cato noted a recipe for making 'Greek wine' by mixing Italian wines and using such flavourings as salt and reduced old wine (Cat. R.R. XXIV). Renowned cooks also prepared fake foods. Apicius tells us how an imitation Liburnian oil can be made with ordinary Spanish oil, and how rose wine could be made without roses (he put in lemon leaves and honey). He also provided a recipe called *patina de apua sine apua*: 'Anchovy omelette without anchovies'. In place of anchovies he used jellyfish. Apicius concludes his recipe:

And no one at table will known what he is eating. (Ap. 132)

Trimalchio's cook served bacon as wood pigeon. Bacon doesn't taste like wood pigeon, but perhaps the cook was able to conjure up the illusion by serving it with a date sauce – dates were traditionally served with pigeon.

The same phenomenon occurs in French cuisine. The French eat

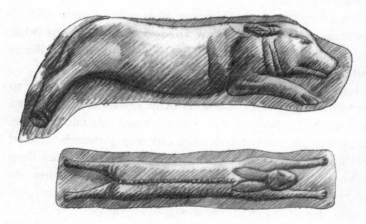

Figure 0.1 – Baking tins

snails with a strongly flavoured butter, parsley and garlic sauce and few French people know how snails taste au naturel. When they eat mussels with the same garlic butter they call the dish *moules à l'escargot*. From there it is but a small step to stuffing mussels into snail-shells and throwing your guests into total confusion.

Birds and beasts were presented whole and carved in the dining room, in front of the guests, so if the cook wanted to pass off bacon as pigeon he had to be a competent sculptor. Judging by the number found in Pompeii, many cooks used bronze baking tins, which have been found in all kinds of shapes, such as chickens, pigs and rabbits. These tins brought food fakery within the reach even of less gifted cooks.

Refined Simplicity

Not all Romans were keen on fakery, and some objected to the use of heavy sauces – for health reasons or because they preferred simple peasant fare. Others preferred subtly prepared food, not out of a striving for simplicity but from a desire for refinement.

By Minerva, how delicious it is when something works so well! What a fresh fish I had, and how perfectly I cooked it! Not buried under cheese, or covered with herbs. No, when I had roasted the fish, it looked exactly as it had done when it was alive. You wouldn't believe how soft and gentle the flame was to which I exposed it.

You know the way a chicken runs about with something in its beak that is too big to swallow? It runs around with it and tries to swallow it as quickly as possible. Then the other birds start chasing after it. That's exactly how it was [at table].

The first man who discovered how delicious this dish was leapt to his feet and ran around clutching the food in his hands, with the other guests hot on his heels. I could have cheered. Some of the guests got hold of a little bit, others got nothing at all, and yet others kept it all for themselves. And all this when I'd used only an ordinary river fish that eats mud. You can imagine what would have happened if I'd had something unusual, like an Attic sea-devil, a wild pig from Argos or a moray eel from Sicyon . . .

(Ath. Deipn. VII-288d)

Apicius

Apicius' volume is the only gastronomic cookery book handed down to us from classical antiquity. For this reason it is an important source. Unfortunately it leaves open many questions. It contains recipes, but precise quantities are given only where the primary function is medicinal, so we have to use our own judgement. Descriptions of preparations are brief. Really, the book consists of no more than 470 lists of ingredients for professional cooks.*

Nothing is known about the author, but the language of the cookery book is 'vulgar', fourth-century popular Latin. This probably means that a cook rather than a noble wrote it, but he must have been highly respected, because 'Apicius' was a nickname that meant something like 'gourmet'. Tertullian wrote:

> . . . just as artists name themselves after Erasistratus, philologists after Aristarcus and cooks after Apicius . . .   (Tert. 3.6)

The legendary M. Gavinus Apicius, who gave his name to cooks and gourmets, lived in the time of Tiberius. Many dishes bear his name. It was he who discovered gastronomic glories like the combs cut from living birds, the livers of drunken pigs, and other such delicacies:

> Apicius, the greatest and most prodigal gourmand of all, proclaimed the view that the tongue of the flamingo is highly delicious.   (Plin. N.H. X-lxviii)

Martial wrote that this Apicius had made a fortune of 60 million HS (*sestertii*). He wasted most of it on gastronomy and had 10 million left when he took poison to kill himself. Apparently he could not get by on such a 'small' fortune, and was afraid of hunger or thirst (Martialis Epigr. III, 22). The story was confirmed by Seneca, a contemporary of Apicius (Seneca, Ad Heviam, 10, 8–9). The original Apicius was not a working man, but a rich and noble lord.

---

* The numbering and the Latin text of the recipes in this book follow Barbara Flower and Elisabeth Rosenbaum, *The Roman Cookery Book*.

Fifty years later Apicius had become a nickname. Athenaeus wrote about an Apicius in the time of Trajan:

> When the Emperor Trajan was in Parthia, many days' journey from the sea, Apicius sent him oysters that were preserved in his special way.   (Ath. 1.7)

The book named after Apicius was published about seventy-five years later, and contains instructions for the preservation of oysters:

> Wash them in vinegar, or wash a pitch-treated pot with vinegar and put them in.   (Ap. 12)

Some experts on Apicius, such as Jacques André, assume that many recipes from other Apiciuses have been included in the cookery book that we have today. Others, like Eugenia Salza Prina Ricotti, doubt this. Ricotti shows that, according to Pliny, Apicius found various varieties of cabbage unpleasant yet devoted his life to finding a suitable recipe for them. He reached the conclusion that cabbage must be placed in salt and oil before being boiled. The cookery book ascribed to Apicius does not pay special attention to the cabbage. The sauces and recipes for cabbage are not very different from those for other vegetables.

We may not be able to tell to what extent the book by the cook Apicius is based on the culinary ideas of his namesake, the noble Apicius, but we should be grateful for the existence of a cookery book from antiquity. It provides suggestions for the direction we must take in our quest to understand ancient Roman cookery.

PART ONE

I

CULINARY HISTORY

We can't really talk about Roman cuisine as though it was a single entity. The classical history of the nation covers a period of more than a thousand years, and cookery changed throughout that period.

The cultural development of Rome is often seen as a negative development; it was not only later Christians, but also earlier pagan Romans who described such a decline, particularly where gastronomy was concerned. They lamented the loss of their forefathers' simplicity, a gradual slackening of moral values and an ever more extreme degeneracy – particularly where gastronomy was concerned.

THE AGE OF KINGS (753 BC TO 509 BC)

The legend of Romulus and Remus, who are supposed to have founded the city of Rome in 753 BC (the year 0 of the Roman calendar), illustrates the first cornerstone of Roman cuisine: soldiers' cooking. The twins, Romulus and Remus, were left in a wood as babies, but a she-wolf took care of them and kept them alive. They were found by a herdsman, who took them away with him. Despite this traumatic childhood, the boys grew up without any noticeable psychological disturbances. Romulus became an excellent soldier, Remus a capable shepherd. They lived in a small community of herdsmen. The years pre-dating the foundation of the city of Rome can be described as a pastoral age. The sole preoccupation of the boys was looking after sheep and cattle. One day, while they waited for their evening meal, they were practising their athletics:

Romulus and his brother were training, naked, in the sunshine on the field. Suddenly the cries of a herdsman echoed from the distance: 'Hey, Romulus and Remus, a pack of thieves are taking your bulls into the wilderness!' They had no time to arm themselves, and the brothers ran off in opposite directions.

It was Remus who drove off the villains and came back with the booty!

Returning home, he drew the hissing flesh from the spit and said: 'Only the winner gets any of this.'   (Ovid. Fast. 15 Feb.)

However, Romulus wasn't happy with Remus' victory. He was the soldier, while his brother was merely a herdsman. He bore a grudge, and in the course of a later argument he killed Remus.

The eating habits of later Romans suggest that the death of Remus ended the pastoral tradition. Herdsmen ate above-average quantities of diary; Roman cooks made moderate use of milk and cheese. Herdsmen regularly ate meat; ancient Romans seldom did. When Romulus became king of Rome, he ate soldiers' food, not pap.

Soldiers' cuisine was no more elegant in those days than it is now. The notion that soldiers should eat poor food to make themselves wiry and hard was derived from the Spartans, who subjected their men in peacetime to a cruel regime: every day they ate black soup, made of blood and water with a few green vegetables and a little meat. It was popular throughout Greece, but the Spartans added bile to it, which made it unpleasantly bitter and torturous to eat. During wartime the food was better, which taught the soldiers to resent peace.

Under Romulus' leadership Rome was filled with fighting men – soldiers and bandits – from the surrounding area. They ate better in wartime, provided they had been victorious: when they plundered either cities or the countryside, they took as much food as they could find. They stole whole herds of cattle, which they led in triumph through the streets of Rome.

In those days there was no talk of refined cuisine. People generally did their cooking in a cauldron of water, which stood on a tripod in the middle of the army camp, just as the Homeric heroes had done in the seventh century BC.

Romulus' soldiers were not popular: none of the neighbouring peoples wanted to give their daughters to them in marriage, and soon it was evident that the city's exclusively male population would die out within a generation. To forestall this the Romans decided to invite their neighbours, including the tribe of the Sabines, to a banquet. When the meal was under way Romulus gave a sign, at which his men grabbed the women and carried them off, leaving behind their drunken brothers and fathers. Today, the tradition of carrying a bride over the threshold recalls that ancient rape of the Sabine women. The Sabine men found the gesture less romantic and declared war on Rome, but the women sided with their husbands. They stepped between the armies and persuaded the men to forge a truce. It was decided that the Sabines would come to live with the Romans in the new city, and that Rome would have two kings: the Roman soldier king, Romulus, and the Sabine farmer king Titus Tatius. It was agreed that the women of Rome, in thanks for their heroic deed, would never have to 'cook or grind grain'.

Once the Romans had married, they became a little more domesticated and began to grow their own crops rather than helping themselves to those of the people around them. In time of war they were still soldiers, but in peacetime they grew vegetables. The second foundation of Roman cooking lies therefore in agriculture.

In later centuries the twofold basis of Roman cuisine, agricultural and military, led to conflict. Some Romans still had the soldier's compulsion to roam, while others preferred simple peasant food. They enjoyed vegetables grown in their own gardens, ripened slowly in the sun then simply cooked.

Clearly the origins of Roman cuisine do not lie in a culture of nomadic shepherds, like that of Jews, Bedouins, Arabs or Dinkas. Romans ate vegetables and pork, rather than dairy products and red meat. Unlike the Greeks, they consumed little fish. The daily food of the early Romans consisted of cereals, pulses and vegetables, and plunder became the exception rather than the rule.

The Etruscans

In 616 BC the first stage of Rome's culinary refinement began with the arrival of Tarquinius Priscus, who was of Greek origin but had grown up in Etruria. He was elected King of Rome because of his exemplary behaviour and his enormous wealth. The Etruscans have gone down in history as a race of gourmets. The Romans describe them as given shamelessly to luxury:

Figure 1.1 – Funeral urn

> Twice a day the Etruscans drape opulent tables with coloured
> cloths and all kinds of silver chalices. Handsome and richly clad
> slaves serve them. Timaeus reports [in book 1 of the Histories]
> that until they are fully grown, little slave girls serve them naked.
>
> (Athn. Deipn. IV 153d)

No recipes survive from Etruscan cuisine, but excavations in
Bolsena have uncovered the remains of beans, peas, chickpeas, nuts,
figs, plums, other fruits, goat's cheese, sheep's cheese and milk. The
only meat of which traces were found was pork, which was considered
a luxury.

The Etruscans were highly skilled in casting bronze. They made
specialized cooking vessels, pots and long-legged tripods, so that food
could simmer high above the flames. Some pans were flat and broad
for rapid cooking. They also roasted on grills over hot ashes and used
rotating spits. The bread ovens introduced by the Etruscans have barely
changed over the centuries: the pizza oven is a direct descendant.

People at the court of Tarquinius Priscus ate luxuriously, in the
Etruscan style. In Etruscan tomb frescoes the theme of banquets recurs
frequently, and from the images we know that they reclined, rather
than sat down, to eat. However, the earliest illustration of an Etruscan
meal is to be found on the top of an urn from Montescudaio from the
seventh century BC: a male figure fashioned from clay sits at a laid table.
Next to him stands a serving girl – fully dressed, incidentally.

In the sixth century BC the fashion for reclining took hold first in Greece and then in Italy. From the sixth and fifth centuries BC onwards, the Etruscan aristocracy was shown lying down to eat and drink, watch dancing and listen to music.

The Etruscans made wine from grapes, which are native to Italy. In all likelihood they passed on their skill in viticulture to the Romans. Wine-drinking, reclining and advanced culinary techniques all lent sophistication to the banquets of the Etruscan kings of Rome, and eventually the Romans adopted and improved on them. We still drink wine today. The Etruscans bequeathed a lasting legacy to us.

THE REPUBLIC (509 BC TO 7 BC)

On 24 February 509 BC Tarquinius Superbus, the last Etruscan king of Rome, was sent into exile and a republic declared. During this period Rome progressed from an insignificant backwater to a cosmopolitan city, and the Romans combined their military and farming capabilities. They conquered territories to turn them into farmland. Originally conquered land became the property of the state, but later it was distributed among army veterans. The army became a good way for a peasant to better himself, and in the end to become a landlord. Gradually all of Italy was turned into Roman farmland.

Unlike the imperialistic peoples, such as the Greeks, who preceded them, the Romans were not concerned with subduing cities, but in land. They were interested in them only because the cities governed the countryside around them. In southern Italy there were a number of Greek cities, such as Neapolis and Tarentum, whose inhabitants lived primarily from fishing and trade. Greek cities ruled the sea rather than the land, and Roman farmers gave them a wide berth.

But confrontation between Greeks and Romans was inevitable, and to fight the Greeks, the Romans had to learn a new kind of warfare, conducted on the seas. Rome quickly built up its first fleet and was soon highly successful. Some Greek cities sided with Rome, and respect grew between Greeks and Romans.

Once they had become seafarers, the Romans came into conflict with another trading and sea-faring people, the Carthaginians, who competed with the Greeks and whose influence stretched across North Africa, Spain and Sicily. The Romans had their eye on Sicily, because the island was famous for its fertile farmland – it was known as 'the blessing of Ceres', a paradise where grain, olive trees and grape vines flourished. Three bloody wars were the result, from which the Romans emerged victorious.

Africa

In 147 BC Rome celebrated its final victory over Carthage, and the North African city was in ruins. A large proportion of Carthaginian culture was also destroyed. Consequently the highly developed cuisine of Carthage had little influence on Rome.

However, Rome now controlled not only the whole western part of the Mediterranean and a large number of 'overseas provinces' – the Carthaginian colonies of Spain, Sicily and Corsica – but also the home of the Carthaginians, which was incorporated under the name of 'Africa' and constituted, more or less, present-day Algeria, Tunisia and Libya.

The Romans had not come to Africa to exchange recipes but to rob and plunder mercilessly, eventually invading Egypt at the end of the republican era. Egypt was enslaved, exploited and pillaged, as was

Figure 1.2 – Bronze sculpture of Africa

the African natural environment, whose fantastic flora and fauna were an inexhaustible source of inspiration for the cook. An African herb, laserpithium, was consumed to extinction. Things weren't much better for animals: many wild beasts were taken to Rome to appear in the circus and were eaten after they had performed (see page 280–2). The variety of meat on the Roman menu expanded dramatically to feature flamingo, ostrich and antelope.

Greeks

Once Rome controlled the western part of the Mediterranean, its rulers turned their attention to the east, which had more influence on Roman eating habits than their conquests in the west. In the course of the republican period, the Romans overran the Greek empire, but the superior Greek cuisine triumphed over their own.

Just as the Greek armies were pitting themselves against the invading soldiers, some Romans tried to stave off the incursion of Greek cookery. Cato the elder (234–149 BC), a celebrated author, stood up for the peasant diets – vegetables, fruits and pulses – against the Greek refinements that the soldiers were importing to Rome.

The Greeks, too, had always stressed simplicity in cookery. Fishermen ate boiled or grilled fish, and herdsmen lived on goat flesh, mutton and cheese. Farmers concentrated on raising olives and grapes. But in 333 BC Alexander the Great conquered the Persian and Egyptian empires, and Greek culture merged with that of the eastern kingdoms.

At the courts of the Egyptian pharaohs and the Persian princes meals were anything but simple. Their tables gleamed with gold, silver and costly fabrics. The guests smelt of expensive and exotic perfumes, the dining room of incense, and dishes were flavoured with Indian spices. The royal ovens in Persia were big enough to roast whole camels. The Greek cuisine that came to Rome was an exotic oriental hybrid.

Spices Versus Herbs

In conquering the western Mediterranean region, the Romans also took control of the trade routes to India and China and spices were introduced to Rome.

In keeping with their agrarian traditions the farmers of Latium, the region surrounding Rome, had always used herbs to flavour their food which they grew in their vegetable gardens. But some cooks shared a sense of adventure with the soldiers, and started to use black pepper, cloves and nutmeg. In one of the plays of Plautus (254–184 BC), a fashion-conscious cook prefers spices to herbs:

> *Cook:* . . . I tend to flavour my meals very differently from other cooks. Others put herbs on my plate. They give weeds to their guests, as though they were cattle. And they flavour their weeds with other weeds. They put coriander, fennel, garlic and parsley on sorrel, cabbage, beet and orache. Then they cover it with half a pound of laser. They grind common mustard that makes the grinder's eyes water before he's finished grinding.
>
> When these lads do their cooking, they don't spice their food with seasonings; they use vampires that eat away the innards of the guests. That's why people here have such short lives: it's because their bellies are full of weeds. It's terrible to discuss such dreadful things, but it's even worse to eat it. People are eating weeds that cattle wouldn't touch.
>
> *Ballio:* And what about you? You're forever complaining about herbs. Do you flavour your food with something divine? Something that makes people live longer?
>
> *Cook:* You can say that again! Anyone who eats the food that I have spiced can live for two hundred years. Because the bodily system warms up when I add a pinch of ciciliander, or cipoliander, or macarosis, or secatopsis.* Everyone heats up straight away.
>
> (Pseudolus 810 ff.)

In Plautus' time, eastern spices were still rare in Rome. Later on in the play the same cook complains that his services are too expensive for most people. However, spices eventually became so established in cooking that recipes began to point out when pepper was *not* used.

* All made-up names.

Sumptuary Laws

Many people besides Cato the Elder resisted the advance of culinary 'hellenization' and luxurious eating. Families began to spend such large sums on food that the state began to worry about this form of capital erosion:

> Recently I read about an ancient decree that was passed by the Senate under the consulate of C. Fannius and M. Valerio, according to which the important citizens who were accustomed to invite each other to dinner on the occasion of the Megalensian games had to swear to the consuls that they would not spend more than 120 AS [25 HS] per dinner, except on vegetables, bread and wine. They were not permitted to serve foreign wine, only local wine, and not more than 100 pounds of silver could be used at table.
>
> (Gell. II-xxiv)

Athenaeus adds that there were restrictions, too, on the number of guests, and Plinius reports that the Lex Fannia prohibited a number of luxurious foods, such as fattened chickens and dormice (see page 289–90).

It is characteristic of Roman attitudes that strict laws were passed to keep citizens' appetites within bounds. And it was entirely typical of the Romans (as, to some extent, of modern Italians) that everyone tried to circumvent the laws, even respectable patricians:

> Although [official] expenditure was kept within limits through [illegal] smuggling, and although some wastrels pushed up the prices of [contraband] goods, the men I mentioned above still managed to enjoy a pleasant life without breaking the law. Tubero, for example, received wild game from his own tenants, and Rutilius bought his fish from fishermen who used to be his slaves, for three obols a pound, including delicacies like dolphin and swordfish.
>
> In the same way Mucius set his own prices for the things that he bought from tenants and slaves. Out of many thousands, these were the only three men who strictly observed the law.
>
> (Ath. Deipn. VI-274d)

The lawmakers were not discouraged by the gluttons' disobedience. Some decades later a new law was passed: Lex Licinia. It was somewhat less strict than Lex Fannia, but even so no one observed it. 'Legem vitemus Licini,' people said – 'Let's sail around the law of Licinus' (A. Gell. II-xxiv). A series of increasingly toothless sumptuary laws was passed, but the wealthy citizens continued to flout them shamelessly. Aulus Gellius described the laws, they were:

> 161 BC Lex Fannia – Maximum: 25 HS on meat and fish on
>   feast days for a maximum of five guests. 7.50 HS on special
>   days, maximum three guests. 2.50 HS on working days.
>   50 kg of silver at table.
> c. 103 BC Lex Licinia – Maximum: 50 HS at marriage feasts,
>   25 HS at major festivals, 7.50 on other days, on dried meat
>   and salted goods, excluding vegetables, wine and fruit.
> c. 80 BC Lex Sulla – Maximum: 300 HS on important feast
>   days, 30 HS on all other days.
> 78 BC Lex Aemilia – No fixed maximum for prices, but
>   controlled quantity and quality of food.
> c. 75 BC Lex Antia – Magistrates may only eat at the homes of
>   certain people.
> c. 00 BC Lex Iulia – Maximum 1000 HS at marriage feasts,
>   200 HS at major feast days.
> Lex Augusta or Tiberia (Gellius is uncertain under whose reign
>   the law was passed) – Maximum: 2000 HS for feast days.

The maximum prices were subject to a degree of inflation, but in the time of Augustus and Tiberius a slave could be purchased for 2000 HS (about the price of a car today) and a dinner that cost so much could hardly be called modest. And this is nothing in comparison with the amounts that were spent on dinners in the Imperial Age.

Religion

Neither the words of Cato, the laws of Fannius nor religion could stop the Romans gorging themselves. On the contrary, the moderation in food and drink that was later encouraged by the Christians contrasted starkly with the excess celebrated by pagan beliefs.

Religious food prohibitions – one related to the slaughter of sacred cows – were lost with the development of religion. The worship of ancestors, who had lived and eaten more frugally, was one of the few moderating influences that Romans took seriously.

The gods themselves had no need of modesty. On the contrary, they were dependent on humans for their basic requirements: lodging, in the form of temples, and food, as offerings. The bigger the temples and the more extravagant the offerings, the better the mood of the gods. That gods needed food may seem strange to modern man – gods never die of hunger, after all – but sharing food was, and is, a fundamental way to acknowledge someone's presence. Anyone sharing a meal became a part of it, so the gods were always asked to join in. They received the first mouthfuls of each meal and the first drop of wine poured in each round.

Feast Days

Almost every feast was dedicated to a particular deity and the Romans observed many, which constantly increased in number. During the reign of Claudius there were 160 each year. The Romans did not have weekends, as we know them, since the week is a biblical unit. They did not have vacations (vacant days), but they took holidays (holy days) – so many, in fact, that they spent more days at leisure than we do with our summer breaks and weekends. On most such days, they ate, drank and partied in honour of the gods.

Sometimes the feast was public, as with the Compitalia, celebrated between late December and early January; the precise date was determined each year. Those who lived in apartments came together on the street corner and roasted chickens in honour of the god of crossroads. This boisterous event lasted three days. At another public festival, Fors Fortuna (24 June) people took boat trips on the Tiber and had picnics on the riverbanks.

Some feasts were celebrated within the private circle, such as the Saturnalia, from 17 to 23 December, comparable to Christmas. Presents were exchanged and slaves were allowed to recline at their master's table. Slave and master alike wore the cap of liberty and during Saturnalia everyone was free. The populace of Rome gave itself up to wild revelry.

There were other festivals outside the communal calendar, such as birthdays and weddings, and there were family feasts like the Paternalia: food was taken to the graves of dead relatives and afterwards the living had a meal together.

The way in which the gods were honoured privately depended on the worshipper's circumstances. A simple peasant, who brought an offering to persuade the god to protect his cattle, performed different rituals from the wealthy intelligentsia in the cities. Cato describes the peasant's ceremony:

> An offering for the protection of cattle is made as follows: by day on Mars Silvanus, sacrifice in the wood 3 pounds of spelt, 1 pound of bacon, 4.5 pounds of filleted meat, 1.5 litres of wine. Put the meat in a pot with the wine. A slave or a freeman may perform this ceremony. Once the sacred rites are out of the way, everything is eaten up immediately on the spot. A woman may not take part in the rituals, or even see how they are performed.
>
> (Cato the Elder LXXXIII)

It is almost as though he is describing a recipe for a tasty stew rather than a religious ritual.

In the cities, private religion assumed a less rustic form. The people of Rome were not content with the 160 public feast days, and foreign gods were introduced, such as Bacchus from Greece.

Philosophy

Decent citizens striving for moderation found more support in philosophical trends than in religion. The philosopher Pythagoras, from southern Italy (530 BC), for example, forbade his followers to eat fish and obliged them to live as vegetarians. Meat-eating was allowed only at sacrifices, because Pythagoras was wary of offending the gods.

The followers of Antisthenes (366 BC) refused even the meat from the sacrificial altar. They were called the 'Cynics' (dogs) and wanted to 'get back to nature'. They rejected superficial pleasures, such as elegant eating and deliberation over a glass of wine. The famous Cynic Diogenes (323 BC) trained himself to starve and thus rise above bodily functions. Unlike Pythagoras he ate fish, but served with as little artifice as possible. He even ate his octopus raw, but was ill afterwards. Mendicant Cynical philosophers wandered about Rome, and were sometimes invited to dinner, but it was generally felt that they made dull guests.

Epicurianism was an entirely different kind of teaching. It was named after Epicurus (341–270 BC), a devotee of hedonism, who pursued a state of bliss. He wanted to rise above pain and shed the fear of god, man or nature, to achieve a state of absolute happiness. His followers understood this to mean that man is on earth to enjoy himself, and that it was permissible to achieve happiness through pleasure. Athenaeus quoted Epicurus:

> I cannot comprehend the Good if I hold myself back from the pleasures of sex and taste.   (Ath. Deipn. VII 278f)

Epicurus' teaching found favour with many Romans and remained influential for a long time, but it horrified the later Christians. St Augustine compared Epicureans to whores, addicted to lust.

> Pleasure alone, Voluptas, leads them to temperance in their consumption of food, although they take pleasure in it. They are afraid of doing anything harmful to the health of the body and thus to their enjoyment, for according to the Epicureans health and pleasure depend on one another. Thus the virtue of modesty remains the slave of pleasure, as is the case of an imperious and lubricious woman. Nothing, it is said, is more disgraceful and perverse, and nothing is harder for good men to behold. And this is right.   (Aug. CD, V-20)

But Christ had not been born at the time of the Republic and his influence would not be felt for many years. For now, with philosophies that underscored sensual pleasure, with gods that enjoyed lavish feasts, with sumptuary laws that everyone could ignore, and with ever-increasing wealth, Rome had all the right ingredients to become the gastronomic capital of the world.

THE EMPIRE (7 BC TO AD 476)

Imperial Rome became a metropolis with a fabulously wealthy upper class, a large number of slaves, free citizens and foreigners all living together. They all had to eat, and even during the Republic, cargoes of grain arrived from colonies like Sicily and Egypt to feed the people. Bread (and games) were free, or almost. This munificence, which was the basis of a kind of welfare state, was politically motivated. During the Republic, the consuls and other magistrates owed their positions to the votes of the people. Although the emperors did not have to worry about election polls, they too distributed free food to gain personal popularity and keep the peace in the capital. Rome should not starve: Rome had conquered the world and should profit from it.

Other foodstuffs were imported, apart from cereals. Roman authors wrote that the colonies 'gave' delicacies to the capital, as though they were presents. Rome exported culture and government but imported food produced by the colonies for the Roman market. Some historians have concluded that Roman expansion ceased in the north because the climate was too cold for grapes. There was no point in conquering land that could not support Roman farms. The promotion of Roman agriculture was an important mission, and many conquered peoples learnt from the Romans how to irrigate their land.

Figure 1.3

The Romans introduced to them new plants, such as fruit trees, herbs and many vegetable varieties, and in northern Europe, birds and animals, such as peacocks, chickens, rabbits and pheasants. After escaping their Roman cages, the last two species survived so well that now they seem indigenous to the areas they inhabit.

The colonies worked hard to satisfy the Roman palate. Rome received ham from Belgium, oysters from Brittany, *garum* from Mauritania (Morocco), wild animals from Africa (Tunisia), laser from Cyrenia (Libya), flowers from Egypt, spices from Syria, lettuce from Cappadocia and fish from Pontus (both present-day Turkey) to name but a few. Rome became the giant stomach of the world, devouring everything.

The Spiral of Luxury

Roman cuisine slowly abandoned the virtues of peasant simplicity, making way for the cosmopolitanism of Imperial Rome. What had seemed strange became commonplace. Some Romans craved rare and exotic foods: just as we pay out hefty sums for caviar, Romans impressed their guests with ibis brains and the livers of rare moray eels. Anything unusual and expensive was thought delicious:

> Luxury has given rise to fresh appreciation of the elephant – the taste of the horny trunk. In my opinion this is because it is a bit like eating ivory.
> (Plin. N.H. VIII-x-31)

At dinner delicacies were literally fought over, apparently to the delight of the host, as though they had special nutritional value. It was a status symbol to spoil one's guests. The wealthy gave food to friends, slaves and poorer citizens. The more extravagant the dinner, the more popular the host became, although he and his guests of honour often received the most exclusive titbits. Each host tried to outdo others:

> It was during the consulship of Cicero* that P. Servilius Rullus
> . . . first served up a whole pig at a dinner. The origin of some-
> thing that is now an everyday affair is as recent as that. This is

* In 63 BC.

reported in the history books, probably to scorn people of today, since we now serve up two or three pigs at the same time, and not even as a complete meal, but merely as a starter.'

(Plin. N.H. VIII-lxxviii)

Apparently the consumption of pigs at dinner parties had trebled over 140 years, and Pliny's observations are supported by other sources. In 35 BC Horace described a meal given by Maecenas, at which a wild boar was the main course. Petronius wrote of a dinner from around AD 60, at which the host served all manner of roast pigs – indeed, as a starter.

The host's need to outdo his rivals produced a kind of inflation. A hundred and forty years after Petronius and Pliny, Emperor Elagabalus (AD 204–222) could not go far enough in indulging his guests:

Following in the footsteps of Apicius, he regularly ate camels' feet and cockscombs that had been cut from the living birds, because this was supposed to leave one immune to the plague. He also served the imperial court with gigantic plates containing the innards of morays, flamingo brains, partridge eggs, thrushes' brains, the heads of parrots, pheasants and peacocks.

(Opilius Macrinus)

Elagabalus also had a knack for making traditional recipes interesting:

Ten days in a row he served the udders of wild sows with the womb attached, thirty per day. With this he served peas with pieces of gold, lentils with onyx, beans with amber and rice with pearls. He also sprinkled pearls over mushrooms instead of pepper.   (Opilius Macrinus)

You might wonder how pleasant it is to find pearls in your rice, but the guests were allowed to keep them so they must have been reasonably happy. The emperor was not stingy: he provided enough delights for everyone – at one meal, he served the brains of 600 ostriches.

Although Elagabalus was finally lynched for his extravagance – which was not only evident in the culinary sphere – his exceptional style of cookery has often been quoted to illustrate the decadence of the late Empire.

He is the inventor of all things that extravagant people use today, such as wine flavoured both with mastic and pennyroyal . . . Pleasure was his sole purpose in life. He was the first to make pâté of fish, mussels and oysters and shellfish of that kind, and lobsters, crabs and prawns.

(Opilius Macrinus)

The daily diet of ordinary people was simpler, but they, too, saw the provision of luxurious dinners something to aim at. Many workers were members of a *collegium*. This was not a trade union, since it did not try to protect its members, nor was it like a guild, since it cared nothing for the quality of goods produced by its members. The *collegium* existed to throw regular feasts, with no expense or trouble spared. Even women and slaves belonged to *collegia* – hardly anyone was excluded from lavish feasting. No one wanted to be.

Decline

Rome did not stay prosperous for ever. After Elagabalus the empire acquired hardly any new territories and therefore no new slaves. No new farms were established; trade slackened; it grew harder to feed the growing population. More and more people became dependent on handouts from the rich, who were declining in number. It was no longer so easy to grow wealthy on the proceeds of a military campaign or an administrative post in the provinces, and all the inhabitants of the empire had been granted citizenship. They formed their own elites and could look after themselves.

Under Emperor Diocletian inflation exploded. In the time of Elagabalus a kilo of wheat cost about 1.60 HS. By the time of Diocletian it had reached 16,000 HS. Many switched to barter. To rescue the currency, the emperor fixed maximum prices, and to exceed them was a crime punishable by death. Many goods vanished from the market. More and more peasants left the land and took up plundering, just as Romulus and his friends had done. To counteract this development Diocletian forbade citizens to abandon their farms, or to change jobs, which meant that they were stuck for ever. When a drastic administrative decentralization took place, the foundations of medieval society were laid.

Christianity

A brief period of confusion followed the death of Diocletian, until Constantine assumed power in the name of Christ. From that point on Christians assumed control.

The first Christians were Jews, and adhered to Jewish dietary laws. They never ate in pagan households, because the food was not kosher. Sacrificial meat was out of the question. In a feasting culture, therefore, careful Jews and, above all, austere Christians were considered antisocial.

Jews were more respected than Christians, because the Romans admired anything ancient, and Judaism was older than Rome. Sometimes the Romans bent their own laws for the Jews. For instance, it was the custom in the East to view kings and pharaohs as gods, and eastern provincials had to honour the Roman emperor in that way. However, Jews, as monotheists, were exempt from this. Jewish food customs were fairly well known, even if not always understood, and kosher products were always available in the markets of Rome.

The secrecy of the Christians aroused suspicion. They celebrated their feasts in gloomy catacombs and the authorities assumed the worst about what went on. It was reported that Christians consumed human flesh and blood.

The Last Supper

The root of this misunderstanding lay in the meaning of the word *hostia*, or host. This meant 'sacrificial offering' – a goat, pig or some other animal that was slaughtered on the altar then eaten. During the Last Supper, Jesus Christ had proclaimed that He was the *hostia*, the sacrificial offering. He took the bread and called it His body. He took the wine and called it His blood. In eating the bread, his followers would be eating His body. In drinking the wine they would be drinking His blood.

The consumption of sacrificial offerings was common in antiquity. The Greeks and Romans did so outside tens of thousands of temples. The Jews had one God and one temple where they assembled once a year to slaughter a lamb as Passover offering. The lamb was immedi-

Figure 1.4 – Reclining at the Last Supper

ately eaten within the walls of Jerusalem. According to three of the four authors of the Gospels Christ's Last Supper took place on Passover evening. Jesus was eating the sacrificial Passover lamb, fresh from the altar, accompanied by four glasses of wine, unleavened bread, eggs, bitter herbs, radish, salt and *charoshet* (a Hebrew-Egyptian sauce of dried fruit and spices), when he announced that He was the Lamb of God. His followers understood this to be symbolic; later it led to confusion.

The Lions

The notion that Jesus had initiated a cannibalistic ritual in the Eucharist caused Christians a great deal of misery. The Romans had always detested the idea of cannibalism, which was forbidden in any form.

It seems curious that the authorities should have taken the accusations so seriously, but some Christians admitted having indeed drunk the Blood of Christ. The Catholic Church still insists on the actuality of transubstantiation. Minucius Felix put the accusation against the Christians as follows:

The story of the initiation of their recruits is very well known, and just as repulsive. Before those who are to be initiated into the rites they place a child hidden under bread, to conceal their true purpose from the unwary. Then the proselyte is encouraged to stab the dough with the knife, a seemingly innocent act by which, unknown to the initiate, the child is killed. Goodness, how horrible it is. They greedily drink the blood and sunder the child's limbs. In this way they are pledged to eternal secrecy, by a mutual consciousness of guilt.   (Min. Fel. Oct: IX-5)

However, Tertullian, a Christian contemporary of Elagabalus, accused the pagan Romans of cannibalism:

And what did you think of those people who, mad for boar and stag, eat the wild beasts from the arena? The boar is drenched in the [human] blood that it has shed. The deer lies in the blood of gladiators. Of the bear even the stomach is considered a delicacy, full as it is with undigested human flesh. In this way human beings devour human flesh. That is how you eat.   (Tert. IX-2)

Tertullian considered absurd the idea that Christians had drunk human blood. He could not understand where the idea had come from, given that the consumption of blood is strictly forbidden in the Bible – Romans already knew that from the Jews. Modern Christians often refer to a revelation that came to St Paul in a dream, in which God declared that all foods forbidden to Jews were edible to Christians. In Roman times, however, this was not as well known. In the third century AD, many still observed old Judaic food laws:

You should be ashamed in the eyes of the Christians, because we do not even eat the blood of animals. We abstain from any animals that have been strangled or died of natural causes, to prevent being sullied by the blood, even if the blood is in the meat. It is also the case that Christians [in legal investigations] are identified by being offered blood sausage, which clearly indicates that you know it is forbidden to us. But you are trying to break our virtues. Why so? Do you think we thirst for human blood while you know that we abhor the blood of animals?   (Tert. IX-11)

The Christians did not help their case when they disagreed furiously with each other – one group called the others heretics and tried to discredit them. They even added rumours to those already in circulation:

> They pull out the embryo as soon as it can be picked up by hand. They take the unborn child and grind it finely in a pestle and mortar until it is fine. To this they add honey, pepper, other spices and myrrh, to overcome their aversion to it. And then everyone, in the presence of dogs and pigs, eats the child pâté.
>
> (Epiphanius Panar. 26.4-5)

Christians became scapegoats for megalomaniac emperors who authorized huge massacres. To some extent this encouraged the spread of Christianity. Many felt sorry for these innocent, mild-mannered people; others were impressed by their brave acceptance of death. But their martyrdom also deepened the perception of Christianity as a gloomy religion. Christians who died in the arena became holy martyrs and their bloodstained clothes and corpses were very valuable. The trade in relics began while the persecutions were still going on.

Dietary Laws

When Constantine took power, the persecutions ended and the imperial court became predominantly Christian. Constantine legalized Christianity throughout the empire but did not convert, although some insist he did so on his deathbed. He observed Christian rituals, but he also continued to perform pagan rites.

The pope was no longer the leader of an underground sect but had become an important statesman, and tried to enforce the revelation of St Paul, abolishing the Judaic food laws. However, Christianity spread beyond the control of the pope: missionaries established monasteries in the remotest outposts of empire, where biblical dietary laws were observed for centuries.

Popes might have had a taste for all sorts of delicacies, but monks preferred to deprive themselves. From the penance books of Irish monks, between the sixth and the twelfth centuries, it would seem that the prohibition against the consumption of blood remained in force. Jewish tradition had little to do with it because the Christians had come up with their own interpretations: they decided that all meat-eating creatures were unclean; herbivores, such as cattle and sheep, were acceptable. Chickens and pigs are omnivores, so the purity of their meat depended on what they were fed. A pig became 'kosher' if it had lived for a year on a vegetarian diet. Only a pig that had eaten human flesh remained impure for ever. The regulations had nothing to do with hygiene: food became 'unclean' if it was bitten by a dog, or if a cat climbed over it, but not if a cowpat landed on it.

In the eighth century, the Irish missionary Boniface, who converted the western Germans, corresponded with the pope about dietary matters. Were horseflesh and salted bacon clean or not? In his reply the pope included a list of the foods he himself enjoyed.

In the seventh century the prophet Muhammad also thought that people should eat what they liked and what they were accustomed to, but he adopted the proscription on blood, as well as abstinence from pork, from Jews and Christians. Muhammad believed that pork was always unclean, not because it didn't chew the cud, which is the biblical criterion, or because it might sometimes eat meat, which worried Christians, but because Allah forbade it explicitly. The Koran provides a similarly easy answer on wine: Jewish wine laws were complicated and difficult to implement; the Christians used wine in an arcane ritual; the Koran simply forbade it.

Throughout the western world, from Ireland to Byzantium and Mecca, dietary laws were constantly debated throughout the Dark Ages. But Christian Romans ate pork and other types of food forbidden by the monotheistic God, just as they had in pagan times.

Unfortunately the suspicion of cannibalism also lived on. By medieval times, however, Christians were no longer its object: Jews were accused of infanticide, which was even more ridiculous than the accusations levelled at the Christians for Jews did not perform a 'cannibalistic' ritual like the Eucharist.

Fasting

Roman gastronomy did not collapse due to dietary laws, and the transformation of a culture that had developed over a thousand years did not happen overnight. As St Augustine wrote:

> After the persecutions peace was sealed, and wild hordes of pagans became Christians, but they were impeded by the fact that they were used to celebrating the festivals of their idols in drunkenness and with excessive feasting. They could not hold back from these reprehensible but deep-rooted pleasures. So our forefathers decided to make concessions for these weaklings and to allow their feast days to continue, although from now on they would be celebrated in the honour of the holy martyrs. These feast days were celebrated with similar luxury, but at least from now on they were not blasphemous.

Figure 1.5 – Anti-Christian Roman graffiti

But now that they are united in the name of Christ, and subject only to the yoke of our authority, the holiness of moderation had to be prescribed. Because of the virtue and terror of these prescriptions no one can object to them.   (Aug. Ep. xxix-9)

Under Christianity, delicacies carried the threat of hell and damnation – hardly a positive omen for gastronomy. And gastronomy was not the only cultural area to suffer: famous temples were demolished so that sacrifices could no longer take place. Libraries were burned down. Traditional feasts were forbidden.

Fasting now replaced feasting. Forty days of fasting were introduced, Lent, which preceded Easter, as well as two additional days of fasting per week. At first these two days were the Friday and Wednesday, but later became the Friday and Saturday. For Catholics, Friday remained a day of fasting well into the twentieth century. A new wind was blowing through Rome. The old order was at an end:

The air is sour with the belch of all the patricians, senators and politicians. When the Salius family goes to eat, they have to take a bank loan. Bookkeepers must take account of high expenses for gala dinners and gifts to Hercules. It is said that cooks are welcome at the Apaturia, the Dionysia and the Attic mysteries.* And the smoke from a dinner for Serapis† brought the fire brigade running.   (Tert. Apol. xxxix-14)

In its place came the Christian model:

We [Christians], frugal from fasting, squeezed dry with self-denial, abstaining from the ordinary enjoyments of life, are forever rolling in sackcloth and ashes.   (Tert. xl-15)

While saints like Augustine laboured to subject the Romans to the Christian yoke, and St Martin embarked on a programme of iconoclasm, Germanic tribes such as the Visigoths, the Suevi and the

---

*   Cults like bacchanales.
†   A fashionable Egyptian god.

Vandals transformed the Roman Empire by plundering and occupying the houses and villas. St Augustine saw in this the hand of God, and viewed the sack of the city as Rome's just punishment for its revelries.

When the Gothic king Alaric came to the gates of Rome at the end of the fourth century, he demanded tribute of gold, silver, silk and three thousand pounds of pepper in exchange for not plundering the city. The Romans paid up.

The city was saved, but Rome was out of pepper. That was the end of Roman cuisine. A few decades later the city was sacked anyway.

II

THE MEAL

Breakfast (*ientaculum*)

Public life began at dawn so the Romans had little time to prepare breakfast. They nibbled a bit of bread, dipped in milk or undiluted wine, the alcohol taking the place of caffeine in modern-day coffee, or curd cheese with honey, olives, raisins, fruit or nuts. A heavy breakfast was considered unhealthy and vulgar.

However, a thriving band of confectioners supplied the city with sweet buns – with honey, honey and cheese, nuts, dates, currants – filo pastries et al. Children who had to be at school at dawn could buy the first sweet-smelling snacks from the oven. Other children, perhaps the better behaved, abstained, like this little boy from the fourth century, who, by his own account, did not have a snack until break-time at school:

I wake up at dawn. I call my slave and ask him to open the window, which he does. I sit up and go and sit on the edge of the bed. I ask for socks and shoes, because it is cold. As soon as I have my shoes on, I take a towel. There is a clean one ready for me. I have a jug of water brought to me to wash myself. I pour water over my hands and my mouth. I brush my teeth and my gums. I blow my nose and dry myself, like a good boy.

I take off my nightshirt and put on my tunic, and then put on my belt. I put lotion to my hair and comb it. I tie a kerchief around my neck. I do up my white coat and leave the room with my pedagogue and the nurse to greet Papa and Mama. I greet and kiss them both. I fetch my writing materials and give them to my slave. So, I'm all ready. I run to the door to go to school, followed by my pedagogue. I greet the friends that I meet on the way, and they greet me in turn. Then we all reach the steps, which I climb in a controlled manner, as one should. In the corridor I take off my coat and cap. I go in and say, 'Good-day, master.' He embraces and greets me in turn. My slave gives me my slate, my pen and the other writing implements.

'Hello, friends, make some room, shove along a bit.'

'Come and sit here!'

'That's my place, I was sitting there first.'

I sit down and start working. When I have finished the lesson, I ask the master if I can go home and eat. He lets me go and I say, 'Goodbye,' and he returns my greeting. I go home and change my clothes. I take some white bread, olives, cheese, dried figs and nuts. I drink some cold water. After lunch I go back to school.

(Anonymous schoolboy, fourth century AD; *La Vita del Bambino nell'Antica Roma*, Museo della Civiltà Romana)

Breakfast was eaten either nonchalantly in the street, or contemplatively at home. At this time of day, one would place some food on the domestic altar to receive a blessing for the day, something similar to what one might have for breakfast oneself: wine, milk, curd cheese, fruit or honey. The ceremonial breakfast of the gods included buns with honey (like *placenta* and *libum*). Even those who made do with dry bread honoured the gods by throwing a few crumbs into the fire; if the crumbs crackled in the flames the day was off to a good start.

Then people hurried to work, or to the *patronus*. The relationship between *cliens* and *patronus*, or protégé and protector, was an important element within the social structure. Most male Romans had dependent wives, slaves and children but in turn depended on someone in a superior position. Consequently nearly every patron was himself a client.

In exchange for favours and protection, clients had to pay their respects to their patron, which they did every morning at the *salutatio matutina*. This did not last long, because the patron often had to visit his own patron. At the *salutatio* the clients received food and presents, often edible, named *sportula* after the little basket in which they were carried. They could be eaten immediately for breakfast or kept until later. Many tried to sell or exchange their presents in the street.

Lunch (*prandium*)

In southern countries it gets very hot in summery afternoons, which is why modern-day Spaniards still have a siesta and Italians spend hours over lunch. So too did the Romans. They started the most important meal of the day, *cena*, at around midday until they discovered that it was more agreeable to spend the hottest hours of the day in the bathhouse rather than at the table. The *cena* was put off until afterwards.

It was normal to have a luncheon snack between the morning's work and the afternoon at the bathhouse – the *prandium* – at which people ate bread, pulses or porridge, cold meat or fish, or leftovers from the previous day's *cena*. Various authors also mention eggs, olives, fruit and cheese. Not everyone went home for *prandium*: many ate it in the inn.

In the bathhouse they practised athletics, swam, bathed and were massaged. Physical activity helped keep the weight down, but it also made people hungry: you could buy food in the bathhouse – biscuits and sweets but also fried snacks, marinated vegetables, fresh and dried fruit, meatballs, fish pâtés and sausages.

Dinner (*cena*)

The anthropologist Desmond Morris has divided the development of modern man's eating habits between the practices of two primal groups: the hunters and the gatherers. Hunters eat nothing all day, but in the evening they enjoy whatever they had caught. The gatherer searches all day for nuts and berries and eats them as he finds them. Of the two extremes, the Romans tended towards the hunter rather than the gatherer. They often skipped breakfast and lunch; only the major meal, dinner, *cena*, was important.

Cena began after the visit to the bathhouse at four or five p.m., the tenth or eleventh hour on the Roman sundial. These days we tend to eat dinner later, but electricity is cheap. By sunset most Romans wanted to go to bed because lamps burned costly olive oil. Rich citizens, however, did not have to worry about the price of oil – they could party all night. Yet they too started their evening meal at four or five p.m.

The wealthy always had enough to eat, and so did their slaves, but the mass of free citizens were not certain to get anything. The proletariat had great difficulties in getting hold of food and money. Manual labour was beneath the dignity of free citizens, and paid employment was in short supply anyway because slave labour was cheaper for employers.

The proletariat was dependent on distributions of grain and meat, and on the *sportula*. Luckily the patrons often invited their clients to dinner. Then the client tried to ensure that he crammed in as much food as possible, which explains the glutton of many guests. Some took food from the meal with them for the following day, or for a wife, child or slave.

Anyone who didn't get an invitation to *cena* from his patron on his morning visit had the rest of the day to find an invitation elsewhere. The daily hunt for a sumptuous dinner had begun. Needy citizens could meet potential hosts anywhere in the city, but the bathhouse was a prime meeting-place between rich and poor. Martial complained:

> You don't invite anyone to dinner, Cotta, apart from your bathing companions. The bathhouse alone supplies you with guests. I've been wondering why you never invite me, but now I understand; you don't like the sight of my bare arse.   (Mart. I-xxxiii)

Those who did not score at one bathhouse could try another – there were hundreds in Rome. However, if the temples and parks yield nothing, one was almost certain to go to bed hungry – unless one had some money in one's purse. Then there was the takeaway restaurant.

Home cooking was not an option for the average proletarian. Plebeian apartment blocks were decorated with frescoes and mosaics, but they lacked running water and were not equipped with fireproof stoves or even chimneys. Home cooking would have been a smoky, risky business.

Bars and Restaurants

Rome had countless bars, restaurants and inns. In the small provincial town of Pompeii 118 bars and 20 hotels have been excavated. On the Via dell' Abbondanza, for example, there was one every thirty metres.

Tabernae, taverns, were found chiefly near the bathhouses, but also near temples, libraries and other public buildings. There were several different kinds. Engravings show that they all had an L- or horseshoe-shaped bar made of stone and cement. In comparison with a modern bar, it was low – just over a metre high.

Four or five clay pots were permanently bricked into the bar, some-times with a mortar. This meant that they were well insulated so food and drink could be kept warm or cold in them for a long time. Near the bar stood a small bronze oven, usually portable, in which water was kept at boiling point. Larger taverns had a separate kitchen and a cellar.

If the space was large enough, low tables and stools were arranged close to the bar; otherwise customers had to stand. More luxurious restaurants had separate rooms in which stone horse-shaped benches stood around little tables, which were used for dining. In some cases customers could even recline.

Food in the taverns was less spectacular than in wealthy houses, but the proprietor prepared it freshly. Typical dishes would have included the popular *puls* (a kind of porridge or risotto) and dishes with beans, peas or lentils. From the time of Emperor Vespasian these were the only dishes taverns were permitted to serve. Claudius and some other emperors had prohibited the sale of boiled meat, and any tavern foolish enough to offer it was closed down. Thus to circumvent

Figure 2.1 – Typical taberna

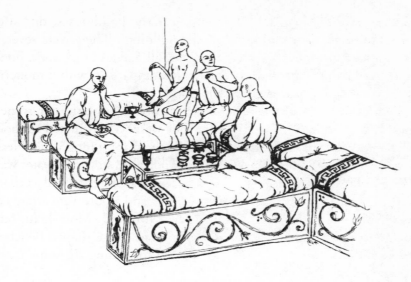

Figure 2.2

the law, meat was usually boiled in the street (Dio Cass. LX 6–7). We can conclude from this that boiled meat was popular. Frescoes, ancient graffiti and other sources suggest that roasted meat was also served, such as ham and pig's head, with eel, olives, figs, possibly sausage, fishballs, meatballs, salads, poultry, marinated vegetables, cheese, eggs, omelettes and all manner of light snacks (think of Italian antipasto and Spanish tapas).

One kind of restaurant, the *oenopodium*, owed its name to the fact that wine was served; the *thermopodium* offered hot water – like a tea-house, perhaps, but without the tea. *Fornax* means 'oven', and this restaurant was a sort of pizzeria. It should not be confused with the *fornix* – brothel.

Popina was the most commonly used word for an inn; in the countryside it was called a *caupona*. *Popinae* were often associated with prostitution. In Pompeii they are to be seen with a little upper room that contained only a bed. The bill would specify not only food and drink, but the company of a lady. An engraved stone from Isernia, now in the Louvre, reads:

– Landlord, the bill please.
– That'll be one HS for the wine, one for the bread and two for the side dishes.

- Fine.
- And eight for the girl.
- That's fine too.
- And two for the hay for your donkey.
- That donkey's going to be the ruin of me!

The *gurgustium*, a place to stuff yourself, was considered inferior to a *popina*, and the *ganea*, a place for gorging, was considered the worst of the lot, but in the eyes of the righteous, all *popinae* and taverns attracted bad company:

Look for [him] in a *popina*, Caesar, because you'll find him there lying with a hit-man, in the company of sailors, thieves and fugitives, among hangmen, coffin-makers, a drunken castrated priest and his abandoned drums. Freedom prevails there, everyone drinks from the same cup, no one goes to bed on his own and no one sits at a separate table. (Juv. VIII-171)

Despite such low-class clientele, these haunts were also frequented by the nobility. In the above quotation, Juvenal is suggesting sarcastically that the emperor should look for an ambassador in a *popina*. Even emperors sometimes went on pub-crawls, or at least so stories about Vitellius, Elagabalus and Gallieno suggest. Suetonius tells us that

The minute darkness began to fall he [Nero] donned a cap* or a wig and set off for the *popinae*, or to wander about in the alleyways. (Suet. Nero. XXVI)

On one such occasion a man whose wife Nero had assaulted struck the emperor. Nero decided not to pursue him. He was in disguise, after all, and the man could not have known that he had hit the divine ruler of the world. But Nero learnt otherwise when the man came to the palace on his own initiative, to offer a trembling apology. Nero was appalled and the man was obliged to commit suicide (Tac. Ann. XIII-25). Citizens began to emulate their emperor. At night the city was thronged with figures disguised as Nero, causing havoc with their gangs of cronies.

Decorous citizens went to more respectable restaurants, *cenationes*,

* The Phrygian cap, or liberty cap, worn by a freed slave.

Figure 2.3

which often had idyllic gardens, pools and fountains. At these establishments they stood at the bar or sat on benches, or lay on a *triclinium*, as they would have done in wealthy houses.

The *Triclinium*

In Greek *triclinium* means 'three beds'. A single bed is called a *kline* or *lectus*. Two beds were called a *biclinium*, three a *triclinium*. The latter was the most frequently encountered. The beds were arranged in a horseshoe shape, each large enough for three to four people. They were originally freestanding constructions of wood, bronze, silver, ivory or some other material. Mattresses, sometimes filled with fragrant herbs, were laid on the frame, covered with an under-sheet, then a multi-coloured bedspread, and topped with a pile of cushions.

> Plato the philosopher said: 'When making bedclothes nowadays they bear in mind whether you are going to recline on them or sleep underneath.'
>
> And the same author has written: 'Then, beautifully adorned, they go and lie on beds with ivory feet, purple mattresses and red cloths from Sardes.'
>
> . . . And Ephippus writes [of bedclothes]: 'Long have I dallied where the bedclothes smell of rose-petals and drip with perfume.' (Ath. II-48)

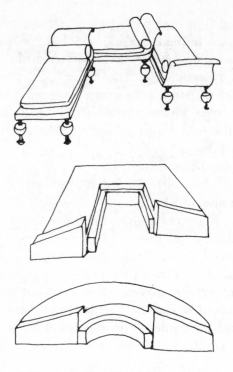

Figure 2.4 – Three kinds of *triclinium*

The *triclinia* that have stood the test of time are solid structures of concrete, cement and brick, permanent horseshoe elevations in the dining room or garden. We also find them near temple sites. They were constructed on a slant, making reclining more comfortable.

There were variations on the *triclinium* theme, of which the *stibadium*, also called the *sigma*, was the best known: this was a sloping semi-circular couch. The standard, angular *triclinium* was designed for nine people. The curving *stibadium* might accommodate only five to seven guests, or could be extremely long, like the *stibadium* that still exists in the Villa Adriana outside Rome on which more than a hundred guests could recline.

The Dining Room

It is confusing that the word *triclinium* referred not only to the couch but to the dining room around it. The location of the dining couches in the house varied from one period to another. In the most ancient times the choice was limited: outside or inside. If it rained, the fire could be lit inside the house and the family sat cosily around it.

Later, houses became larger and developed into the standard Roman *domus*, with a central atrium and smaller rooms leading off it. The atrium was next to the inner courtyard. Like the cottage of earlier times, a hole in the roof allowed smoke to escape, so the domestic hearth was situated there.

Rainwater entered the atrium through the hole in the roof, the *compluvium*, and dripped into a little pond beneath it, the *impluvium*. It supplied the household with water. Until some time around the second century BC, all the cooking and eating took place in the atrium.

Later, the *triclinium* was moved to the *tablinum*, one of the loveliest spaces in the house, between the atrium and the internal courtyard. On one side it looked onto the atrium, with its sculptures or paintings, and on the other, the garden with its flowers, fountains and exotic birds. Either side could be closed off with curtains and wooden panels. The *tablinum* faced the garden in summer and the atrium in winter.

By around 27 BC life was so luxurious that the architect Vitruvius no longer considered one dining room sufficient. A proper home needed several, he thought, for the different seasons of the year, and in the houses of Pompeii there are indeed separate summer and winter *triclinia*. According to Vitruvius, *triclinia* for autumn and winter needed to receive as much sunlight as possible in the morning and throughout the day, but had to be closed off to keep in the warmth throughout the evening. Winter *triclinia* were in closed-off spaces heated with stoves, which produced soot. For this reason, Vitruvius advised against expensive frescoes in them and recommended choosing a surface that was easy to clean. The windows and doors had to face west, for the best of the light from the setting sun.

Summer *triclinia* faced north to avoid the heat of the sun. They were usually placed in the garden, exposed to every minimal gust of wind. In Pompeii summer *triclinia* were often cooled by water. *Nymphaea* were often built near the *triclinium*, domestic altars in honour of water nymphs. They combined religious piety with pleasure in waterfalls and fountains, or the water that flowed from the altar. Shallow marble channels that led the water around and through the *triclinium* are still visible in Pompeii. In some houses there was a pool in the middle of the *triclinium* over which a table could be placed.

Sometimes food was served on the water itself:

> The starters and main courses were placed on the edge of the
> pool, but the lighter courses floated around on trays shaped like
> water-birds and boats.   (Plin. Epist. V 6, 37)

In fact, summer *triclinia* were erected in all sorts of places – on the roof
or in the cellar, in the mountains, in the forest or along the beach. In
Sperlonga in Italy we can admire the remains of a Roman *triclinium*
built in the middle of a fish-pond, next to a grotto by the sea – perfect
for romantic dining.

Varro records that some people cultivated a rustic taste: they
installed their *triclinium* in a barn. In the plainly plastered room, guests
could inhale the fragrance of apples and other fruit spread out to dry
on the floor.

Imagination had free rein in the decoration and location of a *triclinium*, but a strict etiquette grew up around dining. Religion, tradition and snobbery regulated all that went on around the Roman table.

TABLE MANNERS AND ETIQUETTE

Table manners have always been an indicator of social status:

> I cursed my own stupidity and I quickly shut up, to avoid others
> noticing that I am not accustomed to dining in distinguished
> company.   (Petr. Sat. 41)

The table manners of the Romans had a symbolic significance that
went beyond the simple requirements of an agreeable evening: they
were rooted in religion. The Etruscans laid the foundations for Roman
table manners, and the Greeks, with their tradition of conversation
at table, added to them. In his *Moralia* Plutarch discusses how the
Romans were supposed to eat, and refers both to respectable Roman
traditions and to those of the Greeks. This gives us a good idea of
how things were supposed to be done – but the rules were not always
observed.

Dinner Dress

In fashionable circles, men were supposed to appear at dinner in a formal toga, which they also wore to make sacrificial offerings at the temple. There were togas for every occasion, but at a formal dinner the *toga cenatoris* was compulsory. It was white, and made of thin, undyed wool. However, on frescoes in Pompeii dinner guests can be seen wearing all kinds of colours. Most are not wearing formal togas but a much simpler dining outfit, the *synthesis*.

The formal toga, as worn by senators, was woven in an oval shape, slightly broader and three times longer than the height of the wearer. It was usually worn over a *tunica*, a simple rectangular shirt, often with sleeves. The *tunica* could be any length, from the risqué short version to the longer, more ceremonial one. A belt held it all together.

The *tunica* was the everyday wear of the ordinary people. It was suitable for the market, the bathhouse and a snack in the bar, but not for a meal in the *triclinium*. One could attend a formal dinner without a *tunica* (in paintings, sculptures and reliefs it is often absent), but not without a toga. The toga was expensive but those unable to afford their own usually borrowed one from the host.

Figure 2.6 – Toga-wearer with his ancestors

It was almost impossible to work in a toga, and that was partly its raison d'être. A toga conferred dignity: its wearer should be waited upon hand and foot.

There were no permanent rules about what women had to wear at dinner. Their dress was subject only to the fickle dictates of fashion. However, jewels were a different matter. In the early Iron Age metals had been assigned strong, often destructive magic powers. Ancient etiquette forbade weapons at the table, and this was extended to all metals. Later this prohibition was repealed, but Romans still paid lip service to the notion:

> We see that the general custom is to remove one's ring when the table is ready, because this kind of quiet action has a religious value.   (Plin. N.H. XXVIII-V-24)

The *Satyricon* suggests that a ring did not have to disappear altogether: Trimalchio simply switched his from one hand to the other (Petr. 74).

Lararium and *Focus*

On entering the house, the guests passed through the *vestibulum*, the lobby behind the front door, to the large central atrium. Once there, they had to wait until all the guests had arrived. The floor of the atrium was often decorated with mosaics and the walls were painted with frescoes. In the middle, next to the *impluvium*, stood a large rectangular marble table, called a *cartibulum*, on which the family silver, gold and other works of art were exhibited. These tables resembled our modern dinner tables in shape, but they were used only for display.

It was considered appropriate for waiting guests to inspect the atrium, and to worship at the domestic altar that stood there: the *lararium*.

The *lararium* consisted of a niche in the wall or a cupboard in the form of a small temple. Sometimes it was closed off with little doors, but it was always open at important dinners and on holidays. The *lararium* contained small sculptures of the household gods, the *lares* and *penates*. The *lares*, from which the household temple took its name, symbolized the assembled spirits of the ancestors, who acted as guardians to the family. The *penates* were the gods who protected the larder: the *penus*. Every wealthy Roman household had a large store of preserved

Figure 2.7 – Lararium and *focus*

foods – dried meat, salted fish, pickled vegetables, grain, wine, olives and so on – that were originally kept in a niche in the atrium. Later they were moved to cool underground storerooms, the *cisternae frigidariae*, but the *lares* and *penates* kept their place in the atrium, where they protected the treasury, which was also stored in the *lararium*. Apart from images of the *lares* and *penates*, other statues of personally favoured gods were placed in the *lararium*. Valuable objects were kept in it too:

> In the corner I saw a big box where, in a little niche, stood silver *lares*, a little marble statue of Venus and a large golden jar, in which it was said that the first shavings of Trimalchio's beard were kept.
> (Petr. 29)

In front of the *lararium* stood the *focus*. If the *lararium* was built into the wall, the *focus* might consist of a simple four-sided raised-brick construction, against the skirting-board, on which a fire was lit. More often the *focus* was a portable rectangular hearth on stone or bronze feet. Originally the food was prepared on the *focus*, but when separate kitchens appeared the *focus* was used only for religious sacrifices and as a source of warmth. A smaller version of the focus was the *foculus*: a circular tray for offerings that stood on a tripod, in which a fire was also lit.

It was important that the fire on the *focus* was never allowed to go out, since that was seen as a bad omen. The lady of the house ensured that this did not happen. Vesta was the goddess of the domestic hearth, and her vestal virgins kept alight the eternal flame, so that the city would never be without fire. Roman mothers loyal to Vesta looked after the domestic hearth, which became a symbol of the home. A homesick Roman yearned for his *focus* and his *lares*.

Each morning after rising, and in the evening preceding dinner, offerings of incense to Vesta and the household gods spread a spicy aroma through the atrium. Then food offerings were made. Children brought the first titbits from each course to the *focus*, and burned them in honour of the *penates*. Sometimes offerings were simply placed on the *lararium*, under the noses of the gods, who absorbed from them some spiritual quality. At the end of the day the food from the altar was distributed among the slaves.

Washing

On entering the dining room it was customary to step over the threshold with the right foot first, to avoid bringing bad luck. After that the hands of the guests were washed, whether they were dirty or not, in ritual purification – rather like mothers across the world who tell their children to wash their hands before dinner 'even if they're clean!' In ancient Rome, a slave also removed a guest's shoes and washed his feet, with warm water in winter and cold in summer:

When we finally went to dinner, Alexandrian boys poured snow-cooled water over our hands. Others knelt at our feet and with astonishing dexterity cut our toenails. Even when performing such a menial task they were not silent, but sang as they worked.

I was keen to known whether the entire household sang, so I asked for a glass of wine. A boy was immediately at my side, and he sang in an even shriller voice as he took my order. And all my requests were answered in similar fashion.

(Petr. 31)

Feet were always dirty in an age when almost everyone wore open sandals and the streets were muddy. That aside, it is relaxing to have one's feet massaged, which also aids digestion. But, above all, foot washing was symbolic: in removing one's shoes, one was shaking off earthly bonds. One could no longer run into the street but had entered the spiritual sphere of the *triclinium*.

Above the *Triclinium*

The Romans often ate in the open air in front of a temple or a statue of a god. At home the *compluvium* provided direct access to the sky. Thus the heavenly gods were able to peer into the dining room. The ceiling symbolized the heavens, the planets and the celestial gods. When Nero built his golden palace on the forum, he referred to this symbolism in the construction of his dining rooms:

There were *triclinia* with ivory ceilings whose panels opened to rain flowers down on the guests, and with pipes that sprinkled perfume over them. The main dining room was circular and rotated day and night along with the sky.   (Suet. Nero. XXXI)

In the *Satyricon* the ceiling opens and a ring is lowered down, hung with golden wreaths and alabaster perfume-bottles, like gifts from heaven (Petr. 60). Horace describes a dinner at which part of the ceiling and the wall draperies fell to the floor. This was such a terrible omen that the guests immediately went home, ignoring their host who tempted them to stay with exquisite sweetmeats (Hor. Sat. II-viii).

Under the *Triclinium*

The floor on which the couches stood had another function beyond supporting heavy furniture and large numbers of guests. Rubbish and

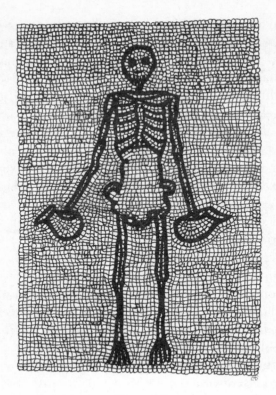

Figure 2.8

large quantities of wine were thrown on it. Some dining-room floors in Pompeii are made of plain cement, and these were probably covered with sawdust and rugs. Others were decorated with expensive mosaics.

The floor symbolized the Underworld, Death and Sleep. References to death might not have been especially agreeable at dinner, but they were always made. Pagan Romans commemorated death in order to remember the value of life and, by extension, of eating. Many mosaics from Roman dining rooms depict skeletons, and skulls appeared on drinking cups and wine-jugs. Statues of skeletons in precious metal have been excavated at various sites. In the *Satyricon* Trimalchio brings to life the concept of death by lying in his grave between courses and pretending to be dead; the slaves burst into floods of crocodile tears.

But the most important symbol of death was the floor. Roman families originally buried their dead in the floor of their house. In the atrium there were graves beneath the *triclinium*. If food fell on to the floor, it lay on someone's grave and belonged then to the ground ghosts. If you were to pick it up and eat it, you risked bringing a curse upon yourself.

Later on, family members were buried in glorious tombs outside the city, but this did not mean that the floor was freed of its ghosts. Children and slaves were still often buried in and around the house. Their spirits, along with those of anyone who had never received a proper burial, were called the *lemures* (see also *lemuria*, page 196). They lived in the ground, and contaminated food that fell to the floor. Even slaves and domestic animals were forbidden to eat it. If a dignitary was unfortunate enough to drop a scrap, it was seen as an extremely bad omen. The dropped food was swept up and burned on the domestic altar.

The removal of fallen food was probably not a task that slaves were keen to perform. *Lemures* did not like it when the floor was swept for food on it belonged to them. It is for this reason that in some Roman villas we find mosaics called *assataros*, floor decorations showing food that has fallen from the table: gnawed bones and fish-spines, nut- and snail-shells. To pacify ghosts, rubbish became art long before twentieth-century artists conceived the idea. However, the *assataros* floor originated elsewhere:

> The Greeks introduced floor decorations. The floors were artfully painted, until mosaics gained the upper hand. The most highly skilled artist in this field was Sosus. He laid a mosaic floor that the Greeks called an 'unswept floor'. Using tiny coloured stones he depicted waste that had fallen from the dining table, along with other rubbish, as though it was simply left lying on the floor.
>
> (Plin. N.H. XXXVI-60)

On the *Triclinium*

Etruscans and Romans lay at table in the same posture in which the dead were buried. The prescribed attitude is well known from sarcophagi: the person reclines on his left side, leaning on his left elbow so that his right hand is free for eating. In this position the most one could do with the left hand was hold a plate or bowl.

Roman works of art seldom show diners in the static pose of

Figure 2.9 – Official reclining posture

Etruscan sarcophagi, and more often in a relaxed, disorderly fashion. Plutarch described how the proper reclining posture was often adopted after eating:

> After this discussion we broach the question of why there is not enough room for the guests at the beginning of a meal, while there seems to be plenty later on. One might expect the opposite to be the case, given that everyone has eaten. Some of us sought the reason in the position of the diners on the couches. Generally, each guest lies almost flat on his stomach while eating, since he has to extend his right arm towards the table. But once he has eaten, he turns more on to his side and then lies in a sprawl, but in more of a straight line.   (Plut. 679)

How could there have been a shortage of space? *Triclinia* were capacious and, according to etiquette, nine was the correct number of guests per couch, symbolizing the nine muses who might inspire the guests: Clio, history, Euterpe, flute-playing and tragedy, Thalia, comedy, Melpomene, song, Terpsichore, dance, Erato, poetry, Polyhymnia, lyre-playing, Urania, astronomy and Calliope, philosophy.

Some hosts departed from custom and found dinners with fewer guests more agreeable, but such restraint was uncommon. Usually there were more than nine and a second *triclinium* would be set up, sometimes even a third.

Figure 2.10 – Reclining posture in practice

Even if the host had invited just nine people, more might turn up. Strict etiquette governed who could lie down and who had to remain seated. The seating arrangement on the *triclinium* followed a hierarchical pattern that reflected relations between people in Rome. Within the symbolic cosmos of the dining room, the guests depicted human society.

Seating Arrangement

A satisfactory seating arrangement was, and is, one in which everyone was comfortable and which promoted sparkling conversation. Here is Plutarch's brother:

> I organize the guests at my dinners in such a way that a wealthy man does not lie next to a wealthy man, a young man does not lie next to a young man neither a magistrate next to a magistrate, nor a friend next to his friend. Such an arrangement is static, and does little to promote sociability.
>
> I try to ensure that people get what they lack. I place those who are hungry for knowledge next to wise men, friendly people next to grumpy ones, the younger, who like to listen, next to the older, who like to talk, the shy next to the bluff, the quiet next to the noisy.

> If I happen to see a guest who is rich and generous, I fetch a
> poor and honest one out of any old corner and introduce them
> to one another, so that the full cup may overflow into the empty
> one.   (Plut. VIII, 1,3)

In practice, Plutarch's brother was not always as successful as he might
have hoped with his informal dinners. 'Sit wherever you like,' he had
once cried, in the hope of making things easy for everyone. An important 'foreign' guest, with a retinue of servants, was a little late and
arrived when everyone else was already reclining. When he saw that no
place of honour was left for him, he refused to join the dinner. Clearly,
not everyone was amused by informality. The rules could not be
ignored. These stated that the diners were first divided into three
groups. Central couch A was for the guests of honour. To the right
stood couch B, for the host and his family. To the left of the centre, the
less favourable side, couch C was for the remainder of the guests.

Couch A

Place 1 was for the guest of honour for whom the dinner was given.
This might be, for example, a friend returning from his travels, an
acquaintance who had won a prize, an important relation visiting the
city. The guest of honour reclined on the 'place of the consul', as it was
called, after the highest office of the Roman republic. If only the family
were present, without noteworthy guests, a senior member, such as the
father or an uncle of the host, would take the 'place of the consul'.

Place 2, next to 'the consul', was the central spot on the couch. This
had originally been the 'place of the king' and in many countries it
remained the most important position. During the Last Supper, this
central spot might have been where Jesus reclined. Rome, however, was
not a monarchy. Since it had become a republic, the consul's place took
precedence over that of the king. In republican and imperial Rome the
king's place was of only minor significance. It was occupied by someone
with whom the guest of honour felt at ease – his wife, his son or a friend.

Whoever sat in *place 3* ranked lowest among Romans but highest
among Greeks. So, any of the three positions on the central couch
might be the most honourable, depending on whether you saw it with
Roman, Greek or monarchic eyes.

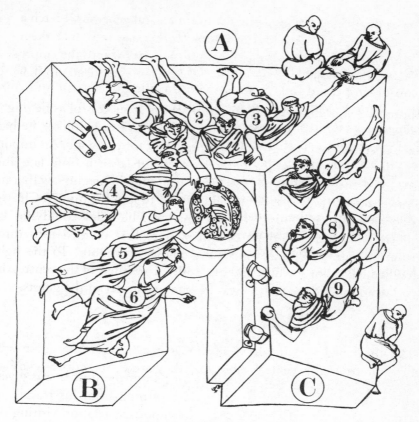

Figure 2.11 – Seating plan

Couch of honour A
1 Place of the consul, or guest of honour
2 Place of the king, or guest of honour
3 Guest of honour

Family couch B
4 Host
5 Place of the hostess or second family member
6 Place of the freedman

Guest couch C
7 Guest
8 Guest
9 Guest

Couch B

Place 4 was occupied by the host. This meant that he lay close to the 'consul' and could thus converse with the guest of honour and check that all was well. Often they shared the best delicacies, which was sometimes resented by lesser guests. Many satirists complained about hosts keeping the best for themselves.

In *place 5*, next to the host, lay a member of his family, usually the hostess. Regional traditions decreed whether or not women might recline. The original Roman tradition had the father reclining on his couch and the mother seated on a chair with the children standing, but later Roman women usually reclined next to their husbands.

Place 6, traditionally the humblest spot, was occupied by one of the family's freed slaves. This was called the 'freeman's place'.

Couch C

The third bed was the least advantageous, because the guests were furthest from the central table but they were not entirely without honour because they had an official place to recline.

Shadows (*umbrae*)

Often more guests arrived than there were places on the *triclinium* because invited guests were allowed to bring their friends. Gate-crashers did not get an official place to recline, and had to sit behind the guest who had brought them. These were called 'shadows', *umbrae*.

The bringing of 'shadows' dated back to the time of Homer (*Iliad*, XVII 575), and Socrates defended the custom: people of consequence never went anywhere alone, he averred, and anyway, it was nice for the host to meet new people. But it caused problems. Some shadows were embarrassed, especially if they knew the host but had not been invited personally. It might also be a nuisance for the host if too many unexpected guests turned up:

> A host should really limit the number of guests that may be
> brought along, to avoid getting himself into the same muddle as

the host who once invited Philippus. Philippus turned up with so
many guests of his own that the host was placed in an embarrass-
ing situation. So Philippus whispered to his friends to leave a little
space for dessert. In anticipation of the sweet course, they ate like
birds, and so there was enough for everyone.   (Plut. 707)

Parasites (*parasiti*)

In Rome witty people might be invited to so many dinner parties that
they could get by on little money. They were called 'parasites'. Originally parasites were citizens selected to eat the offerings after official
sacrifices as an act of worship. They had other tasks too, such as the
selection of the grain to be used in the ceremony. Later the name
'parasite' was transferred to impoverished profiteers who tried to
wheedle a meal, and only much later to insects like fleas and lice. In
general, however, Roman parasites were known as amusing characters,
who earned their bread with entertaining banter:

Let me tell you how we parasites live. Listen to this, for we are
terribly clever in all kinds of situation. First of all someone else's
slave, whom we have been allowed to borrow for a while, always
accompanies us. If I go to the forum, I have these two togas that
I constantly alternate.

When I see a rich fool, I pounce upon him. And if the wretch
should happen to say something, I react in amazement and compliment him in a loud voice, as though impressed by his words.
Then we [parasites] all go our separate ways or off to a dinner, all
just to get ourselves a free piece of rye bread.

Once there, the parasite must immediately begin his clever
natter, or else he will be thrown out the door. I know that this
happened, for example, with Acestor, who went a little too far,
and was chucked out, in irons and everything.   (Ath. VI-236e)

The flattery of the parasites was sometimes taken to unfortunate
extremes:

Hegesander tells of Cheirosophus, a parasite of Dionysius.
Cheirosophus started laughing when he saw that Dionysius was

laughing with some friends, although he was standing some distance away. When Dionysius asked him why he was laughing, he replied, 'Because I assume it must have been funny.'

His son, Dionysius, also had a large number of flatterers, who were known as Dionysians.* At dinner these people pretended to be blind, because Dionysius himself had poor eyesight. They felt around for the food with their hands, as though they could not see, until Dionysius drew their hands towards the dishes. When Dionysius was sick, they let his vomit fall on their faces and licked it up. They found his vomit sweeter than honey.

(Ath. VI-249e)

Flattery was not restricted to parasites. It was an element of client–patron relations. Knights and senators were just as guilty of it, not so much to obtain a meal as political favours or entire estates. Some, however, saw parasites in a more positive light:

If you consider it properly, you will see that the parasite actually supports us in our life and our prosperity. No parasite can ever wish for anything bad to happen to his friends. On the contrary, he prays that they may have eternal happiness, and their life may be one of great wealth. He is absolutely free of jealousy, praying only that he may be a witness of the acquisition of wealth, and may enjoy some of it. He is an honourable and peaceful friend. He does not start rumours and is not easily insulted. He is never unpleasant himself, but can be good at dealing with someone else's hostility. If you make a joke at his expense, he laughs happily along. He is affectionate, amusing and always cheerful. You might even say that he could be a good soldier, provided his ration consists of a ready-made dinner.   (Ath. VI 238a)

Slaves

Apart from 'shadows' and parasites, a man of any importance also had personal slaves and servants in his retinue. This was considered the appropriate entourage of a gentleman:

* A word-play on the followers of Dionysus.

Larensis: 'But as you know, my dear Masurius, every Roman owns countless slaves. Many own even ten or twenty thousand,* or more than that. Not, however, in order to earn money with them, like the wealthy Greek Nicias. No, most Romans have such large numbers to keep them company when they go out.'

(Ath. VI-238a)

The host was not obliged to feed all the slaves, but often found himself doing so. On lesser occasions, slaves often sat at their masters' feet. Otherwise, separate benches were set up for them. With the slaves, all groups of Roman society were represented:

Guests of honour	=	government; kings and consuls
Triclinium guests	=	nobility, knights, the rich
Shadows	=	clients, proletarians, the poor
Slaves	=	slaves

Seder

That slaves did not recline but sat at the table is still remembered at Seder, the Jewish feast that begins Passover. Like the meals of the Romans and Greeks, it is filled with symbolism. The Seder commemorates the exodus of the Jews from Egypt and their flight from slavery. On Seder night, diners used to recline to indicate that they were now free. Nowadays orthodox Jews sit at the table in the modern style, but at Seder it is customary to rest on one's left elbow. Recently an orthodox mother was heard shouting at her children: 'Come on, boys, behave yourselves! Elbows off the table! It isn't Seder, you know!'

The Table in the Middle

The underworld was symbolized by the floor, and heaven by the ceiling. The *triclinium* represented human society. The gods resided in the *lararium*. The only thing missing from this microcosm was the Earth.

---

* These figures are clearly not to be taken seriously.

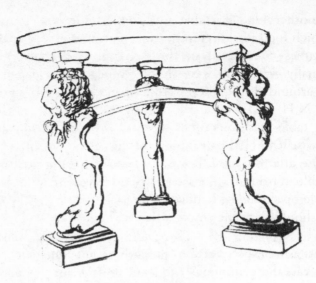

Figure 2.12 – Mensa

> I have a notion that the table is a symbol for the Earth, because
> apart from the fact that they both keep us supplied with food,
> they are also both circular.   (Plut. VII, 4 704)

The Roman dining-table was low, about a metre high, and small:
its diameter was less than a metre. It had three legs. The Romans called
it *mensa*, and the word might drive from the Greek μεσος, meaning
'in the middle'. A square dining-table was a *cilliba*: this was not a
communal table but a kind of side-table, at a time when couches were
still placed far apart. The communal table was always circular. When
referring to a table, the poet Martial uses the word *orbis*, meaning
both 'disc' and 'the world' (Mart. II-xliii). 'Disc' seems an appropriate
word, because most tables were no more than a round tray placed on
a permanent base in the middle of the *triclinium*. Other tables had legs
made of wood, marble, bronze, gold or silver. On several occasions
Martial and Athenaeus describe ivory ones.

Tabletops were prestige objects, made of valuable woods such
as walnut, lemon, maple, cypress, oak and beech. Some men spent
so much on expensive tables that their enthusiasm was compared to
women's love of jewels. Cicero is supposed to have blown 500,000 HS
on one table. At the time you could have bought a whole villa for
that.

Another kind of table was the *repositorium*, a portable buffet on which food was displayed, usually on several different levels. It was sometimes circular, as in the *Satyricon*, but more usually square. Originally *repositoria* were simple display cases made of wood, but from around 80 BC they were also made of silver and tortoiseshell (Plin. N.H. XXIII-lii).

A table was sometimes covered with a tablecloth, *mappa*, but otherwise it was left bare, and was sometimes wiped clean with a cloth, *gausapa*, after the meal. It was not generally considered correct to wipe the table in front of the guests: etiquette suggested that the whole table or tabletop should be removed after each course. Plutarch adds that the table should never be empty when it is taken away:

> Just as we expect Earth to always have something delicious for us to eat, and continuously to produce new things, we also believe that a table should not be seen bare and empty.   (Plut. VII, 4 704)

The table was sent back to the kitchen still laden for two main reasons: first the host should not be made to feel he had served an insufficient quantity for his guests, and second, so that the shadows could eat, and after them the servants and slaves. The last remnants were for the animals. While the guests were at the top of this hierarchical pyramid (just below the gods in the *lararium*), they had to take into account those who were below them. A patron who failed to feed his clients well lost his political support network. An owner who allowed his slaves or animals to starve lost a precious investment. And stingy people lost their friends.

Rude Behaviour

Politeness decreed that guests should be considerate to one another and a certain degree of modesty was considered appropriate:

> People who eat too greedily of the communal dishes irritate those who are a little slower, and who can't quite keep up. I don't consider it a good start to a pleasant evening if there is mistrust, squabbling, pilfering and elbowing among the guests. Such behaviour is ill-mannered and rude. It generally ends in insults

and outbursts of rage, aimed not only at the other guests, but
also at the staff and the host!   (Plut. II-10, 644)

Worse than greed, in Plutarch's opinion, was the waste of food that
others might have eaten.

It is disrespectful to throw away food, after we have had enough
ourselves. Just as bad as it would be to conceal a stream after we
have quenched our thirst from it. Or, when travelling, to destroy
the road signs after we have made our own use of them.

(Plut. IX-VII, 4)

It was also considered rude to spoil other people's appetites. One
should appear at table washed and clean. The passing of wind or
urine was frowned upon. Simple folk might have had no qualms
about belching, but it ill suited an emperor to do so: 'Vitellius
increased his popularity by kissing marching soldiers as they
approached him, even the humblest of them. In the inns and
hotels he was very friendly towards muleteers and travellers,
asking them all if they had enjoyed breakfast, and demonstrating
that he had done so by belching loudly.'

(Suet. Vitell. VII)

Vomiting

The contemptuous Seneca moaned, 'They eat to vomit and vomit to
eat.' But there is no reason to believe that Romans did this any more
than people do today. Of course, there were gluttons, like the Emperor
Claudius:

He did not often leave the *triclinium* before he had eaten and
drunk his fill. Having done so he would fall asleep straight away,
on his back and open-mouthed. A feather would then be put into
his throat, to unburden his stomach.'   (Suet. Claud. XXXIII)

Suetonius reported similar behaviour by the ill-mannered emperor
Vitellius:

Figure 2.13 – Drinking bowl with vomiting Greek

He divided up his feasts into three or four parts: breakfast, lunch, dinner and a carousal. He was able to indulge in all this by using of emetics.

(Suet. Vitell. XIII)

But such practices were unusual. Suetonius describes the manners of these emperors with disgust. However, emperors had to attend many state dinners and should perhaps be forgiven for resorting to the feather.

People vomited much more frequently after an overdose of alcohol. Nowadays we would consider this fairly normal, but in ancient Rome observers were shocked. Pliny reports on the ills of drinking wine in the bathhouse:

Some of these drinkers are carefully boiled in the bath, until they are carried out unconscious. Others never get to the dinner table, because they can't even get into their tunics. Still panting and naked, they clutch an enormous wine-vessel as though to demonstrate their strength. Then they drink this to the dregs, only to vomit it all up and start drinking again. They do this a second and a third time, as though they were born for the purpose of wasting wine. As if we can't throw away wine, save by first funnelling it through a human being!

(Plin. N.H. XIV 139)

The great Cicero was another such drinker. In his letters he writes about vomiting as though it were an everyday matter, but Pliny attacks him and others for their lack of restraint:

Tergilla records that Cicero, the son of Marcus Cicero, was in the habit of knocking back six litres of wine in succession. Once, when he was drunk, he threw his goblet at Marcus Agrippa, as drunks do. No doubt Cicero was trying to beat Mark Antony (his father's murderer) of his drinking records. Cicero even went so far as to write a book about his own drinking.

(Plin. N.H. XIV 147)

Service and Presentation

The theatre of Roman cuisine required a huge team behind the scenes. It must have been an incredible hustle-and-bustle, with slaves constantly running in and out. Slaves did not just serve and clean but also recited poems, sang, acted, danced, fenced and juggled. They had to be skilled in the acrobatic and magic arts, and provide intellectual insights. Each had a speciality, but many were multi-talented.

We might imagine that serving in feasts was one of the most pleasurable tasks of slavery, and from the image we see of slaves in Roman plays, they understood the importance of fun and food. In addition, young slaves had the opportunity to impress their master and his drunken friends, which might eventually lead to freedom.

Food was presented with the greatest care. The cook modelled his creations with the refinement of a sculptor. The dishes in the *Satyricon* are all staged setpieces: roasted birds in pastry eggs, fish that appear to be swimming in a river of sauce and a piglet dressed up as a freedman. Whole roasted animals, hot burning ovens and elaborate still-lifes created from delicacies entered the dining-room in procession, sometimes accompanied by music, dancers and fireworks. Each dish was announced by the *nomenclator*, after which the enthusiastic guests applauded.

The cook himself finished some dishes in the dining room. He often came in to receive compliments or criticism and used the opportunity to boast about his art. Sometimes he had great dramatic skills:

Then Trimalchio looked more and more closely [at the suckling-pig], and said: 'What is this? Has this pig not been gutted? By the gods; it has not! Call the cook.'

When the cook humbly crawled to the table, he admitted that he had forgotten to gut the beast.

'What do you mean, you forgot?' exclaimed Trimalchio. 'As though he had neglected to add a pinch of pepper and cumin! Strip him naked!'

In no time the cook stood sorrowful and stripped between two torturers.

Everyone present started to say: 'Such things happen all the time! Please forgive him. If he does it once more, none of us will vouch for him again.'

I could not restrain myself from leaning over to Agamemnon's ear: 'What a slovenly slave. Who forgets to gut a pig? By the gods, I wouldn't let him off if he had forgotten to gut a fish.' But Trimalchio, his face relaxing into a smile, said: 'Fine, if you're so forgetful, remove the entrails here in front of everyone.'

The cook put his tunic back on, took his knife and cut the pig's belly on either side, with trembling hand. The weight of the pig's content tore the cuts further open and sausages with black puddings spilled out. The slaves applauded the trick.

(Petr. 49)

The cook might have been the first to cut the meat, but then it was the turn of the carver (*scissor*) to chop it up into edible pieces:

> Trimalchio said: 'Carve!' The *scissor* immediately came to the table and, moving to the rhythm of the music, he began to chop the meat, looking like a charioteer, who whips in time to the music of the water-organ.
> (Petr. 36)

The carving of a beautiful roast, or the ruining of a still-life, was a somewhat controversial matter. Guests would exclaim that a dish was 'too beautiful' to spoil, a compliment to the cook and the host, because it meant that the guests had eaten well enough. The host did not insist for too long, instead sending the dish straight back to the kitchen. Plutarch saw the sparing of a beautiful piece of meat as a waste of an animal's life:

How awful it is to have to watch the rich setting their tables, hiring cooks and herbalists to embalm the corpses of animals. And it is even more dreadful to see the dishes carried off again, when more is left than has been eaten! It means that the animals died for nothing! Others refuse to eat the dishes in front of their noses, because it is thought sinful to cut into them. In that way they spare the dead, but not the living animal.   (Plut. 994 E)

Trimalchio sent nothing back: he presented the dishes that had been sent back the previous day, implying that the earlier feast had been even more extravagant.

Generally the *scissor* was instructed to do his work and carve. The sliced meat would then be entrusted to the waiters (*ministratores*). Children often performed this role, walking around with serving bowls and wine goblets. Because they were small, they were able to step over the feet of the reclining guests without causing too much commotion. The youngest slaves had to wash and dry the guests' hands and feet, scratch backs and hand out small items. Children were cute, so mistakes were more easily forgiven:

While he was saying this, a boy dropped a goblet. Trimalchio looked at him and said: 'Hey, clumsy, go and kill yourself.'* The boy's lips began to tremble, and Trimalchio said: 'What are you whining for? As if I would do anything to you. Just try not to be so clumsy in future.' Finally, at our urging, he left him in peace. As soon as he was dismissed, the boy ran around the table.

(Petr. 52)

Styles of Service

Plutarch describes various different types of service.

1. The buffet: tables and *repositoria*, containing beautifully displayed dishes, brought in by servants. Reclining guests helped themselves from such exhibits, without much further assistance.

---

* Note the absolute power, expressed in such an order.

2. Roasts brought in whole and carved in the dining room. The pieces were elegantly displayed on the central table, from which the guests helped themselves.

3. Plate service: each guest was given an individual plate with a set portion, as in modern restaurants. This style of eating was very old, but not much appreciated by fashionable Romans:

> When I held the office of archont, most meals at home were served as plate service, and each person present at the offering was given his portion of the meal. Some thought this was wonderful, while others thought it unsociable and vulgar. After I laid down office, they were going to return to the customary way of eating.
>
> Hagias said: 'We invite one another out for dinner, it seems to me, not so much for the sake of eating and drinking, but in order to eat and drink *together*. Such rationing is unsociable . . .'
>
> (Plut. 642)

4. Not very sociable either, but rather elegant, was the practice of giving each guest their own table. This style was inherited from the Etruscans, and can be seen on ancient frescoes. It was much like traditional Japanese meals, except that Roman gentlemen would recline instead of kneel. Each table looked the same, and carried the same assortment of little bowls and cups. This was also how the nobility ate solitary meals. A slave would stand nearby to fill up empty bowls, or replace them, when required.

5. The Athenian way of serving food was a cross between 1 and 4: not big displays, as in 1, but many little dishes, as in 4, on a central table. This combined a variety of delicacies with the communal aspect of a central table. Not everyone liked it:

> Please listen, cook, my host comes from Rhodes and I'm from Perinthus, and we both hate Athenian-style dinners. There's something revoltingly foreign about those Attic dinners. The cook puts down a tray with five little plates on it. One holds some garlic, the next two sea urchins. Yet another contains a sweet cake, or ten little shellfish, and finally a piece of sturgeon.

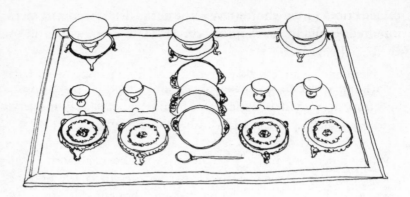

Ill. 2.14: Serving tray with silverware

While I'm trying one snack, the next person along is eating something else, and while he's eating that, I've already finished. I'd like to try everything, but it's impossible. I don't have five mouths and five hands!

Such a presentation is supposed to offer variation, but it doesn't fill your belly. I end up smearing my lips, instead of filling them.   (Ath. 132)

The criticism expressed here seems directed more at the small portions than at the manner of their serving, a common complaint about fine dining. But the Athenian style must have been usual in Italy: archaeologists have excavated silver trays with plates on tripods, egg-cups and tiny bowls that can only have contained the smallest portions of, presumably, the best that money could buy.

Crockery and Cutlery

A visit to any museum of antiquities will demonstrate the great artistry that went into Roman crockery – the Greeks had provided them with a good example in the painting of vases, pots, plates and drinking vessels, but the Romans were masters of the relief, and skilled metalworkers too. Roman crockery was an important form of artistic expression, in which the artists of the day could make a considerable name for themselves.

Some country folk used wooden cups, but terracotta was more

usual. Prices varied enormously, from less than one sestertius to a few hundred thousand sestertii for fine porcelain:

Nero once again outdid everyone, as befits an emperor, by paying a million HS for a single wine-bowl. Let us not forget how seriously the Emperor and Father of the Fatherland took his drink. (Plin. N.H. xxvii 19)

Most pottery was inexpensive, a lot of it disposable, and so much has been excavated today that its value still depends on the artistic appeal – just as it did in antiquity. Bronze, however, had its own status, as did glass. Roman bronze-casting and glass-blowing techniques are still hard to surpass.

Personally I like glass better, which has no smell. I would prefer it to gold if it didn't break, but as it is, it's pretty worthless. There was an artist who made a glass goblet that didn't break. He was allowed in to see Caesar with his gift, and when the Emperor handed it back to him he dropped it on the hard floor. Caesar could not have been more alarmed. But the man picked up the goblet off the floor. It was slightly dented, like a bronze vessel. He took a little hammer from his pocket and repaired the goblet perfectly.

The man thought that he had Jupiter by the balls, especially when Caesar asked him, 'Does anyone else know how to blow glass like this?' But behold what happened; when the man said none knew but him, Caesar ordered that the man be beheaded, on the grounds that if it became known, gold would be worth so much as dirt. (Petr. 50-51)

It would appear the Roman invention of plastic died an early death.

The well-to-do invested their money in silver and gold. In Pompeii, the remains were found of a man fleeing the volcanic eruption, with his silver tucked under his arm.

The smallest amount of silver that a family would have kept in their house was a salt cellar, *salinum*, and a *patera*, also *patella*, derived from the Greek *phiale*, used both for wine and for food offerings.

During the Republic, *patera* became the usual word for a dinner plate. Plates were not always made of expensive materials and cheap pottery was not glazed. It absorbed food smells and stains. After one or two uses it was thrown away. There were deep bowls, like the *catinus*, and cups, such as the *tryblium*, or the *gabata*. *Puls* or soup was served in any such vessels. Unleavened bread was also used as a plate.

Serving dishes were status symbols and could be hired when needed. A serving bowl was generally circular, like the table, and was called a *lanx*. There were also oval containers, called *langulae*, and square dishes for sweetmeats, called *paropsides*. No table setting was complete without a bread basket.

Silver, gold and bronze dishes have been found in the shape of fish, chickens, pumpkins, flowers and, most commonly, shells.

Pans also appeared at the table. The *patina*, a circular or oval straight-sided ovenproof pan, was made of clay or bronze. It was used especially for egg dishes. Many dishes were named after the pan in which they were cooked. Apicius, for example, includes recipes for dishes that he calls 'patina of anchovies' and 'patina of asparagus'. The only similarity between these two dishes is that they are prepared in the same kind of pan.

The *boletarium* was designed for cooking mushrooms, and had little indentations in the base.

Soups were eaten with a spoon. The *ligula* most closely resembles today's dessertspoon. There were straight-handled *ligulae*, and others with a sinuous handle into which a finger was hooked.

The most famous Roman spoon was the *coclear*, about the same size as our egg spoon. It had a long handle with a sharp pointed tip. Originally it was designed to extract snails from their shells and took its name from the Latin word for a snail, *coclea*. The sharp point of the *coclear* was also used to pierce eggs (see page 79) or impale small pieces of food. The *rudix*, another stick-like implement, was originally used for stirring. *Rudiculae* were small ones. Cato used *rudices* during cooking, like chopsticks. He revolved *globi* with them when frying.

Forks were not used. People ate with their fingers. Dirty fingers were wiped on the tablecloth, or on the hair of male or female slaves (cf. Petr. 57). Some slave-boys grew their hair long for this reason. For one household Cato specifies eight mattresses, eight bedspreads, sixteen cushions, ten tablecloths but only three table napkins (Cat. RR X 3); many diners brought their own. A gentleman kept his napkin in his toga throughout the day.

Finally, the fly-swat was indispensable at the table. As Martial writes,

> A fly-swat of peacock feathers: formerly the proud tail of a special bird, it now keeps dirty flies away from your food.
>
> (Mart. XIV-lxvii)

Fingers

Traditionally, food was picked up between the fingertips of the right hand. In many cultures the right hand is still used for eating and the left for washing. Food was picked up only with the fingertips (Ovid Ars Am. III 755). Whole-hand grabbing was considered barbarous.

> After the Celts have strewn hay on the ground, they sit down to eat at a low wooden table. They eat a little bread, but great quantities of meat, boiled, grilled or roasted on a spit. They may eat hygienically, but they do so with bestial greed.

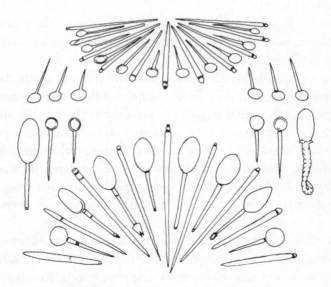

Figure 2.15 – Ligulæ, cocleares and *rudices*

With both hands they seize whole limbs of animal and with
their teeth they tear the meat off the bone. If a piece of meat is
too tough to be gnawed, they use a little knife, which lies to hand
on the table in a special sheath kept in a box.   (Ath. IV-151e)

Athenaeus describes table knives as though they did not exist
in the civilized world, but small ones have been excavated even in
noble Athens. They were not used so much at elegant *triclinium* meals,
where a *scissor* cut everything into small pieces, but in cheap taverns,
where the service left something to be desired.

Logic suggests that dishes eaten with the fingers should not be
served boiling hot or people would burn their fingers. As is so often
the case, history mentions only the exception to the rule:

I remember a glutton so shameless that he used to hold his hand
in boiling water in the bathhouse and gargled hot water, to
become immune to heat. Rumour had it that he persuaded his
cooks to serve the food very hot. Consequently he was the only
one who ate anything, because no one else could.   (Ath. I-5)

THE COURSES

Because a new table was brought in for each course, the word for
'course' and 'table' was the same: *mensa*, a new course, a new table.
Another word for 'course' was *ferculum* (from *ferre*: to bring), which
also suggests the introduction of a new table.

The main course was *mensa prima*, the 'first table' and dessert was
mensa secunda, which shows us that the meal was divided into two
parts. During the first course the food was the most important thing,
although clearly some drinking took place too. In the second part,
drink was central, with morsels of food, not all sweet. During the
Republic, the main course had been preceded by starters to awaken
the tastebuds: the *gustatio, gustaio* or even *gustus*. The three courses
formed a complete meal, a holy trinity. It is to the Romans that we owe
our custom of dividing a meal into starter, main course and dessert.

gustatio	starter (hors d'oeuvre)
mensa prima	main course (food)
mensa secunda	dessert (drink)

From the time of the Emperor Tiberius, aperitifs such as *mulsum* became fashionable, and snacks, called *promulsis*, were served with the strong, sweet drink. These tapas-style dishes were similar to those of the *gustatio* and could be eaten standing.

After the meal came the drinking bout or carousal, the *comissatio*. It was less an extension of dinner than an entirely separate ritual. Guests were invited to the *comissatio* in its own right.

All-night drinking was often interrupted with a meal, the *epula vespertina*, or *vesperna*. In the old days, when the *cena* was still eaten at around midday, *vesperna* referred to the evening meal. Later, *cena* moved to the evening and *vesperna* to the middle of the night. In this way the three basic courses were extended into a feast that lasted from dusk to dawn. 'Who eats seven courses alone?' asked Juvenal (Iuv. Sat. I-94). To count seven courses the main dish was divided in half. The first was called the *cena prima* and the second *cena altera*. Modern Italians still divide their main course into two, which they call *primo piatto*, often a pasta dish, and *secondo piatto*, something less starchy. Here are the seven courses, some of which were meals in themselves:

lustratio	washing
1 *promulsis*	aperitifs (tapas)
2 *gustatio*	starters (hors d'oeuvres)
3 *mensa prima; cena prima*	first main course (*primo piatto*)
4 *mensa prima; cena altera*	second main course (*secondo piatto*)
lustratio	washing
5 *mensa secunda*	desserts with wine
6 *comissatio*	carousal with snacks
7 *vesperna*	supper
lustratio	washing

Starters (*promulsis* and *gustatio*)

The aperitif was supposed to aid digestion. Aperitifs included vermouth (wormwood), spiced wine, mead or mulsum; it was traditionally poured into a communal drinking-bowl and passed from guest to guest. The ritual, called *potio*, consolidated the sense of conviviality.

The *promulsis* might consist of oysters, marinated octopus, marinated vegetables, cauliflower, onion, garlic, snails, sea urchins, wild mushrooms and, above all, *salsamentum*, such as ham, bacon and especially salted fish.

A Roman meal usually began with eggs and ended with fruit. Hence the Latin expression '*ab ovo usque ad mala*', literally 'from egg to apple', which meant 'from start to finish'. Eggs were boiled, baked or sucked raw from the shell. *Patinae* usually involved large numbers of eggs: hot or cold stuffed omelettes, custards, and tarts like quiches. A *patina* that contained more meat or fish than eggs was similar to our terrine or pâté.

Olives were rarely absent. Black or green and salted as they are today, they were served without further preparation. Sometimes they were pitted and ground into a kind of tapenade: *epithyrum*.

> *Epithyrum album nigrum variumque sic facito. Ex oleis albis nigris variisque nucleos eicito. Sic condito. Concidito ipsas, addito oleum, acetum, coriandrum, cuminum, feniculum, rutam, mentam. In orculam condito, oleum supra siet. Ita utito.*

Epithyrum of green, black, or other olives is made as follows: remove black, green or other olives from their oil and pit them. They are spiced as follows: mince them and add oil, vinegar, coriander, cumin, fennel, rue, mint. Place this in a clay bowl and drench in oil. Serve like this.   (Cat. R.R. CXIX)

Dishes such as *epithyrum* were eaten with bread, which was never absent. It was also the base for various *moretum* dishes. *Moretum* comes from *mortarium*, a mortar, and signifies pounded herbs. Many green herbs appeared in *moreta* (mint, coriander, parsley, dill, rocket, aniseed, etc.), and were often mixed with curd cheese.

Rabbit, sow's udder and roast pork might appear as starters, but lighter dishes, like sausages, fish and meatballs, dormice, small fish and birds, were more usual. In the *Satyricon* the fashionable cook knows how to combine game with the traditional egg dish:

On the *promulsis* table stood a bronze Corinthian donkey with two baskets on its back, black olives on one side, green on the other. Two plates stood against the donkey. Their weight in silver and Trimalchio's name were engraved along the rims. Little bridges welded to these plates contained dormice in honey and poppy-seed. There were also sausages on a silver grill, and beneath that plums and pomegranate seeds . . .*

While we were still enjoying our *gustatio*, a *repositorium* was brought with a basket upon it. This contained a wooden hen with its wings spread out, as chickens when hatching eggs. Then two slaves came running in and the music grew louder. They began to examine the hay beneath the hen, and suddenly pulled out pea-cocks' eggs, which were distributed among the guests. Trimalchio pulled a comical face, and said, 'Friends, I have put peacock eggs under a hen. And, by Hercules, I fear they are about to hatch! However, let us try one to see if they are still fresh enough to suck.'

We took our *coclear*, which weighed half a pound at least, and pierced the eggs, which were made of pastry. I was tempted to throw mine away, because I thought I detected a hatched chicken. But then I heard a convivial dinner guest saying, 'I wonder what delight might be in here.' So I peeled away the shell with my hand, and found a fat little fig-pecker in peppered egg yolk.   (Petr. 33)

Main Course (*mensa prima* or *caput cenae*)

The main course, *mensa prima*, was also called *caput cenae*, literally 'head of the dinner'. Its name implied that however splendid the starter might have been, the main course would be better. If the starter was plain, an egg with some cheese and garlic, or bread with tapenade, the main course might consist of a hearty soup with vegetables and boiled meat, a plain *puls* or a dish of legumes.

---

* Imitating glowing charcoal.

A *minutal* was a more refined main course, and consisted of vegetables cut small and baked with little meat- or fishballs and pieces of ham, reminiscent of Chinese stir-fry dishes.

If the starters had been spectacular, the cook had to tie himself in knots to exceed expectations, perhaps with expensive delicacies such as parrot-brains, moray eel livers or sows' wombs. He could present sensational roasts, such as pelican, crane, giraffe or bear, or resort to theatrical effects:

> The next course was brought in. The quantity did not match our expectations, but it was so original that we could hardly believe our eyes.
>
> It was a deep, circular dish, with the twelve signs of the zodiac around the rim. Over each constellation there was food related to the sign. Over Aries there were 'ram' peas [*cicer arietinum*], over Taurus a piece of beef, over Gemini a pair of kidneys and a pair of testicles, over Cancer a wreath of flowers, over Leo an African fig, over Virgo a barren sow's womb, over Libra scales with a cake in one disc and a muffin in the other, over Scorpio a small sea-fish, over Sagittarius a magpie, over Capricorn a lobster, over Aquarius a goose, over Pisces two gurnards. In the middle of all this was a piece of grassy turf with a honeycomb upon it.*
>
> Meanwhile an Egyptian slave-boy carried around bread on a silver platter, while singing a distorted version of a mime-song from 'The Asafoetida-Picker', in a most appalling voice.
>
> As we started rather disconsolately on this substandard fare, Trimalchio said, 'Now let's have dinner.' As he said this, four dancers ran forward to the rhythm of the music. They removed the top of the bowl and revealed beneath it plump game, delicious sow's udders and a roast hare with wings fastened to its back, making it look like Pegasus.
>
> We also saw four sculptures of Marsyas, holding leather bottles that poured out *garum*. The sauce flowed over the fishes,

---

* The connections between the star-signs and the food are sometimes a little personal. Trimalchio provides the interpretation. The crown of flowers is over Cancer because he himself was born in that sign and became successful. He considers Sagittarius a traitorous sign, which he symbolizes with the thieving magpie. A lobster has claws on its head, like the horns of a goat. The piece of turf was supposed to symbolize Mother Earth and the honeycomb the richness of her gifts.

which appeared to be swimming in a river. We heartily applauded along with the slaves and, still laughing, helped ourselves to all these oddities.   (Petr. 35)

Dessert (*mensa secunda*)

After the main course everything was cleared away and bread was passed round for the guests to wipe their mouths and hands, then given to the dogs, who were dedicated to Hecate, the goddess of night and witchcraft. After the main course the sun would have set: it was time to ward off the evils of the dark and thus to feed Hecate's familiars.

According to ancient etiquette wine was not drunk during the starter and the main course.

As the *mensa secunda* was brought in, the host asked for silence, which interrupted the lively chatter of the guests. Sacrifices were made in silence, and at this point children would take some of the dessert and burn it in front of the *lararium*. Then conversation would pick up, and the guests could start on their apples, pomegranates, pears, quinces, figs, dates, peaches, apricots, plums, cherries, raspberries, strawberries or, of course, grapes. Nuts, such as walnuts, hazelnuts, beechnuts, almonds, pine kernels, pistachios and sweet chestnuts, were served with the fruit. Sweet nut cakes were offered, too, such as marzipan, sesame-seed or poppy-seed buns with honey, and filo pastry with crushed nuts.

Ancient sweets were based on honey and curd cheese, like *placenta* and *libum*, or on cheese and dried fruit, like *hypotrimma*. But sweetness was not reserved for dessert: honey-cakes were served among the starters, and snails and tripe among the desserts. Sometimes the order of things was deliberately reversed, as Seneca describes:

> The desire for luxury extended to the courses. An attempt was made to render them more attractive by serving increasingly exotic recipes. The normal sequence of dishes was reversed. The meal started with dishes that are normally offered when people are leaving.   (Sen, Ep ad Luc. XIX-114)

It was not easy to turn a dessert into something special. How can you make something spectacular out of a few apples and some grapes? Trimalchio did his best:

Figure 2.16 – Priapus

A tray with some cakes had been brought in. At the centre stood
a pastry figure of Priapus, with all kinds of fruit and grapes in his
lap, as is the convention. When we reached out our hands for the
fruit, our jollity began all over again. At the slightest touch, all
the fruit and cakes began to squirt saffron. The nasty stuff even
got into our faces.   (Petr. 60)

The *Priapus* described here was the god of garden plants, fruit-trees
and fertility (see also page 207), easily recognized by his excessively
large penis and often shown lifting up his apron, which contains a
quantity of fruit. Sometimes, however, the penis represented the deity.
It was often made of pastry and was intended for eating. Martial jokes:

> A Priapus of bread:
> you can satisfy yourself by eating my Priapus.
> Nibble at him and remain respectable.
>
> (Mart. XIV-lxix)

By the end of the main course night had fallen, and an aphrodisiac
was required. The god Priapus fulfilled this function, too, with the aid

of fruit and honey. The grape was under his especial protection.
Martial writes that anyone who damaged a vine would be punished by
Priapus with cancer:

> Be careful with those vines, if you cherish your prostate.
>
> (Mart. VI-xlix)

Wine, too, was considered an aphrodisiac, and Priapus is sometimes identified with the god of wine (see Osiris page 110–11).

THE MENU

Sometimes written menus were issued:

> It was customary at banquets for every guest, after taking his place
> at the couch, to be handed a tablet with a list of the things that
> were being prepared, so that he knew what the cook was planning
> to serve.   (Ath. 49d)

Unfortunately no such tablets have been excavated, but many dinners
have been described in classical literature. Here are some examples:

Menu for Pliny the Younger

Gustatio	Salad
	3 snails
	2 hard-boiled eggs
Caput cenae	*Puls*
	Baked courgettes with sauce
	Wild flower-bulbs in vinegar
Mensa secunda	*Mulsum* ice
	Fresh fruit

(Plin. Ep. I-15)

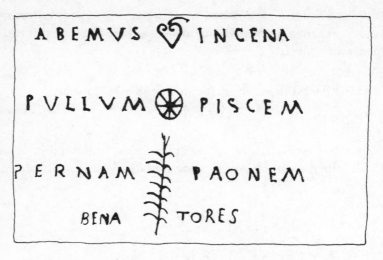

Figure 2.17 – Menu inscription on the wall of a taverna

Menu for Toranius

Gustatio	Salad from Cappadocia
	Leek
	Tuna with boiled eggs
Caput cenae	*Patella* with broccoli
	White *puls* with sausage
	Green beans with bacon
Mensa secunda	Raisins
	Pears from Syria
	Roast chestnuts from Neapolis
	Olives from Picenus
	Chickpeas
	Flower-bulbs

(Mart. V.-78)

Menu for Philemon and Baucis

gustatio	Green and black olives
	Salted dogberries
	Chicory with horseradish

Cheese *moretum*
Eggs cooked in ashes
caput cenae   Boiled loin of pork
Choice of vegetables
mensa secunda   Nuts, figs, dates, plums, apples, grapes
Honeycomb and old wine

(Hor. Ep. I-5)

Menu for Habinnas

gustatio   Pork topped with herbs
Honey-cake
Livers and kidneys
Beets
Wholemeal bread (Habinnas:
    'Personally I prefer it to white')
caput cenae   Cold pie with honey and Spanish wine
Chickpeas and lupins
An apple
Bear-steak
mensa secunda   Soft cheese marinated in *sapa*
Snails
Little dishes with liver
Pieces of tripe
Hooded eggs
Turnips with mustard
Marinated olives

(Petr. 66)

Menu for Julius Cerialis

gustatio   Salad
Leek
Small tunas with egg and rue
Eggs roasted in ashes
Cheese from Velabra
Olives from Picenum
caput cenae   Fish

	Mussels and oysters
	Sow's udder
	Fattened poultry
	Marshland game
mensa secunda	Unknown

(Mart. XI-52)

Menu for Stella

gustatio	Lettuce, 'aphrodisiac herb' [rocket?]
	Marshmallow, garden herbs
	Leek with peppermint
	Anchovies with rue and boiled egg
	Sow's udder with *garum*
caput cenae	Young kid stolen from the claws of a wolf
	Charcuterie
	Garden beans and sprouts
	Chicken
	Ham
mensa secunda	Ripe fruit

(Mart. X-48)

Menu for Nasidienus Rufus

gustatio	Unknown
cena prima	Wild boar from Lucania
	Black salsify, lettuce, rampion
cena alterna	Small birds and shellfish
	Plaice
	Flounder
	Moray with razor clams
mensa secunda	Crane with goose-liver
	Saddle of hare
	Blackbird and pigeon
	Wines from Cecubus and Chios

(Hor. *Serm.* II-8)

Menu for Trimalchio

gustatio	Roast dormice in honey and poppy-seed
	Sausage on plum and pomegranate seed
	Figpecker in peppered mayonnaise
	Black and green olives
caput cenae	Ram's peas, beef, kidneys and ram's testicles, barren sow's womb, African fig, scorpion fish, goose, magpie, cake and muffin
	Fattened poultry
	Sow's udder
	Roast hare
	Small fish
	Bread
	Pork stuffed with live birds
	Pork stuffed with sausages and black pudding
mensa secunda	*Placenta* cake
	Priapus with fruit and grapes
	2nd dessert (unspecified)
	Imitation goose, poultry and fish made of pork
	Snacks at dawn

(Petr. *ibid.*)

THE CAROUSAL (*Comissatio*)

The Romans adopted the practice of the drinking bout from the Greeks, who called it the *symposium*. The word still implies a high level of intellectual pursuit. The Roman *comissatio* followed much the same rules as the *symposium*.

At the end of a meal the dining-tables were removed and hands were washed. Some people put on a clean toga. Then the attributes for the *comissatio* were brought in: wreaths, perfumes and the wine table.

Wreaths

The wearing of wreaths served a primarily religious purpose. Various plants were dedicated to particular gods, and wreaths were woven from them to honour those gods and ensure their protection. The oak, for example, was dedicated to Jupiter, the king of the gods. The vine belonged to Bacchus, of course, but so did ivy. Vine wreaths were supposed to promote tipsiness, but cooling ivy protected against it. With ivy around the temples, you would not lose your head.

In ancient times, the origin of the custom for wearing wreaths was vigorously debated. According to Aristotle, wreath-wearing began as a remedy for drunkenness. He maintained that the forefathers of the Greeks wrapped bandages, later decorated with leaves and flowers, around their heads to combat the hangover headache (Ath. XV 677a).

> But Sappho has a simple interpretation of the reasons why we wear wreaths. She writes: 'With your delicate hands weave anis, my Dica, for the graces who bestow their blessings love the sight of a girl wearing a wreath, but turn away from unwreathed maidens.' She is obviously referring to the wearing of wreaths by girls making a sacrifice, because something decked with flowers is always more acceptable to the gods. (Ath. 674e)

Wreaths were made from any material. Laurel and olive wreaths are familiar to us, but prickly fir twigs, in honour of Pan, and exotic plants, such as lotus and papyrus in honour of Egyptian gods, were also used. Everyone wore flower wreaths although some men found them a little girlish. The fragrance of the flowers was pleasant and thought to do the body good. Wreaths of roses or violets, for example, were believed to soothe headaches. Hazel, crocus and henna flowers were thought soporific and calming, with the power to restrain drunken garrulity. The poppy was considered a narcotic. If someone wore a broken wreath, he was said to be in love (Ath. XV 670C).

Christians refused to wear wreaths, and when they came to power they outlawed the ancient pagan custom.

Perfume

Men did not only crown themselves with flowers, they also wore perfume. Socrates had taken a dim view of this, but most men saw nothing effeminate in it. In defence of the practice, it was suggested that perfumes, or the oil contained in them, kept the head cool and were beneficial to health. According to one Hicesius, the perfume of roses was suitable for a *symposium*, as were the scents of myrrh, quince blossom, oregano, thyme and crocus, as long as they were not mixed with excessive quantities of nard. Fenugreek was also highly esteemed, and the scent of cloves was supposed to be good for the digestion (Ath. 689C).

At the same time, all of these scents were important as olfactory offerings to the gods. Sometimes incense was burned at the same time. We might find such a mingling of fragrances overwhelming, but the Romans were used to it. They enjoyed complex perfumes as much as they relished complex sauces.

The Wine Table (*mensa vinaria*)

Along with the wreaths and perfumes the wine-table, the *mensa vinaria*, was carried in. The Romans had many more types of vessel for drinking than for food, and more than three hundred names for their wine pots, cans and beakers. The wine itself was brought into the room in 26-litre amphorae, with the date when the wine had been 'bottled' and the name of the vineyard written on the side. After an amphora was opened, the wine was scooped out with a long spoon, a *trulla*. The wine was filtered through a sieve (*colum*), perhaps containing aromatic herbs to add flavour, because it still contained lees and

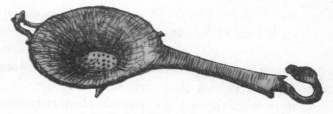

Figure 2.18 – Column

other impurities, into a jug (such as a *stamnos*). At this point a perfume
– myrtle oil was popular – might be added. It was sometimes cooled in
a sieve with snow (*colum nivarium*), then decanted into a snow-cooled
vat (*psykter*).

The drinking of undiluted wine was thought risky:

> After Dionysus had introduced wine to Greece from the region
> around the Red Sea, men drank it in shameless, unlimited quan-
> tities. Some, in their lunatic frenzy, went mad, while others
> appeared to sink into a stupor. But on one occasion men were
> drinking on the beach when a rainstorm broke out, falling upon
> the feasting crowd and filling the vessel in which the wine was
> held. When the weather cleared and everyone came back, they
> tasted the mixture of wine and water, and thus discovered a safe
> and agreeable pleasure.
>
> Consequently, if the Greeks drink undiluted wine with their
> meal they do so in honour of the divinity who invented wine,
> Dionysus. But whenever they drink diluted wine after their meal,
> they are invoking Zeus the Saviour, because he, the bringer of
> rainstorms, was responsible for the safe mixture of water and wine.
>
> (Ath. XV 675a)

Undiluted wine was called *merum*, and today in some Italian dialects
wine is still known as *mero* rather than *vino*.

The decanting of wine from one vessel into another was a responsible job performed by a wine waiter, the *cetarius*, who also diluted it.
In summer the water was cooled with snow; in winter water was boiled
in a kettle-like samovar and the wine was served warm. The wine
waiter poured the water into a mixing vessel, the *krater*, then scooped
in the wine. The host or one of the guests determined the precise
proportions.

Master of Revels (*magister bibendi*)

At the beginning of the *comissatio* the guests elected a master of revels:
the *magister bibendi*. In this they were following the Greeks, who
called the king of drinking the *symposiarch*. He was responsible for
the quantity of alcohol consumed by the guests so he had to know

who could hold his drink and who could not. If he was not well acquainted with guests, he had to rely on generalizations – for example, that old men get more drunk than young men, the impetuous more than the calm, and the pessimist more than the optimist. The authority of the *magister* was beyond dispute. For that reason it was important that he should be neither too strict nor too liberal:

> For the drunkard is arrogant and rude, but the complete abstainer is more suited to looking after children than presiding over a symposium.
>
> (Plut. 1-4-620C)

Because he was in charge of alcohol consumption, the *magister* also had overall responsibility for the carousal. He had to decide whether a subject was appropriate for discussion, and select the speakers. Then if the conversation became too trivial or too heated, he had to interrupt and propose another topic.

But the *magister*'s most important task was to decide the correct proportion of water to wine. His options ranged between pure wine, and wine diluted with six parts water. Usually the mixture was two or three parts water to one part wine, but one to one was not uncommon. In all circumstances the water was poured into the *krater* first, followed by the wine. Once the wine was mixed, it was poured into a small wine jug, a *lagona*, and from there into the cups.

Drinking Cups

The oldest wine cup was the *phiala*, called *patera* by the Romans, a shallow circular bowl without handles or stem. Its most important characteristic was the little round relief in the bottom that symbolized the sun. *Phialae* have been excavated in large quantities in Thrace, where the art of wine-making was developed.

The Romans used the *patera* principally at sacrifices. The *lares* were always shown holding one in their left hand, and in their right a drinking horn, the *rhytium*.

Different gods had their own drinking cups. For example, Hercules is often shown with a *scyphus*, a small personal beaker, and Bacchus with a large ceremonial *kantharus*, with tall handles. The *kantharus* was particularly popular among the Etruscans, who made them out

Figure 2.19 – Drinking vessels. A: *phiala*; B: *kantharus*;
C: *kylix*; D: *scyphus*; E: *poculum*

of magnificent black clay. The shape has lived on to this day in many sports trophies.

The Greek *kylix*, which the Romans called the *calix*, a word used for wine cups in general, was a hybrid of the *patera* and the *kantharus*. It was a flat bowl with two handles, usually supported by a stem, the *symposium* drinking vessel par excellence. Museums in Greece and Italy are full of them. Most *kylices* are between 20 and 30 cm in diameter, but there were smaller ones of not more than 8 cm, and very large ones of 50 cm. Many households had a collection of *kylices*, displayed hanging from a stand in the dining room. The *magister bibendi* chose which size of *kylix* was to be used in the carousal.

The *kylix* was shallow, so impurities in the wine or water were immediately apparent. It was difficult to drink from – in downing the last drops of wine, the drinker's face was obscured behind the bowl. The Greeks often painted two eyes on the underside of the *kylix* to symbolize the eyes of the drinker.

The later Roman *calix* was a small beaker with two handles, made of bronze, silver or gold. A simpler version was made of clay, wood or glass, and called a *poculum*. It had no handles, was fat-bellied and narrow at the rim, which meant it captured the aroma of the wine, like a brandy glass, and retained its warmth in cold weather. Many *pocula* have been found in what were northern Roman provinces.

Individual beakers differed from communal drinking bowls. In the taverns, on public occasions and at informal dinners, each person was usually given his own cup, but for ceremonial wine drinking it was normal for everyone to drink from the same bowl, just as it was in carousals and the *potio*.

Libations

The wine-pourer (*ministrator* or *pocillator*) poured the wine into the beakers and handed it to the guests. It was the most prestigious post a slave-child could occupy. In earlier times the job had been performed by noble youths, and the most famous wine-pourer of all time was Ganymede, a Trojan prince, with whom Jupiter fell in love. The king of the gods transformed himself into an eagle, flew to Earth and abducted the child. Back on Olympus he granted Ganymede immortality and entrusted him with the solemn duty of pouring the wine at the banquets of the gods.

In the days when couches were still placed far apart, the wine-pourer also had to carry the drinking bowl clockwise from one guest to the next. Later on, when the guests reclined around a communal table, they passed the wine bowl to each other. One would hold the beaker in his left hand by one handle, while the next took it with his right hand.

Once a guest had the cup, he would perform a libation (*libatio*): he took one of the handles of the drinking bowl between two fingers, and made the wine swirl inside the bowl, as wine-tasters still do today, and allowed some to splash over the edge as a sacrifice. Sometimes sawdust was scattered over the floor to protect it against frequent libations. It was customary to dedicate at least one libation to Jupiter or Apollo, but Neptune, Bacchus and many others were likewise honoured.

The Hymn of Praise

According to etiquette, the libation was paired with a hymn of praise to the gods. A flautist (*tibicen*) accompanied the singing guests. The hymns were sung in three different ways (Ath. 694b):

1. By everyone together in chorus.
2. By everyone singing in turn.
3. By only the best singers in the company.

Athenaeus provides a few examples of short Greek hymns, some of which sound religious. Others were of a more secular nature.

> I sing of the Olympian Ceres, mother of Pluto, in the season when wreaths are worn. And of you Flora, daughter of Jupiter. Hail to you both, and guard our city . . .

> O Faunus, king of glorious Arcadia, you dance in the company of pretty nymphs, smile upon my cheerful song . . .

> Health is the first blessing, beauty the second. The third is honest money and the fourth is youth spent among friends . . .

Drink with me, play with me, love with me, wear wreaths with me, be angry when I am angry, or be sober when I am sober.

O, that I were a big, new, golden jewel so that a lovely woman would wear me upon her pure heart.

(Ath. 695)

Games

The *comissatio*, or *symposium*, did not consist solely of singing and drinking. In accordance with the best Greek tradition, the guests entertained one another with intellectual diversions such as solving riddles and inventing rhymes. Telling a story or reciting a poem met with approval, as long as it was done with a modicum of talent.

A game arose out of the libation, which retained its popularity for centuries. It came from Sicily and was called the *cottabus*. A vessel was set in the middle of the players, then wine was splashed from a *kylix* and a toast raised to a lover. If the wine landed in the vessel it was seen as a good omen for the couple.

Figure 2.10 – Cottabus

In a variation on this game, little boats floated in the central vessel, and the guests had to sink them with wine. In yet another version metal discs were set spinning on sticks. The aim was to hit the discs with wine to create interesting sounds, without making them fall to the floor.

There were other games, such as forfeits, in which the penalty involved some form of physical exertion. The *magister's* task was to prevent such games getting out of hand:

> He must ensure that the drinkers beware of those superficial games that rampage into parties like crowds of drunks. He must not allow careless members of the party to spoil the feast with rude suggestions (bitter like the henbane in their wine), when they become obnoxious, asking stammerers to sing, demanding bald men to comb their hair, or calling cripples to dance on oiled wine-skins.   (Plut. 621e)

There were other games, too, such as draughts, backgammon and dice. Gambling for money was considered vulgar. Honour was highly valued, and a higher stake in games than money could ever be.

Conversation

Many parasites (see page 61–2) were good at rhyming, singing, wine-throwing and other party games. If they were also intelligent and learned, they received frequent invitations to carousals because such an occasion offered a fine opportunity to present interesting theories and hold learned debates. The Greeks had set a good example with this. Plato's *Symposium* is still one of the most important philosophical works ever written, and accounts of what was said at *symposia* became a philosophical genre.

The Romans tried to maintain the elevated tradition, but their conversations were not always of the same calibre as those of the great Greek thinkers. Plutarch lists the kinds of subject that were under discussion in first-century Rome (Plut. *quaestiones conviviales* and *quaestiones romanae*).

– Why is A the first letter of the alphabet?
– Which came first, the chicken or the egg?

- Why do Romans carry their brides over the threshold?
- Is philosophy a proper topic of conversation for a *symposium*?
- Why do the Romans forbid human sacrifice?
- Why is a priest of Jupiter forbidden to eat raw meat?
- Why does sound travel better at night than by day?
- Can new diseases come into being, and if so, how?
- Why does drink satisfy hunger, while food makes one thirsty?
- Was Alexander the Great an alcoholic?
- Why are people hungrier in the autumn?
- Is wrestling the oldest sport?
- What is the best time of day for sexual intercourse?
- Why are very drunk people less mad than someone who is just tipsy?
- Does sea or land produce the greater amount of delicacies?
- Which god do the Jews worship?

Everyone present could voice his ideas. While one speaker was setting out his argument, the others kept silent. Everyone was entitled to support previous speakers, with more arguments and some elaboration, or dispute their theories when his own turn came to speak, but interruption was not permitted. Each speaker was rewarded with applause:

> When Cynulcus failed to win any applause after he had spoken, he lost his temper and cried, 'Mr. Magister, these gentlemen do not hunger after my words because they themselves suffer from verbal diarrhoea.'
>
> (Ath. 159d)

Other Amusements

The more serious the *symposium*, the greater the need for diversion. Acrobats and jugglers displayed their arts with knives and flaming hoops. Comedians and dwarfs charmed the company. Dwarfs were so popular (and valuable!) that the limbs of some slave-children were bound at birth to create artificial dwarfs. Some Romans even staged gladiatorial combats during dinner, but others were shocked:

> It often happened that someone invited his friends not only for the sake of conviviality, but also in order to witness two or three

pairs of gladiators engaged in combat. Once they were seated
with food and drink, in came the gladiators. And their masters
applauded enthusiastically as they cut each other's throats.

(Ath. 153)

There was always music at a *comissatio*. The flute sometimes played
uninterruptedly 'from egg to apple' in the background. The lyre
was also popular. Professional singers were often hired. The flute and
the lyre addressed the emotions, and the words of the songs spoke
to the intellect:

The lyre has existed since the most ancient times, from the days
of Homer right through to the present. Such an old tradition
should not be broken. We should only try to persuade the singers
to leave the yelping and whining out of their repertoire, and to
sing happy songs in accordance with the mood of the feast.
    And we cannot do without the flute, even if we wanted to. It
is just as important for our libations as the wreaths. And it accompanies the hymn of praise to Apollo.   (Plut. VII 8 713)

Not all music was so delicate. With the support of cymbals, drums
and other percussion, the flautist could produce rhythmic music to
which naked dancers would gyrate. These dances might be compared
with Bacchic orgies and present-day raves. Nowadays it is considered
entirely appropriate if guests start to dance at a party but the Romans
frowned on such behaviour:

At first the music was pleasant, but all of a sudden the musician
filled the echoing dining room with sound. When he realized he
could hypnotize his listeners he intoxicated them with music; with
his piping and his ribald motions, he revealed his true character
and demonstrated that music could make people even more
uninhibitedly intoxicated than wine. The guests were no longer
satisfied with clapping and shouting, but sprang to their feet and
made movements that fitted with this kind of rhythmical music,
but are scandalous for decent folk. When it came to a stop and
everyone went to sit down again, they felt as though they had just
emerged from an attack of insanity.   (Plut. VII 5 704)

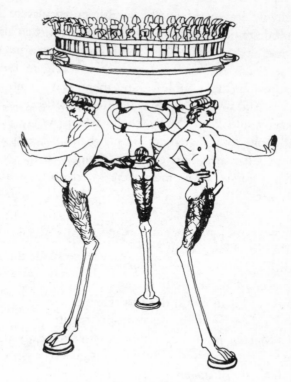

Figure 2.21 – Bronze *foculus* on tripod

Gifts (*apophoreta*)

Aside from the pleasures of food, wine, scent, music and entertainment, it was customary to spoil the guests with little gifts, called *apophoreta*. They often consisted of food, so the parasites had something delicious to take home for their wives and children. Cleopatra used the tradition to win over Mark Antony:

> When she met Antony in Cilicia, Cleopatra organized a royal *symposium* in his honour. The artful table setting was all in gold and jewels. Even the walls, Socrates* records, were hung with tapestries of purple with gold thread. After twelve *triclinia* had been set up, she invited Antony and the friends of his choice.

* Not the philosopher.

He was highly impressed by the wealth on display. Cleopatra laughed modestly and said he could take it all away as a present.

The next day she invited him and his officers to dinner again. On this occasion she presented such an extravagant *symposium* that the previous day's table arrangement was as nothing in comparison. And once again he was allowed to keep everything. Each officer could keep the couch on which he lay. Even the sheets and tables were shared out among them. When it was time to go home, Cleopatra donated sedan chairs with carriers to the high-ranking guests, while most were given horses with pretty silver harnesses.   (Ath. 148b)

Few would have gone quite so far as the Queen, whose dinners were paid for by the Egyptian treasury.

The traditional way to give *apophoreta* was as a raffle. A vessel was filled with pieces of paper with verses written on them. Each guest fished one out, and read aloud the text. Each poem contained a riddle or a joke, and a slave brought the appropriate gift.

The poet Martial published a whole series of ready-made poems, useful to the less inspired host. The subjects give us a good impression of the great diversity of *apophoreta*:

Food

A flour penis, cake, pepper, *garum*, honey, vinegar, oil, *alica, passum, mulsum,* a goat, beans, lentils, spelt, rye, grain, beets, turnips, sprouts, leek, lettuce, asparagus, grapes, figs, dates, plums, quinces, pomegranates, peaches, jujubes, pine-cones, rowanberries, flower bulbs, lemons, eggs, a young goat, a suckling pig, ham, sow's womb, sow's udder, goose-liver, mice, rabbit, bear, a pig, wild boar, deer, antelope, chamois, gazelle, fig-pecker, duck, turtle-dove, wood-dove, capon, partridge, peacock, pheasant, flamingo, goose, crane, swan, mushrooms, truffles, oysters, parrot-fish, prawns, sea urchin, mussels, sturgeon, gudgeon, sea-bass, turbot, moray, gurnard, all kinds of sausage, cheese, wine.

Objects

A notepad, writing paper, a pen-case, a shell, a ruler, a book-roll bag, a wallet, a savings bank, dice, knucklebones, draughts pieces, a board for a game, a hoop, a discus, a ball, a toothpick, an ear-pick, a hairpin, a comb, a brush, a tooth-stone, soap, a bottle of oil, perfume, incense, shaving implements, a first-aid box, a hunting knife, a sword, a shield, a dagger, an axe, a whip, a staff, a broom, a rattle, a flute, a bell, a guitar, cymbals, a lamp, a lantern, a table, table-cloth, a couch, a cushion, a blanket, a bedspread, a drinking-cup, plates, a serving-bowl, a mushroom pan, a vase, a sieve, an ice-bag, a water carafe, a spoon, a snail-spoon, a basket, a belt, a boxing belt, a cap, a parasol, a hood, a ring, a toga, a dinner suit, an over-jacket, a cape, a brassiere, socks, a neckerchief, a *tunica*, a floor-cloth, wool, cushion stuffing, feathers, hay, a birdcage.

Art

Books by Homer, Virgil, Menander, Cicero, Propertius, Livy, Sallust, Ovid, Tibullus, Lucan, Catullus or Calvus. Gold statues of Victoria, Brutus' little boyfriend in clay, Hercules in bronze, Apollo in bronze, a hermaphrodite in marble, Minerva in silver, a hunchback in clay. Paintings of Danaë, Hyacinth, Europa.

Animals and slaves

A parrot, a crow, a magpie, a nightingale, a hawk, a hunting-dog, a lapdog, a pony, a donkey, a monkey, a slave-boy, a slave-girl, a sausage-maker, an amanuensis, a dwarf, an actor, a cook, a confectioner, a buyer.

III

WINE AND OTHER DRINKS

WINE (*vinum*)

For some seven thousand years people have made wine, but the enjoyment of alcohol goes back further into the past. Even some animals, like elephants and monkeys, eat fermented berries and fruit to get drunk. The ancients wrote little about the first viniculture, but they constantly discussed the origins of the wine god. His identity and significance are still relevant today, because he has survived the ages in the form of Jesus Christ.

A study of the wine gods also helps us to understand the polytheist Romans. Orgies and bacchanals in honour of Bacchus gave their culture a bad name – which may not be entirely justified.

Who Is the Wine God?

There are many wine gods. Or are they, perhaps, different manifestations of the same god? The question often arose in antiquity. Pagan Romans, were fascinated by the *Who's Who* of the invisible world.

Cross-identification of gods was a normal thing. The Greek Herodotus, the first historian, travelled to Egypt and encountered the cults of the Egyptian gods. He did not dismiss the Egyptians as praying to false idols, or doubt the existence of the Egyptian gods: he simply identified them with Greek gods, as was the custom. In the Egyptian Osiris, Herodotus recognized Dionysus, or Bacchus, the wine god. His female equivalent was Isis in Egypt, Demeter in Greece and Ceres in Rome.

Identifying several gods as the same deity is one thing, but cults are more complex. One god may be worshipped by several different

Figure 3.1 – Procession

religious groups. Muslims, Jews and Christian, for instance, worship the same God, but the cults differ to such an extent that this is sometimes hard to accept.

Now, back to Rome: the Romans had a wine god called Liber. The Greeks had a wine god called Dionysus, who had many nicknames, of which Bacchus was one. When the Romans were introduced to the Greek god they did not identify him with their own Liber. The stories the two peoples told about their wine gods and the rituals associated with them did not match: the religions were too different. So now we have two wine gods: the Latin Liber and the Greek Dionysus/Bacchus.

Romans had no qualms about worshipping foreign gods, which was seen as a sign of respect for unfamiliar cultures. Also they were afraid of offending unknown gods. In most provinces of the Roman empire local gods were honoured. The Romans identified foreign gods with their own and built magnificent temples to them, which pleased and impressed the local peoples. Roman soldiers stationed abroad were sometimes initiated into foreign cultures, which they brought home with them. In this way many new religions came to Rome. The Roman authorities had to set limits on the practice: the worship of foreign gods must not take place at the expense of Roman gods. However, if the gods could be identified with Roman gods they could be given their own temples in Rome; otherwise the cult had to remain private.

The cults of Bacchus and later Christianity both remained private. For a long time the religions remained underground, but in the end

Bacchus was accepted as one of the Roman state gods (and finally identified with Liber). Later, Christianity, following a similar path to the cult of Bacchus, became the state religion.

The Greek Cult of Bacchus

In prehistoric times the cult of Bacchus probably consisted of wild fertility dances. The dancers wore masks and the hides of sacrificed animals, and carried a pole, also decorated with sacrificed animals and topped with a mask. The pole represented the deity and is the forerunner of the *thyrsus* staff, a piece of reed topped with a fir-cone and decorated with ivy and vine leaves, with which Bacchus was later depicted.

The dance was the predecessor of Greek theatre. Masks were worn in both Greek and Roman theatre, but a chorus replaced the original dancers. For the Greeks, Bacchus/Dionysus became the god of wine *and* the god of theatre.

At the feast of the Great Dionysia, which was held in the spring in honour of Dionysus Eletthereus (Bacchus the Liberator), plays were performed for three days in a row – a long sitting for the audience, but a religious duty, for which they were paid.

At the Dionysia a statue of Bacchus in the form of a phallus was carried around the streets in procession. Herodotus noted the same ritual for the rites of Osiris, when he went to Egypt:

> Apart from the absence of choric dancing, the Egyptians celebrate the feast of Dionysus in much the same way as the Greeks do, but in place of the phallus they have puppets, about a yard tall, with phalluses almost as big as their bodies. These are pulled up and down by strings, as women carry them around the village. A flautist walks at the head of the procession, with the women behind him singing a hymn to Dionysus. Why the penis should be so large and why it is the only part of the body that moves is unknown. (Her. II-48)

He goes on to state in his report that the Greeks must have adopted the Dionysus cult and the phallic procession from the Egyptians, but the origins of the rituals were lost in prehistoric times. From archaeological evidence it appears that the fertility gods Dionysus and Demeter were much more important in the old Greece of the Bronze Age, but that their cults were suppressed around 1000 BC by the Dorians, who introduced the Olympian gods.

This is not, however, how Greek myth describes the arrival of Bacchus.

Greek Myth of Bacchus

In myths, fiction and fact run alongside each other. According to the official Graeco-Roman religion, Bacchus was the result of one of Jupiter's adulterous affairs. His mother was a mortal, Semele, princess of Thebes. Jupiter's jealous wife, Juno, wanted to prevent the birth of the illegitimate child, so she burned the pregnant Semele, but Jupiter flew to the aid of his unborn child and he transplanted the foetus into his own thigh.

After Jupiter gave birth to little Bacchus from his leg, he entrusted the divine baby to Mercury, with instructions to hide him from the vengeful goddess. Bacchus was taken to the nymphs of Nysa, who laid him in a cradle of ivy leaves, hence the connection between Bacchus and ivy. The young god grew up in the wild with satyrs, the male equivalent of nymphs and nature-spirits with a strong animal instinct, as his playmates. They could predict the future and symbolized male sexuality, with donkey's ears and a constant erection. Their chief occupations were music, dance and sex. They made love with each other, with nymphs and with animals.

The satyrs taught Bacchus how to predict the future, but he taught himself how to make wine. The satyrs and nymphs were impressed by this, and the first to acknowledge Bacchus as a god. Bacchus made wine from sunshine and water – which is essentially how the vine produces grapes. Basically, Bacchus *is* the vine. He and his disciples, the *bacchantes*, moved from country to country, but encountered opposition wherever they went. The reason for this was their outrageous ritual: the *orgia*.

THE ORGY

The basis for the orgy was not wine or sex, but dance. Women in particular, but also men, nymphs and satyrs got carried away by music played on drums, cymbals and the double flute. They began to dance wildly and worked themselves into a trance-like state, in which the soul left the body, the *extasis*. Ecstasy was dangerous: a spirit might easily possess someone in this condition, which, of course, was the point of the orgy. The spirit of the wine god should possess the disciples and a condition starts called *enthousiasmos*.

Once the god had entered a human, he became man. Now he could nourish himself. He could fill his belly with sacrificial meat, quench his thirst with wine, make love or avenge himself on his enemies.

Bacchus was able to rouse his followers into a frenzy, called *mania*, which endangered everyone around them. In this state, the *bacchantes* tore sacrificial animals to pieces with their bare hands, then devoured the flesh and dressed themselves in the skins. Human beings, too, were the victims of *mania*. In the tragedy by Euripides, *The Bacchae*, the impious King Pentheus of Thebes is torn to pieces by his mother and other female relations, who, in their manic ravings, see him as a sacrificial beast. Euripides calls the women *maenades*, which means 'the possessed'.

Bacchus in India

According to Ovid, Bacchus proceeded through Thace, Phrygia, Asia Minor and even India, where he was believed to have discovered cinnamon and incense. According to myth, he celebrated a victory at the Ganges and returned home triumphant on the back of a tiger; artists often depict him in this pose.

Not in myth, but in real history, when Alexander the Great went to India, he established an Indo-Hellenic community. The Greeks discovered the Indian god Shiva, who is dedicated to wild dancing, like Bacchus, and is also capable of manic destruction. As well as being the god of destruction, Shiva is also a god of rebirth – again, like Bacchus.

In India Bacchus and Shiva were identified as the same god. So on Roman mosaics, when we see Bacchus riding a tiger he is really Shiva, the resurrection god.

Back to myth: when Bacchus returned to Europe the Olympian gods recognized him as their equal. Apollo offered him a job: for nine months of the year Apollo divulged the future to the priests at the oracle of Delphi but for the three winter months, when the vines stood bare, Bacchus made the predictions, which he had learned from the satyrs how to do. The priests of Delphi treated Bacchus as an equal of Apollo, the great sun god, which was recognition indeed.

The Latin Gods: Liber and Bona Dea

Meanwhile, in Italy, Pater Liber, 'the Free Father', was worshipped as the god of wine. He was a fat, good-natured little chap, much less formidable than his slender Greek counterpart. Liber was credited with the discovery of honey: when his disciples made music with cymbals, a new species of insect appeared – the bees had mistaken the music for buzzing. Liber felt sorry for the homeless insects, and stuffed them into a hollow tree. Out of gratitude for their new home, the bees rewarded him with honey.

It was customary, therefore, to sacrifice honey to Liber, or the honey-cakes that bore his name: *libum*. In Latin, *liber* means 'free', so the notion of freedom was linked with him too. On his feast-day, *liberalia* (17 March), everyone had a holiday and sixteen-year-old boys were granted their 'freedom' or citizenship. The Latin word for a libation, *libamen*, also derives from Liber's name. The existence of a Latin wine god, who was separate from the Greek Bacchus, indicates that the Romans had made wine before they came into contact with the Greeks.

At first the Romans were not as lavish in their use of alcohol as the Greeks. The founding father of their city, Romulus, performed his libations with milk. In addition he decreed that wine was forbidden to anyone but free men over the age of thirty-five. Slaves, youths and women were not allowed to touch it.

The women of Rome were not allowed to drink wine. The wife of Egnatius Maetennus drank wine from the vessel and was for that reason bludgeoned to death by her husband. Romulus acquitted him of murder. Fabius Pictor wrote in the Annals that a housewife who had broken open the box holding the keys to the wine cellar was starved to death by her family for that crime. And Cato writes that a woman's closest family had the right to kiss her on the mouth* to find out whether she had been at the wine jug . . .

The jurist Cn. Domitius imposed a fine equivalent to her dowry on a woman who had clearly drunk more wine than she had been medicinally prescribed. For a long time, wine was treated with the greatest thrift.   (Plin. N.H. XIV-89)

In practice women drank wine anyway – even the best families didn't always uphold the law. Neither did the gods set a good example: the goddess Bona Dea (the wife of Faunus, see page 159–60) was an alcoholic. Early in December, but not on any fixed date, the ladies of Rome celebrated her feast-day and men were excluded from the revels. There are no writings by female historians from the period, so we don't know exactly what happened, except that the house was decorated with garlands and the ladies wore hairbands and wreaths. We know that the flesh of a sow was eaten, and that a large vessel was filled with a ceremonial drink. The women called it milk, but many men (such as Juvenal, Sat. II-83) assumed that it was wine.

During the Republic attitudes changed towards wine drinking. It became normal for women to drink wine, and eventually even slaves were allowed to do so – farmers made a cheap wine especially for the latter. When children were given wine as medicine, Liber had finally gained respectability.

Bacchanalia in Rome

Just as mistrust of Liber and wine was fading in Rome around 200 BC, a new wine god arrived to cause havoc: the Greek Bacchus. Only the initiated could take part in the rituals dedicated to him and they were pledged to secrecy. Herodotus wrote about the mysteries of Osiris (alias Bacchus) and Isis (alias Demeter):

* The kissing law: IUS OSCULI.

Figure 3.2

In the evening, in the lake, the Egyptians perform plays about his adventures, which they call mysteries. Although I know still more about how it all occurred, I must remain silent. And I must also keep silent about the initiation ceremony of Demeter . . .

(Her. II-171)

His pious silence has ensured that we will never know what happened during the *bacchanalia*, or at the *orgia*. However, on the walls of the Villa dei Misterii in Pompeii, there are depictions of a Bacchic initiation, and we can make out a few details. The frescoes were drawn as a kind of cartoon strip. In the first picture a girl is coming in with a brown sacrificial cake – or perhaps a piece of pork – cut into slices.

Mystery rituals, such as those dedicated to Demeter, consisted of three parts:

1. *Legómena*, or 'things spoken': prayers were uttered and hymns sung. In the Villa dei Misterii a little boy sings from a papyrus scroll.
2. *Deiknúmena*, or 'things shown': something of sacred significance was displayed, just as priests in the Christian Church hold the bread aloft during the Eucharist, so that everyone can see it. At the mysteries of Ceres, the goddess of agriculture, an ear of corn was shown. In the case of Bacchus a phallus was revealed. In the

Villa dei Misterii we see a girl creeping on her knees as she lifts a corner of the dark blue cloth covering the phallus. This symbol, both sacred and obscene, has led to doubts about the chastity of the Bacchic mysteries.

3. *Drómena*, or 'things done': this last category was kept even more secret than the others. One of the last pictures in the Villa dei Misterii shows a naked girl initiate being whipped in ritual purification. Afterwards she pirouettes, while striking together two small cymbals over her head.

The dance of ecstasy was a significant part of the Bacchic orgy, but it is not clear whether it brought the 'things done' section to its conclusion. Sadly we can only guess, which leads us to think the worst: the word 'orgy' is used nowadays to mean uninhibited group sex, while a 'bacchanal' is over-indulgent revelry. Roman legislators were influenced by the gossip that circulated about the orgies: in 186 BC the Senate forbade the rites. None of this proves that the *bacchantes* actually were hell-raisers, and it should be borne in mind that Christians were rumoured to engage in group sex and to eat children. In any case, Romans did not have to join an underground religion for sex – they had plenty of willing slaves in the privacy of their homes.

Osiris

According to myth, the Egyptian god Osiris was the brother of Isis. He ruled Egypt with his sister, and taught mankind agriculture and oenology. A golden age prevailed until Seth, Isis' and Osiris' evil half-brother, cut Osiris into pieces and scattered parts of his body across the whole of Egypt. Isis gathered them up but was unable to find his penis. She then prepared the body for its resurrection, when Osiris will usher in a new golden age. Until then he rules the dead.

The torment of Osiris points to his significance as wine god and the vine symbolizes him, as it does Bacchus. In autumn it, too, is hacked to pieces, and left apparently dead throughout the winter. In spring it comes back to life. All of the wine gods symbolize destruction/resurrection – Bacchus, Shiva and Osiris.

The Egyptian cult of Isis and Osiris attracted many devotees among the Romans, and Osiris was quickly identified with Bacchus. Many

Roman emperors were initiated into Egyptian rituals: a giant statue of Osiris stood in the palace of Hadrian and Caligula was a fanatical follower of Isis. Yet acceptance in Rome was not so easy for the next wine-and-resurrection god on the list: Jesus Christ.

WINE PRODUCTION

The wine gods have been successful. Many narcotics are now illegal, but the wine gods, whether Christ or Bacchus, have sanctified alcohol consumption, although medical science has categorized it as a danger-ous substance. Pliny himself was astonished by the efforts that went into wine production when its effects were so questionable:

> If we consider the matter carefully, no area of human life is so laborious [as wine production], as though nature had not given us the healthiest of drinks, water, which all animals drink, apart from the fact that we even make our beasts of burden drink wine.*
> So much work, so much toil, so much money is put into wine, and this despite the fact that it perverts the mind and leads to madness. It is the cause of many crimes, and yet it is considered so attractive that much of mankind can see no other reason for living . . .
> (Plin. N.H. XIC-137)

Pliny's criticism of wine consumption did not prevent him writing many books about wine production, which had become fundamental to Roman agriculture. In climates where the vine would not grow, the land was deemed fit only for barbarians. The borders of the Roman Empire, north and south, coincided with zones where the vine was viable.

The Romans did not learn wine-making techniques from the Greeks, but Greece was the centre of viniculture. The most expensive and prestigious wines came from Greece, and Romans planted many Greek vines in their gardens, just as modern Italian farmers often

---

* Some remedies against bovine illnesses required cattle to drink wine.

Figure 3.3 – Crushing grapes

use French varieties. And just as modern Italy produces more wine than France, ancient Italy yielded more than all Greece. However,

> Democritus, who claimed to know all the grape varieties in Greece, was the only one who thought they could be told apart. Everyone else thought them countless.   (Plin. N.H. XIV-20)

Vines were planted in many different ways. In Africa and Gallia Narbonensis (the South of France) they were allowed to creep over the earth, with the grapes lying on the ground like strawberries. These grapes had an unusually thick skin. In Italy the vines were trained upwards along reeds, or along wooden frames. Sometimes two, three or four vines were planted side by side, or in a small circle, so that they supported each other. Some people grew vines up the walls of their houses. Pliny describes villas overgrown on all sides by a single vine, and one ornamental vine over the colonnades in the gardens of Livia in Rome that produced 312 litres of wine every year (Plin. N.H. XIV-II).

The finest method, however, was to allow the vines to grow into the trees, as the wild grape does. Nowadays it would be far too expensive to do this but it was popular with the Romans, who used slave labour to pick the grapes. In Campania the vines grew so high in the poplar trees that those who harvested them were guaranteed the cost of a funeral and a grave in their contracts. Since ancient times vines have grown in elm trees throughout Italy. The chestnut was also popular, because of its sturdiness and ease of pruning, as were the willow, the olive and the ash.

Grapes were harvested in late summer if a light, dry wine was required, and in the autumn for a riper, sweeter wine. In some cases they were left on the vine or dried on reed mats until they became raisins, for raisin wine (*vino passito*). The harvest ended up in a vat where the slaves crushed the grapes, after their feet had been inspected to ensure that they had no wounds. It was of crucial importance that they didn't drop anything into the grapes because, apart from spoiling the flavour, this would have rendered the wine impure for religious purposes. The same was true of grapes from an unpruned vine, or if a man had been hanged somewhere near the vineyard.

As today, the crushed grapes underwent their first fermentation in a large open vat, where they remained for anything from a few days to a few weeks. Then additives might be mixed in to the 'must', such as tree-resin, vinegar or the must of an earlier season, as a fermentation starter. Seawater was sometimes added, not only because it was thought to improve the flavour, but also as a preservative. Unfortunately, though, seawater rendered wine unclean for religious purposes.

Then the must was tapped and sieved. Not all of it was made into wine: various recipes called for must, which is sweeter than wine, and some was boiled down to a syrup, which was the basis of many sauces (see page 148) and also used to sweeten wine. Yeast was made from must. The Romans stored must in wide clay vessels, made watertight with resin, clay and ashes, then buried them in the ground to maintain a constant temperature. The method of maturing wine in wooden barrels was Celtic rather than Roman, but some Celts lived as close to the Empire as northern Italy:

> In the area around the Alps wine is put in wooden barrels, and a construction of tiles is built up around them. In the winter fires are lit to protect them against the worst of the frosts. It was thought impossible but the casks have been known to burst in the cold, leaving the wine standing in a frozen block, something of a miracle, since wine by its nature does not freeze. Usually it is only thickened by the cold.

In warmer climates wine is stored in jars, which are partially or entirely buried in the ground to protect them against the weather. Otherwise the vessels are stored in a roofed structure. One side of the wine cellar, or at least its windows, must face north-east or, failing that, east. Dunghills and tree-roots, especially figs or wild figs, must be kept at a distance, since wine easily absorbs others flavours. Space must be left between the jars to prevent the spreading of infections, to which wine is extremely susceptible.

In addition, the shape of the jars is important; fat-bellied and very broad vessels are not ideal. Immediately after the rising of the Great Dog the jars must be covered with pitch, then washed with seawater, or salted water. They must be sprinkled with ashes from vine-cuttings or white clay, then brushed clean and smoked out with myrrh. The same must be done regularly with the wine cellar itself.

Weak wines are stored in buried jars, but jars with strong wines should be open to the air. The jars must never be filled to the brim, and the inside of the vessel above the level of the wine must be smeared with raisin-wine, or reduced wine mixed with syrup, or with new wine and ground iris. The lids are treated the same way, with the addition of mastic or tar from Bruttia.*

(Plin. N.H. XIV-132)

While the wine was maturing, the lid was removed every so often to check progress and remove undesirable fungi. After a year or more, it was ready. It was sometimes filtered before transferring it to amphorae, the Roman equivalent of bottles. Today bottles usually contain no more than three-quarters of a litre; an amphora held twenty-six litres. It always had two handles for lifting and carrying, and was filled to the neck with wine, then sealed. The date and the producer's name were marked on the outside.

* Southern Italy.

Old Wine

As with bottles, wine matured further in the amphorae, and the longer the better. The Romans enjoyed aged wines: they were not only more delicious than young ones, but thought beneficial to health. They were supposed to be strengthening, to improve the circulation of the blood and give it a deep red colour, aid digestion, ensure a good night's sleep.

Nowadays few wines survive beyond twenty years, and their last years aren't their best. Among the Romans, the price of wines rose dramatically until their twentieth year, after which it began to decline, but there are frequent accounts of thirty-year and even older wines. Did they make more durable wines than we do? Perhaps: short-term profit was less of an issue then than it is now. It is also possible that the Romans enjoyed flavours we would find over-mature. Pliny wrote about a wine from 121 BC, the most famous vintage of classical antiquity. Wine from that year was given the name of Consul Opimius, who had been in power at the time, and was still available in Pliny's time:

> This wine has now lasted for 200 years, but it is coarse and has assumed the thickness of honey, as is the way with very old wines. It cannot be drunk neat, and neither can it be diluted with water, because the bitterness of the fermentation predominates, but we can recommend mixing it in very small quantities with other wines in order to improve them.   (Plin. N.H. XIV-55)

In the time of Caesar this wine already cost eighty *sestertii* per litre. 'How much money we have stored in our wine-cellars!' Pliny exclaims.

Types of Wine

The Romans distinguished between sweet and dry wines, and Pliny identifies four colours:

Albus – white, a light white wine, such as a Moselle

Fulvus – golden yellow, like a heavy Sauterne, or a dessert wine
Sanguineus – blood red, like most young red wines
Niger – black, probably used for aged red wines and red *passito*
  wines

It is not always clear which ancient wines belonged to which colour group, because in literature the colours are mentioned only sporadically. When wines are named, the sole reference is usually to the place of origin.

When Apicius used wine in his recipes, he made no specification as to type, and usually wrote 'wine', or on one occasion 'old wine'. We think of white and red wine as different drinks, with different culinary properties. Once Apicius puts wine into a 'white sauce', from which we may conclude that he uses white wine. On another occasion he writes, 'Add wine to colour,' from which we may also draw our own conclusion. Usually we have to guess.

The number of vine varieties was countless, and the same was true of the wines, but here are some examples:

Albanum, of which there were two kinds, dry and sweet. The wine was matured for fifteen years. Athenaeus, Horace, Pliny, Martial and Columella praise its excellent quality.

Calenum, a favourite wine of the patricians, lighter than Falernum (Ov. IV-xii-14).

Falernum, one of the most famous wines of antiquity, and frequently mentioned in literature. It was best drunk after ageing for ten to twenty years. Any older, it gave the drinker a headache. The wine came in two colours: white and peach (rosé).

Fundanum, a strong wine, which made you drunk quickly (Ath. I-27a). According to Martial, this wine existed in the time of Opimius (Mart. XIII-113).

Massilitanum, a heavy, smoked wine, which, according to Galen, was healthy and delicious. Martial thought it disgusting. He recommends giving it to beggars to poison them (Mart. XIII-123). In addition, it was cheap: Martial remarks that it was not cooled with snow, because the snow was more expensive (Mart. XIV-118).

Nomentanum, a mediocre wine which, according to Martial,

you should not give to your friends, and which was only
drinkable at five years old (Mart. XIII-19 and Ath. I-27b).

Opimianum, not a type of wine but wine from a famous vintage,
named after the consul of the year, Opimius (121 BC).

Sorrentinum, a light wine, drunk young. It was sour, however, and
tasted of earth. It owed its fame principally to the gorgeous
clay drinking bowls that came from the same region and
from which the wine was traditionally drunk. Nowadays
some people like drinking sake because it is served in such
elegant Japanese porcelain (Mart. XIII-110 and Plin. N.H.
XXXV-46).

Spolentinum, a sweet, golden-coloured wine (Ath. 27d), which,
according to Martial, was better than young Falernum (Mart.
XIII-120). It was served mixed with water that had been
boiled then cooled in snow (Plin. N.H. XXXI-40).

Tarentinum, according to Galen, was a wine with a light taste and
low in alcohol. This is surprising when we consider that the
wines which come today from that part of Italy, Puglia, are
among the world's heaviest. Martial thought they were terrific
(Mart. XIII-125)

Trifolinum, a wine comparable to Sorrentinum, because of its
earthy taste. Martial put it seventh on the list of good wines
(Mart. XIII-114), but Pliny thought it suitable only for
plebeians (Plin. N.H. XIV-69).

Additives

Vinology was still relatively primitive. Wine spoiled quickly, and crude
media were often added to correct it. Cloudy wine was cleared with
albumen or chalk. The taste could be 'improved' by smoking it.

Smoked wine is often bitter, and the colour suffers in the process,
but the Romans remedied this by dyeing it with aloe, saffron or
elderberry. It could also be sweetened with reduced must. All kinds
of flavourings were added, such as myrtle, rush-flowers, nard, roses,
violets, lilac flowers, coriander, celery, anis, almonds, pepper, cinnamon, etc.

Some wines were flavoured with resin, like modern-day retsina.
The custom of adding seawater also came from Greece. Heavily

flavoured wine was called *conditum*. Apicius gives two detailed recipes for it, the principal ingredients being pepper and honey. He also gives recipes for absinthe and rose wine:

Absinthe

Apsinthium romanum sic facies; conditi camerini praeceptis utique pro apsinthio cessante. In cuius vicem absenti pontici purgati terendique uniciam, thebaicam dabis, masticis, folii, costi scripulos senos, croco scripulos iii, vini eiusmodi sextarios xviii. Carbones amaritudo non exigit.

Take spices for Camerinian wine, if you have no wormwood. Otherwise: 27g cleaned and chopped wormwood, 1 date, 7g mastic, 7g aromatic leaves, 7g costum, 3g saffron, 10 litres good wine. Charcoal against bitterness is not required.   (Ap. 3)

The best-flavoured wormwood comes from North Africa, but it can also be cultivated in northern climates. In the nineteenth century an extract from this herb was used in absinthe, an anise liqueur, which was popular among fashionable Victorians. It was supposed to cause hallucinations and therefore prohibited, but in retrospect, it seems that its dangers were exaggerated.

Mastic is the resin of the mastic bush *Pistacia lentiscus* and can be found in Asian food stores. 'Aromatic leaves' possibly means plants like bay, citrus and myrtle. Costum is often translated as costmary. Little more is known about it, except that it came from India.

Put the wine and spices, in the quantities suggested by Apicius, into a bottle and leave it for several weeks. The Romans sometimes sieved spiced wines through charcoal to remove bitterness, but absinthe is intended to be bitter.

Rose Wine and Violet Wine

Rosatuum sic facies: folia rosarum, albo sublato, lino inseris et sutilis facias, et vino quam plurimas infundes, ut septem diebus in vino sint. Post septem dies rosam de vino tollis et alias sutiles recentes si similiter

*et tertio facies, et rosam eximis, et vinum colas, et, cum ad bibendum
voles uti, addito melle roasatum conficies. Sane custodito ut rosam a
rore siccam et optimam mittas. Similiter ut supra et de violatum
facies, et eodem modo melle temperabis.*

Rose wine is made like this: lace rose petals, with the white part
removed, on a thread, and immerse in wine for seven days. Then
remove the petals from the wine and put new rose petals in, laced
in the same manner. Do the same thing for a third time and
remove the petals. Sieve the wine, and when you want to drink it
add honey, to get rose wine. Be sure to use only the best roses, and
ensure that they are free from dew. You can make violet wine in
a similar way. Again, flavour with honey.   (Ap. 4)

This recipe requires some interpretation, since Apicius writes
elsewhere that 'as many rose petals as possible' should be used. In all
likelihood the quantity that we could gather from our own gardens
would not have been enough for Apicius. It is possible to make a cheap,
inferior version by mixing rosewater with white wine – one part
rosewater to ten parts wine. Dessert and raisin wines are best suited
to this.

OTHER DRINKS

Aperitif (*mulsum*)

The apéritif of choice was *mulsum*. This was wine to which honey was
added, either during the production process or afterwards. Columella
championed the first method:

The best *mulsum* is made as follows: collect *lixicum* from the press.
Lixicum is grape pulp before it has been completely crushed by
the feet. Use grapes from a vine that has been trained around a
tree, which have been harvested on a dry day.
Take 5 kilograms of the best honey for each 13 litres of must.

Mix well and pour into a wine vessel. Seal it tightly, and have it placed in the wine cellar. If you want to make a larger quantity, add honey in the above proportions.

The vessel is opened after 31 days. The must is filtered and poured into another vat, which is sealed in turn. Then it is placed in the smoke. (Col. R.R. XII 41)

Pliny disagreed: he thought a dry wine should be used and mixed with honey – 'Sweet wine does not mix well with honey' (Plin. N.H. XXII-24,53). His version is easier to imitate.

Mead (*aqua mulsa*)

An older and simpler drink than *mulsum* was *aqua mulsa*, or mead. It was seen as inferior to wine and more suited to the simple honey god, Liber, than to sophisticated Bacchus. Because it did not contain grape juice, just honey and water, it could also be made in the bleak northern provinces, and is still popular in Scandinavia. Mead is made by combining water, honey and yeast and leaving the mixture, like wine, to ferment. Mead has a wonderful golden colour, a high alcohol content and the subtle fragrance of honey, but it lacks the impressive concert of flavours found in wine.

Sweet Wine (*passum*)

Passum is a sweet white raisin wine, to which no honey is added. It is made with half-dried grapes, which contain relatively large amounts of sugar and little juice. The high fructose content ensures a sweeter taste, and more sugar is converted into alcohol – it may reach 18 per cent proof. We know *passum* as 'raisin wine'. In Italy it is sold as *vino passito* (from *uva passita*, a raisin) – the Tuscan Vin Santo is a famous example. Some countries, like modern Greece, use the term 'liqueur wine'. The Romans made it like this:

Collect the first fully ripened grapes. Remove any mildewed or damaged fruits. Stick rakes or poles into the ground, two metres apart. Link them with sticks. Lay reeds over them and spread the

Figure 3.4 – Drinking vessels

grapes out on these in the sun. They should be covered at night to prevent them being covered with dew. Once the grapes have dried out, remove the stalks and put them in a wine vessel. Pour the best possible must over them, so that the grapes are completely covered.

If they are saturated by the sixth day, put them in a basket, and press them in the winepress to extract the *passum*.

(Col. R.R. XII. 39)

After this the *passum* was treated like any other wine. A variant on this method of preparation was to soak raisins in must then press them again. In all the methods described by Columella the grape stalks are removed, which implies that raisin wines were white. Today most raisin wines are white – deep golden, really – but red varieties are produced in Italy and Greece.

Lora

An inferior wine was made with the leftovers of wine production: grape pulp was mixed with water and pressed for a second or third time. This was how slaves made wine for themselves.

Syrups (*defrutum, caroenum* and *sapa*)

Three boiled must syrups, which were alcohol-free. Mixed with water, and sometimes vinegar, they made refreshing drinks for children. They were used chiefly in cooking (see page 148).

Beer (*cerevisia*)

Beer is the oldest alcoholic drink in the world. The Mesopotamians and the Egyptians were the first beer-drinkers of ancient times. The latter brewed it from rye bread crumbled in water, which was left to ferment with date juice, myrtle, cumin, ginger and honey. It was sometimes drunk warm.

Upper-class Romans did not drink beer. It cost half the price of bad wine and, consequently, was not for the sophisticated. In Italy and Gaul beer was made from rye. The Spaniards discovered how beer could be kept under pressure, which was when it acquired a foamy head. Pliny valued the foam for the yeast it contained:

Beer-foam is used by women for cosmetic purposes.

(Plin. N.H. XXII-164)

Hops, which give beer its bitter taste, were not used until the thirteenth century.

Alica

A cheap drink made of coarsely ground spelt or other grain and water, light in alcohol content, not unlike Russian kvass.

Posca

Posca was a refreshing drink made of vinegar and water, popular with travellers. They carried the tangy vinegar in a flask, ready to dilute when they found water. Vinegar has a disinfectant effect, a bonus when the only available water came from an unreliable source. The vinegar was sometimes flavoured with spices and honey. When a Roman soldier gave the crucified Jesus Christ 'vinegar' (posca) to drink, it was not an act of cruelty. Jesus thanked him, and meant it.

Snow

Snow was eaten on its own, and sometimes flavoured with spiced wine and *mulsum*. Melted snow was drunk for its purity, and snow was used in cooking as a cooling agent.

In winter, snow and ice were stored between layers of straw in well-insulated cellars. During spring and summer Romans fetched their ice, in small but rapid horse-drawn carts, from the Penniculus mountain thirty-five kilometres away, as long as it was snow-covered. If there had been a thaw, consumers paid dearly for ice cream: prices went up as summer progressed. Only the rich had their own ice cellars.

Water

Most people drank water from wells or collected rain. Nero had hit upon the idea of boiling it then cooling it in snow, which we would consider a sensible hygiene precaution, but the Romans found this absurd and decadent.

Mineral water was held in high esteem, and some springs became the sites of spas: a bathhouse and often a little town grew up around them. The city of Rome is blessed with six natural springs, but that wasn't enough for an ever-growing populace that bathed every day and demanded fountains on every street corner. Monumental aqueducts were erected to carry water from the mountains into the towns and provide the citizens with an endless supply.

Milk

Milk was drunk by children, but rarely by adults, who might take a cup at breakfast on a doctor's advice or a herbal infusion with milk. In the kitchen, it was used in several desserts, but Roman cuisine was not dairy-oriented. Most milk was made into cheese.

According to Pliny, camel milk was the most delicious kind, and it was drunk diluted with three parts water to one part milk. Only wealthy Romans could afford it. Goat's and sheep's milk were easiest to obtain. Cow's milk was not popular as a drink, but it was well suited to cheese-making. The milk of horses and asses was not only for drinking:

> It is thought that asses' milk contributes something to the white-ness of the female skin. At any rate Nero's wife brought 500 female donkeys with foals with her wherever she went, and soaked her whole body in a bath full of the milk of asses. She believed it smoothed her wrinkles.
>
> (Plin. N.H. XI-xcvi)

Apart from these excesses, milk's primary use was as nourishment for babies, who were not given cow's milk – Athenaeus was horrified that the Scythians (the ancestors of the Russians) did this. If a Roman matron had no wish to press a screaming infant to her breast, or if she produced too little milk, she bought a wet-nurse (*nutrix*). If the woman produced more than necessary, the surplus was sold. Other mothers might buy it, but human milk was considered beneficial to adults and used in all kinds of medicines.

Melca

Melca was a kind of yoghurt, thought to aid digestion. It was made of sheep's and goat's milk. The *Geoponica* (18, 21) describes how the Greeks made it: 'Add some fermented milk to fresh milk to make it sour. Always save some without throwing it away, because if it is all finished you will not be able to make any more.' That is exactly how yoghurt is made today. Apicius suggests serving *melca* with pepper and *garum*, or with coriander and salt.

IV

THE COOK AND HIS CONDIMENTS

THE COOK (*coquus or cocus*)

The Roman matron didn't cook. In all other countries and provinces
a woman's place was in the kitchen, but in Rome cooking was a slave's
job. In theatrical plays most cooks are male, and we know that noble-
men sometimes cooked, as had Homeric heroes.

> I have nothing but condemnation for the table of Achilles, which
> always seemed to be empty. When Ajax and Odysseus came to
> visit, he had nothing prepared in the house, and had to start from
> the beginning by slaughtering and roasting a cow. Once, later on,
> when he wanted to show Priam his hospitality, he jumped up,
> slaughtered a white sheep, chopped it into pieces and roasted it.
> That in itself took up the greater part of the evening.
>
> (Plut. VII-703)

Roman householders sometimes honoured their friends in a
similar fashion. Conservative men, like Cato the Elder, would fetch
vegetables from the garden to cook them in the atrium. On feast days
it was the householder's duty to sacrifice animals. He would then
cut the meat into pieces, roast it on the altar and serve it as dinner. So,
barbecues have always been a male preserve.

Famous gourmets, like Lucullus and Apicius, were a dab hand
with the pots and pans but so too were emperors, like Vitellius
and Heliogabalus. True gourmets found cooking too important to
leave it to slaves:

> Alexis also makes it clear in the play *The Pot* that the art of
> cooking is a fitting occupation for the freeborn. For the cook

Figure 4.1

in that play is far from being a bumpkin. Indeed, the cookery writers Herakleides and Glaucus of Locris also clearly state that the art of cookery should not be left to slaves or even to ordinary freedmen.

(Ath. XIV-661e)

But not everyone had time to cook:

It is said of [the writer] Antogoras: King Antigonus once saw him at army camp wearing a cook's outfit, and in the act of boiling a conger eel, and asked him, 'Do you think Homer would have had time to describe the deeds of Agamemnon if he'd spent all his time cooking conger-eel?'

Antagoras aptly replied, 'Do you think King Agamemnon would have had time to perform his heroic deeds if he had worried about who cooks the conger-eels at his army camp?'

(Plut. XIV-668c)

On special occasions a hired cook came to demonstrate his arts. The plays of Plautus, from the third century BC, feature many commercial cooks. They are independent-minded, humorous figures, with a tendency to boast. As freelance businessmen they sometimes had their own retinue of slaves – kitchen helpers, but also waiters, flautists and dancers – so that they could provide a complete party service. The chef was called the *archimagirus*, or *magirus*, the sous-chef was the *vicarius supra cocos*, and there were other cooks below him. Some rich people owned hundreds of cooks, whom they took with them when they travelled. Others hired additional cooks only for parties. Most cooks, however, were slaves, with all the restrictions that that implied:

A: What have we here? A cook strolling outside the city walls?
B: That's right, if I'd stayed inside the walls I'd never have been able to get a dinner together.
A: Does that mean you've been freed?
B: No, not exactly, but I've been bought by a free colleague, and I'm working for him as a buyer. (Ath. XIV-659c)

Cooks were for sale in the slave market as bakers, grinders, buyers, carvers, chefs and so on. It was a question of finding the right person for the right job. This was no simple matter, because the slaves were in competition with each other:

When buying a cook I have heard all the insults that the cooks hurl at their opponents. Of one they will say he has no sense of refinement, of another that he has terrible taste, another is said to have ruined his tastebuds with his excessive enthusiasm for seasonings: too much salt, too much vinegar, too much nibbling from the various dishes, and the meat is roasted for too long. One is said to be allergic to smoke, another can't stand the fire. After moaning about the fire they move on to the subject of knives. But despite all this the cook that I've bought has made it unscathed through fire and knives. (Ath. XIV-662a)

Heavy demands were made of a cook: the playwright Nicomedes insisted on an understanding of astrology, mathematics, medicine and art (Ath. VII-291a), but he neglected to mention the most important thing of all:

I am a gourmand, and that is the basis of my art. Anyone who cherishes a great love of the ingredients entrusted to him will never spoil them. The cook who places great importance on his own taste will not be bad at his job. You don't make mistakes easily if your tastebuds are clean.

Keep tasting your food as you cook. Not enough salt? Add some more. Does it need anything else? Keep tasting until it's exactly right. Tune the taste like a harp until it's perfectly harmonized.

Then, when everything is in tune with everything else, serve up the whole concert of dishes.   (Ath. VIII-346c)

COOKING

Two opposites are required for cooking, water and fire, and both were to be found in the atrium, where food was prepared from ancient times until the late Republic.

Water

The Romans originally took rainwater from the *impluvium*. However, once aqueducts had been built to bring great quantities of water to Rome, households were increasingly connected to the city water supply. This provided the opportunity for running water in every kitchen, as well as the installation of bathrooms and toilets (*latrinae*). Latrines were often situated next to the kitchen so that kitchen rubbish could be dispatched direct to the sewer, which had been built in the time of the kings.

Less affluent Romans collected water from the fountains on street corners and in squares, which contributed to the health of poor and rich alike: the spring water they supplied was rich in minerals, such as calcium, unlike rainwater. It was a mixed blessing, though, because the pipes were made of lead, and lead poisoning soared among Rome's inhabitants (see also page 148).

Fire

The lady of the house, the *matrona*, was responsible for the hearth. She did not have to cook, but it was seen as her duty to throw a log on the fire. The custom dated back to prehistoric times. Early campfires protected women and children against wolves while the men were out hunting and it was the woman's task to keep the fire alight: if it went out the whole group might succumb to cold, hunger or the depredations of wild animals.

Concern with fire was symbolized by the goddess Vesta, the protector of the family. In Rome the temple of Vesta stood in the middle of the old forum. It was here that the Vestal Virgins lived – priestesses who kept alight the holy eternal flame of the city. If a housewife had let her fire go out, she might ask the virgins for a light. The holy fire of the Vestals was primarily symbolic, because in time fire and hot water became available everywhere (in the *tabernae carbonariae* and the *thermopolia.*

The city had the legal power to punish its citizens' misdemeanours with *interdictio ignis et aquae*, which meant that no one could give them fire or water – a form of death sentence. Later, tinder-boxes and, finally, matches were invented.

Fire was considered sacred, and it was thought sinful to extinguish it:

> Caerenius was of the opinion that the ancestors refused to extinguish fires out of religious conviction, because of their relation to the Holy Eternal Flame.
>
> Like mankind, fire can die in two ways. It can die by violent means, if doused, and by natural means. The Holy Fire was protected against both types of death. It was continuously guarded and tended. A normal fire was allowed to go out by itself . . .
>
> 'For nothing,' he went on, 'so closely resembles a living being as does fire. It runs by itself and finds its own food. Its radiance, like that of the mind, casts light everywhere and clarifies everything. Particularly when it is being extinguished we see something resembling the force of life. It sputters against

the water and resists being doused, like a living creature suffering an act of aggression.'

(Plut. IX-VII, 4)

As though fire itself were a living deity, offerings were made to it. The cook, dependent on the blazing god, threw a little of his cooking into the flames to satisfy the fire and prevent it claiming the food.

That is why Hesiod rightly forbids the serving of bread or meat from unconsecrated pans. We must throw a little food into the fire as thanks for the service that the fire has given us.

(Plut. IX-VII, 4)

The Kitchen

The domestic fire burned on the *focus* (see page 52). Portable stoves and ovens were also in use. Water pots were built into some, and grills were laid on others so that meat and vegetables could be cooked over them, as on a barbecue. This kind of oven was traditionally placed in the atrium, but even when Roman houses were equipped with a separate kitchen, portable ovens were used in the dining room.

In Pompeii (AD 79), most houses had separate kitchens, many of which were no larger than a few square metres. Larger kitchens have also been excavated, such as that in the Villa dei Misterii, which covers an area of nine metres by twelve.

Several kitchens in Pompeii were roofless, more like courtyards than rooms. Open to the sky, they were light and the smoke was not a major nuisance. A little wooden shed was built over the oven to shield the fire against rain. Other Pompeiian kitchens probably had roofs, but no chimneys. At best there may have been a high window or a hole in the roof to provide ventilation. The ancients used smoke-free charcoal, but some of those kitchens must have been appallingly smoky. The food hanging in kitchens such as these must have tasted smoky, which, fortunately, appealed to the Romans.

The Stove

Every kitchen had a solid built-in stove made of cement or clay, also called a *focus*. A *camminus* was a stove with a chimney above it. The stove consisted of a square structure between 1.10 m and 1.30 m high, and about 1.20 m deep. They varied more in length (the oven in the Villa dei Misterii is 2.40 m long). Wood and charcoal, stored in a shed, were burned on the *focus* barbecue fashion.

Unlike a barbecue, however, no grill was placed above the embers. Instead, each pan was placed on the flames on an individual tripod. Grills (*retiacula*) were generally no larger than 25 cm square. They had handles and little feet, so that they could be placed above the hot coals.

The *focus* was large enough for different kinds of fire: licking flames, glowing coals and hot ashes.

Fierce flames were for searing meat, which was exposed to the side of the flame, and for roasting whole animals and hams on a spit, again to the side of the flame, never above it. Fierce flames heated cold liquids quickly, and were necessary for stir-frying.

As on the modern barbecue, glowing cinders were the most versatile heat source. Delicate pieces of fish, meat and vegetables were cooked on metal grills directly over the heat. The Romans also put hot cinders under pans for long boiling and stewing.

Hot ash was used in many ways. Roman stoves were full of it. It could be used to smother fire when it was burning too fiercely. Many dishes were buried in ash to cook slowly. Vegetables and eggs were sometimes cooked in ashes – ash eggs were especially popular.

The Romans also adjusted oven and stove temperatures by changing the height of the pan over the fire. Some pans had legs, others were placed on tripods of varying heights. Apicius used a simmering system: he brought a dish to the boil, removed it from the fire to cool, then put it back to return it to the boil. He writes: 'Bring to the boil two or three times.' The principle of the bain-marie was also employed: many pans fitted into other pots so that food could be kept warm above boiling water.

The spit (*veru*) came in all sizes, from small skewers on which pieces of meat, vegetables or a chicken were impaled to poles for full-grown pigs.

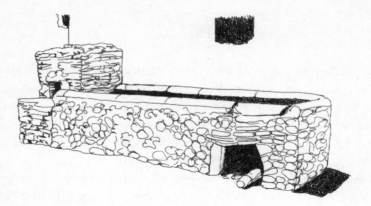

Figure 4.2 – Oven and furnace at the Villa dei Misterii

The Oven

Many kitchens had an oven, *furnus*, sometimes called a *fornax*. Some, like the kitchen in the Villa dei Misterii, had two. The oven consisted of a square or dome-shaped hollow construction of brick or stone, with a flat floor, often made of granite, sometimes lava. It was filled with dry twigs then lit. When the fire was spent, the glowing embers were swept aside. The first heat of the glowing oven was suitable for baking unleavened or thin breads. Pizzas are still cooked in this way, and this type of oven is still considered best for baking top-quality bread. Thin breads go in first, then large round loaves go in, or meat dishes, and the door is closed. After an hour or so, these are removed, but the oven is still hot, so finer pastries follow, then dishes that require the least heat, such as meringues.

Cooking Equipment

On the wall of the Roman kitchen there were hooks and chains for hanging equipment like knives and choppers, meat forks, soup spoons, sieves, graters, spits, tongs, cheese-slicers, nutcrackers, measuring jugs, pâté moulds and all kinds of pots and pans, such as:

> the *pultarius*, the stewing pot, for *puls*
> the *caccabus*, a pot used for simmering

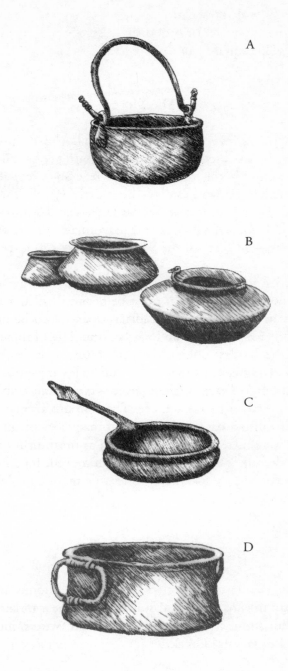

Figure 4.3 – Pans A: *pultarius*; B: *caccabus*; C: *padella*; D: *patina*

the *padella*, a shallow pan
the *patina*, a circular or oval dish
the *angulis*, a square pan

The Mortar

The mortar (*mortarium*) occupied a prominent place in kitchens and restaurants, and was used not only to grind salt, pepper and hard spices but also to pound herbs into pastes and vegetables to pulp. Meat and fish were mashed and minced in the mortar for all kinds of dishes, such as terrines and meatballs. Sauces were blended in it too. You can emulsify and blend vinaigrettes and mayonnaise in a mortar, without any whipping – in fact, all the work of modern food-processors and blenders!

The order in which ingredients are put into the mortar is of some relevance. Anything that must be ground to a fine powder then sieved goes in first, when the mortar is dry – coriander seed with bits of husk, cumin, fennel and cardamom. Then follow the smallest seeds and the hardest spices, such as lovage, rue, rocket, mustard, poppy and fenugreek. Dried herbs, the stalks removed, follow, and then sturdier ingredients, such as garlic – coarse salt helps to reduce it and other vegetables to a fine paste. The Romans also used the mortar to crush nuts into a paste as the base of many sauces, and dried fruit. The pastes were mixed with liquids, such as broth or brine, vinegar or wine, water or oil or a combination, to make sauces.

MEDICINAL THEORY

The culinary uses of herbs and spices cannot be separated from their medicinal functions. The Romans dealt with two important medical traditions: Roman and Greek.

Roman Medicinal Theory

Roman remedies were based not on scientific research but on centuries of experience, passed from father to son.

The head of the household, the paterfamilias, was also the doctor and the priest for the family, which included the slaves, and these two functions blended into each other. Some aspects of this style of medicine resemble the magic of a witch-doctor rather than the science of a doctor. Here are some remedies from Cato:

> 149. To prevent blisters when travelling, hold a twig of worm-wood beneath the anus.
> 150. If a limb has become dislodged from its socket, it can be healed with this spell: take a piece of green reed and split it lengthwise. Have two men to hold it against the injured hip and sing, 'Motas uaeata daries dardares astataries dissunapiter'* while moving the reeds towards each other. Wave a knife over them. Where the reeds meet, grab them by hand and cut them off to the right and left. If these pieces are held to the broken or dislocated limb, it will surely cure. But be sure to sing, every day, the following: 'Huat huat huat istasis tarsis ardannadou dannaustra.'†
>
> (Cat. R.R. CLX)

Sometimes the magic prescriptions seem reasonable. Romans deemed that a medicine that fell on the ground lost its potency, which isn't far removed from our own notions of hygiene. Sometimes the need for spiritual purity took precedence over practical hygiene:

> If a cow falls ill, give it a raw chicken egg to eat, and make sure that it swallows it whole. The following day, grind the white part of a leek with a quarter of a litre of wine. Make sure that the cow drinks it all up. The grinding must be done standing up, and the ox has to be fed from a wooden cup. The ox itself and those who administer the medicine must all have fasted.   (Cat. R.R. LXXI)

---

* Untranslatable magic spells.
† Ditto.

It is hard to see why the doctor should fast for the healing of a cow. For a priest, however, fasting is a normal route to spiritual purity.

Other remedies had a clear practical, rather than religious, function, such as this cure for constipation:

> The patient must eat no dinner. The following morning grind 4g incense, 4g reduced honey and a pint of oregano wine. This is given to the fasting man. For a child, regardless of age, use 2g and half a pint of wine. Make the patient climb a pillar ten times and jump down again. After that, make him go for a walk.
>
> (Cat. R.R. CXXVII)

Cato the Elder was a perfect example of a paterfamilias who knew everything and had no need of Greek doctors. He had learnt it all from his father, traditional knowledge that did not follow a rational system.

Pliny the Elder, who lived some two centuries later, had a great deal of sympathy for Cato. He, too, liked to collect his medicines from his own garden. He questioned the wisdom of doctors, who were believed to have death and torture on their consciences and against whom there was little legal protection. Nevertheless, in Pliny's day Greek medicine had become widely accepted as the best available.

Pliny wrote a wide-ranging work in which he listed all the healing plants. Although he was clearly influenced by Greek science, many of his remedies, like Cato's, drew on Roman traditions. He believed that certain forms of scrofula could be cured by touching the hand of someone who had died prematurely. He advised applying mouse droppings to the bladder of those who had difficulty in urinating. He fed his patients hedgehog meat, baked grasshopper and millipede. His comments on diet are more acceptable:

> Simple food is best for humans. An accumulation of different flavours is unhealthy and even more harmful than the sauces we tend to eat. It is difficult to digest all that spicing, all those innovations, all that artistic originality . . .
>
> Sweet and fatty foods make people fat, but dry, lean, cold food helps one shed that fat again . . . In any case, no one dies after seven days of starvation. Strong people will not die after twelve days, or more. Man is the only animal to suffer from such an insatiable hunger and an unconquerable desire to eat.
>
> (Plin. N.H. XI-CXVII-282)

Greek Medicine

Greek medicine was not based on magic but on all-encompassing rational theories. The Greeks had established links between herbs, illnesses, planets and the cosmos.

The Humours

ELEMENT	TASTE	TEMPERATURE	HUMOUR	STAR-SIGN	GOD
fire	bitter	warm and dry	*choleric* (yellow gall)	Aries Leo Sagittarius	Mars Jupiter Vulcanus
earth	sour	cold and dry	*melancholic* (black gall)	Taurus Virgo Capricorn	Saturnus Pluto
air	salt	warm and moist	*sanguine* (blood)	Gemini Libra Aquarius	Mercurius Apollo Sol
water	sweet	cold and moist	*phlegmatic* (mucus)	Cancer Scorpio Pisces	Venus Neptunus Luna

The founder of Greek medicine, and therefore of all scientific medicine, was Hippocrates (fifth century BC). He was a priest in the service of Aesculapius, the god of healing, around whose temples a kind of spa had developed, where people sought cures with rest, therapy, healthy food and warm or cold baths. Hippocrates was something of a rebel among priests: he wanted to divorce medicine from religion and criticized many so-called cures.

In those days snake bite was 'healed' by rubbing the wound with the excrement of a boar and filling the patient's nose with wine. Hippocrates, however, preferred to use as little medicine as possible, and encouraged patients to recover on their own strength. The doctor merely prescribed the healthy conditions in which the restorative power of nature was optimized.

Hippocrates believed that the life force, or soul, strove for good physical balance, and that illness meant that the balance was disturbed. He called the life force *pneuma* (*spiritus* in Latin), and distinguished three kinds:

1. Life (*spiritus naturalis*)
2. Instinct (*spiritus vitalis*)
3. Consciousness (*spiritus animalis* or *anima*)

These three elements were supposed to flow through animals, humans and gods. The heart pumped the soul through the body. Hippocrates was not aware that it had anything to do with the circulation of the blood. He saw the heart as an organ of the spirit – and today the heart remains our symbol for feelings and emotions.

According to Hippocrates, four fluids flowed through the body. Each had certain qualities, or 'humours':

1. Yellow gall (*chol*), active fluid that dissipates poisons (male)
2. Black gall (*melan chol*), thick fluid that slows down the body (old)
3. Blood (*sanguis*), fluid that promotes growth (young)
4. Mucus (*flegma*), nutritional fluid (female)

Like the life force, the humours had to be in equilibrium with each other. A doctor might encourage this by prescribing baths, because each humour had its own temperature. A phlegmatic humour, for example, was seen as cold and wet. Someone who was phlegmatic might therefore take a sauna, which provided hot, dry air.

The cook and the pharmacist could influence the humours with food and herbs. All plants had their own qualities: oak was melancholic, ivy was sanguine, peppermint phlegmatic and stinging-nettle choleric. Therefore a stinging-nettle could dissipate poison.

The taste of food was also important. Sweetness was seen as nourishing and phlegmatic, so sweet dishes were given to children and pregnant women. Salt was good for the blood and recovering wounds. Sourness was cold, dry and melancholic, so sour dishes were used to reduce fevers, or as tranquillizers. Spices and toxins like wine were called 'bitter': they could increase the energy of a listless person. Old people with 'thick blood' were often diagnosed as 'melancholic', and wine was prescribed.

Any cook would have known the significance of the tastes and in the design of his meals he tried to achieve a balance between all of the elements. Salty and tangy flavours predominated in the starters, to whet the appetite and set the saliva flowing, while sweetness, a rich conclusion to the meal, was dominant in the dessert. Peppered snacks, spicy enough to be tasted by the inebriated, were served at the carousal. In the main course all the tastes were brought together, sweet, salt, sour and bitter, in almost equal measures. This kind of balance was thought both delicious and healthy.

The theory of the four humours remained the basis of medical science throughout the Byzantine empire. In the Middle Ages it was appropriated by Arabs and Europeans and survived into the eighteenth century. Today it has made a comeback in the herbal theories of various alternative healing systems.

FLAVOURS – SOUR

To increase the piquancy, or sourness, of a dish, we add vinegar, lemon juice or yoghurt. The Romans were familiar with yoghurt (see *Melca*, page 124): it was eaten as a dessert, but not used in sauces.

Citrus

The early Romans didn't use lemon juice, although the wild citrus tree was native to the region. The fruit looks like the lemon but is bitter and has a thick peel. The juicy lemons that we know today were not developed until the third century AD. Later Romans were surprised to learn that their ancestors were unfamiliar with the lemon (Ath. III-83f).

Early Romans used citrus juice as a mouthwash, and also, because it was so sour, to strengthen vinegar. In cooking, the leaves of the citrus tree, used like bay leaves, were more popular than the fruit.

Vinegar

A heavy, popular vinegar was made from figs, but most kinds came from grapes. The Romans produced large quantities of wine, and hence vinegar. Good wine makes good vinegar; bad wine makes bad vinegar. Columella describes different methods of preparing it:

> How to make vinegar from a weak wine: take 27 litres of wine and grind 3 ounces of yeast, 80 grams of dried figs and ½ litre of (sea) salt. Rub well, and add half a pint of honey dissolved in vinegar. Add this mixture to the above quantity of wine.
>
> Some people add 4 pints of roasted barley and forty hot walnuts and fresh mint to the same quantity of wine.
>
> Others heat lumps of iron until they are red-hot, and throw these into the wine. Then they remove the iron, set five or six pine-cones alight and throw them ablaze into the wine. Others do the same with burning fir cones.   (Col. R.R. XII-V)

The first method seems less strange than the rest. Salt, figs and honey provide flavour and feed the wine. The yeast is added to start fermentation, although it seems superfluous, since the required bacteria culture is already present in the added vinegar. The use of fire is mysterious: the quantity of burned material is scarcely enough to leave a smoky taste. Perhaps this was some kind of spiritual sterilization. In any case, people were aware of the sterilizing properties of vinegar once the process of acidification was complete. Soldiers and travellers always carried vinegar to purify water (see *Posca*, page 122). Wounds were washed clean with it; it was used to soothe insect bites. Pliny gives a long list of applications:

> If drunk, it drives away sickness and suppresses hiccups. The scent helps against sneezing. It has cooling properties if held in the mouth during a hot bath. If drunk with water, it is good for the stomach of recuperating patients. The gargling of vinegar and water is good against sunstroke. It is also very healthy as an eye-bath.   (Plin. N.H. XXIII-xxvii)

Et cetera, et cetera. Pliny goes on to observe that vinegar is so powerful it can split rocks where attempts with fire have failed and, if poured on the ground, causes the earth to seethe. Powerful stuff indeed. He does not neglect to mention that there is no better sauce for flavouring food. If the vinegar was too sharp, it could be blended with toasted breadcrumbs or cumin to make it less so. According to Pliny, salt had the same effect.

FLAVOURS – SALT

By our standards, the Romans consumed a great deal of salt, partly because food was preserved in it. In addition to this, or perhaps because of it, the Romans loved salty food. Apicius cooks 'Suckling-pig à la Trajan' in a pot with its own weight of salt.

If we measure salt consumption by the amount Cato gave to his slaves (16 pints per year), it amounts to about 20 grams per day, or more if the salt crystals were finer than coarse sea salt. It seems unlikely that a slave would have eaten that amount. Perhaps he was allowed to exchange or sell part of it. Salt probably served as a kind of pocket-money. Originally magistrates were paid in salt – *sal* in Latin, hence our word 'salary'.

Salt had always been considered sacred. The master of the house kept it in a silver salt-pot (the *salinum*), which he used to banish the spirits that spoilt food or caused it to rot. The exorcism appeared to work for salt indeed prevented decay. For that reason everything offered to the gods had first to be strewn with salt. The Romans mixed spelt flour with salt to make *mola salsa* and all sacrificial animals were dusted with this mixture before slaughter.

Simple offerings might consist of bread or cake, but salt had to be present. This was not only true of the Romans for the Jewish and Christian Bible decrees:

> And every oblation of thy meat offering shalt thou season with salt; neither shalt thou suffer the salt of the covenant of thy God to be lacking from thy meat offering: with all thine offerings thou shalt offer salt.
>
> (Leviticus 2:13)

Salt for consumption was available in several forms. Sea salt was popular, but there were also salt mines inland. Each type had its own market value. According to Pliny, only *sal tarentinus* was pure white. A golden-coloured salt came from Cappadocia, and had a magnificent aroma. Darker varieties had been dried on wood and absorbed its flavour. The most delicious salt was obtained by drying fish sauce. Salt was also flavoured with herbs, or dyed with saffron (Col. II 131).

Brine (*muria*)

Brine was indispensable for salting cheese, olives and ham. Rainwater was poured into a large vessel, then a basket was placed in it and coarse sea salt added until the water was saturated and the crystals ceased to dissolve. Then the basket was removed and the vessel placed in the sun to remove mustiness and provide a 'good fragrance'.

Another method was to mix salt with water then drop in some cheese or a boiled egg. If it floated, the brine was salty enough. Although it was simple enough to make, not everyone made brine at home: it was available commercially from many different countries.

Seawater (*aqua marina*)

Apicius cooked ham from the wild boar in seawater. Centuries before, Cato had left an account of how seawater should be prepared for cooking:

> Fetch 25 litres of seawater from the deep sea, where no fresh water flows into it. Grind 0.7 kilo sea salt finely. Add as much of this to the seawater (stirring with a stick) until a boiled hen's egg floats in it. At that point add no further salt. Into this pour 7.2 litres of old wine from Aminoea, or diluted white wine. Pour it into a jug treated with resin. Seal the jug.   (Cat. R. R. 106)

Fish Sauce (*garum*)

Garum was a highly salted fish sauce, comparable with and related to soy sauce, made from fermented fish. Rotten fish smells disgusting and, in ancient Rome, *garum* factories stank. That ancient Romans used *garum* in nearly every dish gave later historians the impression that Roman cuisine must have been revolting. However, the anchovies we eat today are fermented, and a variety of *garum* is still eaten in Italy, *collata*. It is a by-product of the anchovy factories along the coast of Amalfi. In the Far East the ancient sauce is still popular: in Thailand it is called *nam pla*, in Cambodia *tuk trey*, and in Vietnam *nuos nam*. It is used in the same way as soy sauce or *garum*.

A similar fish sauce, *gyoshô*, used to exist in Japan, but it has now become as obscure as *garum* in Europe. Its vegetarian counterpart, soy sauce, ousted it, under the influence of Buddhism.

In 1908 the Japanese scientist Kikunae Ikada discovered what makes these sauces so popular. The Chinese and Japanese recognize not four but five flavours. In search of the fifth, Ikada isolated monosodium glutamate, which he identified in fermented products and observed its taste-enhancing effect. Glutamate is an amino acid precipitated by the process of decay. We now know why the Romans were so fond of *garum*: it contains a high level of glutamate. The substance is naturally present in soy sauce, miso products and fermented fish, but is also added to stock cubes for soups and sauces.

Roman *garum* was prepared in various ways. The *Geoponica* (a late Roman collection of ancient manuscripts on agriculture) describes four methods:

> *Garum*, also called liquamen, is made as follows: fish-guts are placed in a vessel and salted.

> 1) Take small fishes: chiefly *atherinae*,* or anchovies, or any kind of small fish. Salt them all and leave to mature in the sun, but turn regularly. When they have completely fermented in the sun, *garum* is extracted in the following way. Place a deep, fine-woven basket in a vessel and pour in the fish. Press the *garum* out of the basket. Catch the fluid that escapes from the

---

* Untranslatable.

basket. This is called *liquamen*. What remains in the basket is called *alex*.*

2)   The Bithyri make it as follows: they select anchovies, or whatever is available, small fish or larger, anchovies, or mackerel, or *bonito*, or even *alex*, in whatever combination. They place these in a vat, which usually also contains flour; to every nine litres of fish they add one litre of salt, then mix the fish with the salt. This is left to rest for one night. Then they put it into a clay pot, which they leave open in the sun for two or three months, stirring occasionally with a stick. Only then is the lid placed on top. Some people add one litre of old wine to each half-litre of fish.

3)   If you prefer to make *garum* for immediate use, not by leaving it in the sun but by boiling it, this is done as follows: take brine, carefully prepared, and test it by floating an egg in it; if it sinks the brine is not salty enough. Pour the brine and the fish into a new clay pot, add some oregano and put it on a very high flame until it boils, and cook for a while (some people add *sapa* at this point). Then leave to cool and filter several times until clear. Then replace in the jar and seal.

4)   The best *garum*, called *haimation*, is made as follows: take the innards of a tuna, with the gills, the juice and the blood, and scatter with salt. Place everything in a vessel. After about two months pierce the vessel and the *garum* that flows from it is called *haimation*.   (*Geoponica*, XX, 46)

There were many more kinds of *garum* (and *allec*) than those listed above. Spanish *garum* was particularly famous, but *garum* factories were found in every outpost of empire. The sauce was made from prawns, sardines, mackerel, anchovies, tuna, salmon, red mullet and oysters among other sea creatures. It was sometimes flavoured with herbs (like the oregano mentioned above) and spices. It was also mixed with wine or vinegar.

There was even a kosher version, *garum castimoniarum*. *Garum scombri* was made with mackerel, roe and blood. Apicius' *garum* was made with expensive red mullet livers. But the most famous of all

---

*   Or *hallec*, or *allec*.

was the *garum sociorum*, made of fish drowned in *garum*. Its name means '*garum* of companions'.

'Nowadays a *garum* of mackerel from the fisheries of Carthage is the most highly prized. It is called *sociorum*: 1000 HS are paid for 6 litres of it. Hardly any other liquid commands such prices, apart from perfume.'

(Plin. N.H. XXXI-xliii)

This was indeed a considerable price, given that the same quantity of Falernian wine, the Châteauneuf du Pape of its day, cost only 60 HS. The Romans took their *garum* seriously, and its quality was clearly of enormous importance. That makes it difficult for us to assess Roman cuisine properly. Nowadays the range of *garum* is narrow, despite the array of fish sauces from the Far East. The best Roman brands, such as *sociorum*, no longer exist. Consequently *garum* is one of the most problematic ingredients in the evaluation of Roman recipes.

Liquamen

Liquamen is another word for *garum*. J. D. Vehling, who made a pioneering translation of Apicius in 1926, denies this, believing that *liquamen* had a broader meaning. He consistently translated it as 'stock' because Apicius occasionally writes 'boil in *liquamen*'. Vehling could not imagine that this might refer to super-salty *garum*. It is possible, however, that Apicius meant a solution of *garum* in water. Apart from this, some kinds of *garum* were mixed with wine and thus were considerably less salty. Also, if pigs are boiled in salty seawater, why not in salty *garum*? Above all, the *Geoponica* clearly states: '*Garum*, sometimes called *liquamen*.'

Allec

A by-product of *garum*, as described on page 143–5 in the *Geoponica*. It was cheaper, and used by the poor in place of *garum*. In Pliny's time *allec* was made from anchovies, which he does not consider fit for any other purpose. *Allec* is something like English anchovy sauce, or Italian anchovy paste.

Apart from cheap *allec* made from anchovies, there were also expensive kinds, made from mullet livers, sea anemone, or sea-urchin roe.

Salsamentum

Salsamentum or *salsa* originally meant whole salted fishes, which were eaten as a starter. Gradually all salted foods became known as *salsa*. *Salsa* is also the root of the word 'sauce'.

FLAVOURS – SWEET

The Roman love of honey has often been mocked. In Apicius, we often find it used with meat, vegetables and fish as well as in desserts. Apicius lists thirty-four sauces for fish, of which only two are entirely savoury: honey, syrup or preserved fruit is added to the rest.

Of the four flavours we distinguish, sweet is the most popular. Animals, children and gods love sweetness, so why should adults pretend to outgrow it? Some might turn up their noses at a sauce that contains a pinch of sugar, but many a cook knows it gives a lift to many savoury dishes. Sometimes even the French combine salty dishes with sweet flavours – ham with honey, or cheese with fruit, for example. The Romans used sweet tastes to counter overpowering saltiness. Apicius writes:

If it is too sweet, add *garum*. If it is too salty, add syrup.

Honey (*mel*)

Bees make honey from flowers, and honey was seen by the Romans as a gift from heaven, closely related to the nectar drunk on Mount Olympus.

One Greek myth has it that Jupiter transformed the lovely Melissa into the first bee. According to another, the bee is descended from the horse-fly, which was ennobled with the help of the sun.

There was disagreement among the Romans about the reproduction of bees. Some thought that bees were able to reproduce, while others believed they were born from rotting beef. Still others were convinced that they came into being in both ways, or that bees were born from flowers. That the queen in each swarm is the mother of all its members was not discovered until the seventeenth century. In Rome one could buy bees, receive them as presents or plunder them from newly conquered territories. A beehive could not be carried on a cart over long distances because it wouldn't survive the jolts. Instead a slave carried it carefully by night.

You could also steal bees from nature. Country folk had a clever way of doing this: the peasant would close off one end of a hollow reed and pour in some honey, then place it near a spring where bees came to drink. When bees had crept into the reed, attracted by the honey, he closed off the opening with a finger. Then he allowed a single bee to escape and followed it on foot for as long as he could. Once he was sure of his trail, he let a second bee escape, continuing until he found the bees' nest. If they lived in a hollow tree, he felled it, wrapped it in cloths and carried it back to his home.

Every farm had a few beehives, made of clay, tree-bark, woven twigs or broom, for the pollination of fruit trees and vegetables. Some farms specialized in honey production, and plants were grown for the benefit of the bees rather than their owner. Honey farmers planted roses, thyme, rosemary, oregano, savory, basil, poppy, lilies, saffron, celery, beans, lentils, peas, ivy and clovers, such as alfalfa, to keep their bees supplied with nectar. They also planted trees, such as lime, peach, almond, oak and pine for aromatic nectar. Honey from farms that grew mostly vegetables was considered inferior:

> One flower results in a thin honey, like skirret, another in a thick honey, like rosemary. While the fig supplies poor honey, a good quality comes from alfalfa, and the best from thyme.
>
> (Varr. R.R. III-xvi, 26)

At the market, honey cost about the same as olive oil. The two products were divided between similar price-ranges: just as oil is available from the first and second pressings, and so on, honey that ran freely from the honeycomb was the most expensive.

Unlike many other ingredients of Roman cuisine, we know what their honey tasted like because bees still produce it exactly as they always have.

Syrup (*defrutum*)

Defrutum was a syrup, made from must, and was not the same as the grape-juice syrup we can buy today, although it makes an adequate substitute. Neither was it the full-bodied, savoury residue from reduced wine, as used in the kitchens of modern French restaurants (another delicious substitute). It was obtained by slowly reducing a quantity of must until it had the thick viscosity of treacle, which is how Palladius describes it; other authors suggest that it was thinner. According to Varro and Columella the must had to be boiled down to a third of its original quantity, but Pliny stipulated half.

Traditionally must was boiled down in lead pans, but lead is poisonous, and the slow boiling process dissolved a great deal of the metal into the syrup. An abnormally high level of lead has been found in the bones of Romans and some have suggested that the Roman Empire collapsed due to lead poisoning either from these pans or, as mentioned above, from Roman water pipes. A symptom of it is a declining sense of taste, which may be why the Romans used such strong flavourings.

Caroenum

Caroenum resembles *defrutum* in that it is sometimes prepared from must but, according to Palladium, it was reduced to only two-thirds of its original quantity. Some commentators describe *caroenum* as reduced wine rather than reduced must: the word *caroenum* derives from the Greek word for wine, '*oinos*'. One major culinary difference between must and wine is that the former is sweet, while the latter is not.

Sapa

According to Palladium, *sapa* is also made from must, which is not reduced to the same extent as *defrutum*, but more so than *caroenum*, to a third of its original volume – which is what Varro and Columella describe as '*defrutum*'. Consequently the difference between *sapa* and *defrutum* is not entirely clear, especially since other authors refer to the syrupy nature of *sapa*, a characteristic of *defrutum*. If we keep to Palladium's instructions for clarity's sake, we can differentiate the three types as follows:

sapa	=	one-third reduction
caroenum	=	two-thirds reduction
defrutum	=	syrup

We can assume that all three were made from red wine, because Apicius uses them to colour dishes. Palladium also remarks that plums should be added when boiling down *sapa*, and the fire stoked with fig-wood.

Fruit (*poma*)

Many of Apicius' sauces include a finely ground paste of dried fruit to add a sweet note, and to bind sauces. Dates and plums were used more frequently, then figs and raisins.

Sugar (*saccharon*)

Sugar was almost unknown. Now and then a ship loaded with sugar cane pulled into harbour, but the Romans failed to see its culinary potential:

> Sugar is made in Arabia as well, but Indian sugar is better. It is a kind of honey found in cane, white as gum, and it crunches between the teeth. It comes in lumps the size of a hazelnut. Sugar is used only for medical purposes.　　　　(Plin. N.H. XII-xvii)

FLAVOURS – BITTER

Bitter is not the most popular taste. A cook seldom uses flavourings to intensify bitterness. If anything he masks and softens it. One famous exception to this, of course, was the blood soup of the Spartans.

The Latin word for 'bitterness' is *amaritudo*, but the same word also meant the 'sharpness' or 'heat' of spices, which was highly esteemed: cooks were liberal in their use of hot spices. Apicius noted the herbs and spices that a Roman larder should contain.

List of the spices that one must have in the house that nothing may be wanting:

SPICES	SEEDS	DRY HERBS
saffron	poppy	laser root
pepper	rue	mint
ginger	rue berries	catmint
laser	laurel berries	sage
aromatic leaves	aniseed	cypress
myrtle berries	celery	oregano
costmary	fennel	juniper leaves
chervil	lovage	shallots
lemon grass	rocket	thyme
cardamom	coriander	coriander
spikenard	cumin	Spanish camomile
	dill	lemon leaf
	parsley	parsnip
	caraway	Ascalonian shallots
	sesame	dill
		garlic
		elderberry
		Cyprian rush
		silphium

(Ap. Excerpta 1)

The list is not complete: savory, mustard and fenugreek are not mentioned, although they appear regularly in recipes. Also absent are herbs that are only used fresh, and therefore not kept in the larder. The number of herbs named in Latin literature is so enormous that it would be impossible to mention them all. In the following section only the most commonly used herbs are described, more or less in order of the frequency with which they are used.

HERBS

Lovage (*ligusticum, levisticum*)

As we couple pepper automatically with salt, Apicius mentions it, almost automatically, with lovage. Lovage has a pronounced taste that gave every dish a typical Roman note.

Lovage is easily grown, even in harsh climates. It is curious that it has fallen into disuse in Italy. Its place has been taken by parsley and celery leaves, which are related to it but have a milder flavour. Apicius does not specify whether the root, the leaf or the seed should be used. All three are possible, but in all likelihood the seed was used most frequently, since Apicius nearly always mentions it in conjunction with pepper.

Cumin (*cumminum*)

After pepper and lovage, cumin seed was one of the most used spices. It is often briefly roasted in an oven or a dry pan before being ground to a powder. It is very popular in Asian and Middle Eastern cuisine, but has disappeared from Italian cooking.

These days, cumin is used primarily as a seed, but the green leaves are also tasty. It is easy to grow in temperate climates. According to Theophrastus one should curse and shout when sowing cumin (Theo. VII-iii-2) to encourage the seed.

Cumin is supposed to encourage human seed: according to Pliny, women became pregnant more quickly if the scent of cumin can be smelt during sexual intercourse (Plin. N.H. XX-lvii). In addition, it was rumoured that cumin made the complexion deathly pale. Julius Vindex, who lived at the time of Nero, ate it in great quantities to give false hope to flatterers waiting like vultures for their inheritance.

Rue

Rue is rarely used now, except in some alcoholic distillates, herbal bitters and liqueurs, but it is often mentioned in Latin writings. Alternative healers still sometimes prescribe it as a restorative and Pliny recognized it as an important medicine. It was chiefly employed as an antidote to poison – for example, if a person had eaten poisonous mushrooms or been bitten by a snake. A dinner guest who expected to be poisoned with aconite would take rue beforehand. The juice was also injected into the ears to combat earache. Painters and sculptors ate it on bread or with watercress because it was supposed to be good for the eyes, and it was eaten with cheese to combat dysentery. Combined with rose-oil, it had a deodorant effect (Plin. N.H. XX-li).

> Against headaches caused by a hangover, one should drink an infusion of rue leaves, but rue is also a healthy foodstuff, either raw or cooked.   (Plin. N.H. XX-li-136)

Healthy perhaps, but dangerous too: Pliny writes,

> Similarly, rue is taken against premature ejaculation and wet dreams. Pregnant women should abstain from rue, for I have observed that it kills the foetus.   (Plin. N.H. XX-li-143)

Apicius mentions rue in many recipes, both the seed and the leaf, dried and fresh. It was used to spice wine, and to flavour pickles or olives. Rue had a strong aroma reminiscent of pine trees, but be careful with the quantities: depending on the season and the soil, it can be bitter.

Rue is easily grown, and hardy. The Romans harboured the superstitious notion that it was tastier and more effective if it was stolen rather than bought.

Coriander (*coriandrum*)

Coriander is among the spices that have given ancient Roman cookery a bad reputation in modern Italy, and Italians no longer use it. It also had its place in Roman medicine. A weeping eye, for example, could be soothed by bathing it in human milk with coriander. According to Xenocrates women could postpone menstruation by a day by swallowing a single coriander seed. Two seeds would defer matters for two days, and so on, but Pliny doubted this. Varro maintained that coriander mixed with ground cumin would prevent meat rotting, and the combination of the two spices is still popular around the world today.

Mint (*menta*)

Today Italians use mint as they have for millennia, both fresh and dried. There are dozens of different varieties: green mint, white mint, peppermint, spearmint, corn mint, water mint, pennyroyal, and so on. Pliny first distinguishes *mentastrum*, which he describes as 'mint from the forest, whose leaves look like basil' – perhaps our peppermint. It was supposed to be a good cure for jaundice and cholera. An anti-dandruff shampoo was made by mixing it with vinegar then washing the hair with it on a sunny day (Plin. N.H. XX-lii).

What Pliny usually calls *menta* is probably our green mint, or spearmint. It was taken against sickness, a swollen uvula or tonsils. Its juice was inhaled to ease nasal congestion or chest conditions. But its most important function was in cooking:

> The very scent of mint revives the soul, its flavour whets the appetite. That is why it is used so often in sauces. Mint prevents milk going sour, or curdling and thickening, so it is added to milk that is going to be drunk.
>
> (Plin. N.H. XX-1iii)

Pliny also writes of *puleium*, our pennyroyal, which is also a kind of mint. Apicius mentions it specifically in nine of his recipes. Pliny knew that both pennyroyal and mint could revive people who had fainted. Varro recommended hanging garlands of pennyroyal rather than roses in the bedroom, to avoid hangovers. Roses were said to have a tranquillizing effect and pennyroyal to act as a stimulant, which suggests that Varro had more trouble in getting up than he did in going to sleep.

A wreath of pennyroyal was believed to protect the head against heat or cold, and a sprig behind each ear ensured that one would not be tormented by thirst. It disinfected water and counteracted fatigue, thus was valuable to travellers.

Mint is easy to grow, hardy and prolific. It soon covers the garden if not cut back. Columella recommends taking a cutting of wild mint and planting it upside down in the garden:

> For in that way one removes the wildness from the herb: one tames it.   (Col. XI-iii-37)

Basil (*ocimum*)

Basil should not be included in a list of the most-mentioned herbs, but many people associate it with modern Italian cuisine and might expect it to have played a large part in ancient Roman cooking. Not so! Apicius mentions it only in one recipe: he adds the fresh leaf to boiled peas.

Although basil is described in Columella and Athenaeus as a common plant frequently encountered in herb gardens, it had a bad reputation. According to the *Chrysippus* it interfered with the stomach, the eyesight and the bladder. It caused madness, malaria and liver complaints. It also attracted vermin – scorpions and worms especially. Anyone who ate basil and was stung by a scorpion on the same day would die. And people who ate it regularly would probably get head lice. So, be warned (Plin. N.H. XX-xlviii).

Celery and Parsley (*apium*)

Celery was another high-risk herb because it was dedicated to Pluto, the god of the underworld and the dead. Funeral wreaths were woven of celery leaves, and it was served at funeral banquets. Yet its culinary benefits could not be denied:

Celery is generally well liked, for all over the country sprigs of celery float in milk, and the herb is particularly welcome in sauces.

(Plin. N.H. XX-xliv)

Pliny identified other plants from the umbellifer family as varieties of celery, such as *apiastrum* (wild parsley or mock parsley), *petroselinum* (garden parsley), *helioselinum* ('sun celery'), *oreoselinum* ('mountain celery'), *buselinum* ('cow celery') and *hipposelinum* ('horse celery').

The last is *olastrum*, known in English as alexanders (the scientific name is *Smyrnium olusatrum*). It was believed to cure the bite of a mad dog. However, in the Middle Ages, it was thought to have properties associated with black magic, and consequently disappeared from the kitchen.

Marjoram (*origanum*)

Apicius mentions marjoram, or oregano, in many of his sauces, but never specifies whether it should be dried or fresh, although the former seems more likely. Columella points out that the Romans also salted it. It was washed in water or wine before use. Oregano was supposed to be good for colds, chest infections and pleurisy.

Laserpithium

Laserpithium, or *silphium* as the Greeks called it, is extinct, and this is the Romans' fault. The herb used to grow abundantly in North Africa, in the province of Cyrenaica (Libya). It was the country's main export, and became a national symbol, appearing on coins and reliefs. The plant itself was eaten, the stem boiled or roasted, but the juice extracted from the roots was more important. It was called *laser*.

Sadly the plant could not be cultivated, and had to be gathered in the wild. It was worth its weight in gold. Apicius, who was generally happy to pay considerable sums for his food, provides a cooking tip to make a little *laser* go a long way. He stored it in pine nuts, which absorbed its flavour. When a recipe called for *laser*, Apicius used the flavoured pine nuts.

With full-scale plunder of *laser* for Roman gourmets the herb became increasingly scarce. For some decades it appeared to have died out, but then one more plant was found. Rather than leave it alone in the hope it might propagate itself, it was picked and sent to Rome, where it was given to Nero. The last *laser* plant vanished into the fat emperor's belly.

From that point on the Romans fell back on substitutes. *Silphium parthicum* grew in Persia and Armenia. Pliny suggests that this variety was greatly inferior. It still exists, known as *ferula asafoetida*. An extract is made from the root juices and can be bought from Indian grocers as a liquid, paste or powder under the name *asafoetida* or *heeng*. It is a popular ingredient in India, Afghanistan and the Middle East, but its strong, garlicky aroma has never appealed to northern European palates.

Asafeoetida – which means 'stink root' – has a penetrating flavour. The tiniest amount enriches a dish, while too much makes it inedible. It is not used in Italy, where it failed to become an accepted substitute for the real thing. Modern Italians use garlic where Apicius called for *laser*. In a way garlic has always been a laser substitute. Even when *laser* was still available, it was too expensive for the poor, who used garlic (Plin. N.H. XIX-xv).

Thyme (*thymum*)

Thyme was – and is – important in honey production. The burning of thyme was supposed to keep pests at bay, and it was thought to bring relief to those bitten by sea creatures.

Dill (*anetum*)

Both the fresh leaf and the seed of the dill were used. According to Pliny, it cures diarrhoea (Plin. NH. XX-1xxiv).

Fennel (*feniculum*)

It was believed that snakes ate fennel before they sloughed their skin to improve their eyesight, and that therefore it must be good for human eyesight. The seed and the leaf were both used as herbs in cooking. Large fennel (*ferula*) was also eaten as a vegetable with honey and brine. It was beneficial to the stomach, but too much might cause headaches (Plin. N.H. XX-xcv).

Anis (*anesum*)

The Romans chewed aniseed in the morning to freshen their breath, then rinsed their mouths with wine. They rubbed anis extract into their faces to make themselves looked younger. Aniseed and the fresh leaf of the plant were used in cooking and, according to Pliny, 'could even substitute for lovage' – a big compliment, considering how important lovage was.

If one wished to vomit after eating, one took an emetic composed of ten finely ground bay leaves and 70 millilitres of anis in water. At night the herb was hung from the pillow to promote a good night's sleep, and clothes were stored with it as a protection against moths.

A pleasant-tasting cough medicine was made from honey, fifty finely ground almonds and 70 millilitres of anis – a kind of marzipan was the result.

Babies with epilepsy were smeared with fresh anis. Pythagoras even records that one cannot have an epileptic fit if one holds anis in one's hand. He also records that the smell of the herb makes an attack pass more easily, and that immediately after childbirth an aniseed drink with a little barley in it should be given [to the mother] to drink.   (Plin. N.H. XX-1xxiii)

Laurel/Bay (*laurus*)

The bay tree, a member of the laurel family, was a sacred tree dedicated to Apollo. It also enjoyed the protection of Jupiter, the thrower of lightning-bolts. Emperor Tiberius had the good sense during storms to wear a laurel wreath. Pliny believed that triumphant generals crowned themselves with laurel because of the divine protection it afforded against lightning.

Masurius points out that the bay was used in many purification rituals: in ancient times the blood of the enemy was purified with the perfume of the bay. In this way the tree came to be associated with victory. Soldiers decorated their lances and spears with it, and at the end of every triumphal procession, the general laid a sprig of bay in the lap of the statue of Jupiter on the Capitol. Associated with the end of war, the bay became a symbol of peace.

The imperial family also had a personal connection with the tree:

When Livia Drusilla, named Augusta after she married the emperor, was sitting one day, an eagle dropped a strange white chicken into her lap. Livia was not frightened, but was still in amazement, when she discovered another miracle: the chicken held in its mouth a sprig of bay with berries.

The priests determined that the chicken and its descendants had to be saved, and that the sprig must be planted and protected with religious rites. This was done at the imperial villa on the Tiber, about nine miles from the via Flaminia. Since then the villa has been called 'Chicken Villa'. A glorious bay tree has grown there.

Since that time the emperor, at his triumphs, has held a sprig of the bay tree in his hand, and worn a laurel wreath on his head, and every emperor after him has done the same.

(Plin. N.H. XV-xl)

Bay wood was so sacred that it was forbidden to light a fire with it, even on the sacrificial altar. But it was employed in cooking in other ways: bay berries were never missing from the larder. They were stuffed whole into sausages, or ground into stews and sauces. Bay leaves were cooked whole; young shoots were finely ground for sauces or fillings. They were wrapped around certain dishes, such as suckling pigs, and around a pastry served on wedding days, called *mustaceum*. This dish also required the ground bark of the bay tree. The dough was baked on a bed of bay leaves, from which came the Latin expression '*laureolam in mustaceo quaerere*' (to look for the wreath of bay leaves in the cake), meaning something along the lines of 'to win honour without over-exerting oneself'.

Myrtle (*myrtus*)

Myrtle was almost as sacred as bay and was dedicated to Venus, the goddess of love. In a sense myrtle was the predecessor of bay. Like the bay, the Italian myrtle (*myrtus communis* is the scientific name) has aromatic leaves that will flavour a soup or sauce but are too tough to eat. Myrtle berries are used in the same way as juniper and bay berries. Pliny observes that the Romans scattered myrtle berries over their food like pepper, before Indian spices were known.

In triumphal processions myrtle crowned the victorious hero before laurel took on that role. The first triumph ever held in Rome came shortly after the rape of the Sabine women. The war had been averted by the intervention of the women, and a great deal of myrtle grew in the field where the peace was concluded. Women had procured peace near myrtle, the plant of Venus, goddess of love. The Romans made wreaths from it and returned to the city in triumph, attributing their victory to love.

Thereafter triumphant generals crowned themselves with myrtle wreaths, and high-ranking men wore them when watching the games. Laurel wreaths were first used when Crassus celebrated his bloody victory over Spartacus. Marcus Valerius wore a laurel wreath and a myrtle wreath at the same time, but in the end myrtle vanished from military ceremonies.

Myrtle continued to play a part in Roman politics, though. Two myrtle bushes stood in front of the temple of Romulus, one for each of the two political parties: the patricians and the plebeians. When the patricians were in power their myrtle bush flourished, while the plebeian bush withered. When their roles were reversed, the opposite was the case. The myrtle even anticipated political developments, leading Pliny to speak of 'prophetic fortune-telling' (Plin. N.H. XV-xxxvi). With the dawn of the imperial age both myrtle bushes had died.

Myrtle might have vanished from the army camp and politics, but it continued to play a role in love. Sweethearts and wedding guests wore myrtle, and the plant was revered for its amorous reputation. When the women of Rome celebrated the festival of the Bona Dea, nothing of a masculine nature could be present, because the goddess had a poor relationship with her husband Faunus, who beat her for her alcoholism (see page 108). The Bona Dea wanted nothing to do with love or men so myrtle was banned as her festivals and women made wreaths and garlands from other flowers and trees (Plut. Mor. Rom. Quest 268 d).

Today myrtle has even disappeared from the kitchen, except in Corsica and Sardinia. It is practically unknown as a spice, but bay leaves are found in nearly every kitchen.

Mustard (*sinapi*)

Just as it does today, the word mustard referred in Roman times to the plant, its seeds and the hot sauce made from them. The Romans made mustard in much the same way as we do:

> Mustard seed is carefully cleaned and sieved. Then the seed is washed in cold water and soaked for two hours. It is then taken out and the water is squeezed out by hand. Put the seed into a new, cleaned mortar, and pound it finely with a pestle. Once the mustard is finely ground, put it in the middle of the mortar and press it down with the palm of the hand. Once it has been pressed flat, make some incisions in it. Place a few burning coals on top of it, and pour over soda water, to draw out all the bitterness and pallor from the mustard. Then lift the mortar and pour out the soda water. Add strong vinegar and mix it through the mustard with the mortar.   (Col. XII, 57)

Columella recommends that the mustard is mixed with ground almonds and pine kernels.

Poppy (*papaveris*)

Poppy seed is not mentioned in the recipes of Apicius, although it is first on his list of indispensable seeds – perhaps because in a hand-written document, it was easier to add something at the top, or because poppy seeds were used in desserts for which his recipes have not survived. Other sources suggest that they played a major part in cooking as decoration. Black poppy seeds were scattered over bread as they are today, while white poppy seeds were roasted with honey and served in pastry. But much more important than its culinary use was the poppy's role in medicine, because it yielded opium:

> The best way is to make an incision beneath the head and the calix. In no variety of poppy should an incision be made in the head itself. The sap is collected on a little wool, as is done with other plant-juices, unless there is only a small quantity of sap, in which case it is scraped off the following day when it has dried, with the nail or the thumb, as one does with lettuce.*
>
> If the poppy yields a large amount of sap, allow it to thicken, roll it into pastilles and allow these to dry in the shade. It is a tranquillizer, but if you take too much, you will die in your sleep.
>
> It is called 'opium'. The father of P. Licinius Caecina took it to commit suicide in Bavili in Spain when an unbearable illness made his life miserable, which caused some controversy, but many others have done the same Diagoras and Erastistratus condemned opium as a deadly poison, and forbade injections because they were thought to be bad for the eyesight.   (Plin. N.H. XX-lxxvi)

However bad injecting opium might be for the eyes, it was widely used in medicine. When modern scientists consider Roman medicine they recognize only opium as an effective ingredient.

Spikenard

Spikenard is an aromatic grass that enjoyed great popularity with the Romans, and remains popular in the Far East. The Romans imported the eastern version from India, and called it *Spica indica*, possibly lemon grass.

There is a European variety of spikenard, which the Romans called *saliunca*. They found it in the Alps, and in Pannonia and Nordicum (both in the Balkans). The quality was so good that it became a goldmine for the local population (Plin. N.H. XII-xxvi).

---

* Indeed a weak type of opium could be harvested from wild lettuce.

Spikenard was important to the perfume industry, and Pliny recommended scattering it over one's clothing for a bright fragrance (Plin. N.H. XXI-xx).

Garlic and Onion

Garlic and onion were used not only as herbs, but also as vegetables.

Other Herbs

The above herbs are the most important in Roman cuisine, but others appear in recipes. In decreasing order of frequency, they are,

caraway (*careum*)
savory (*satureia*)
saffron (*crocus*)
hyssop (*hysopus*)
sage (*salvia*)
fenugreek (*foenum graecum*)
rosemary (*ros marinus*)
juniper (*iuniperus*)
elder (*sambucus*)
wormwood (*apsinthum*)
sumac (*rhus*)
cypress (*cyperus*)
costmary (*costum*)
wild spikenard (*asarum*)
borage (*borago*)
sesame (*sesamum*)
mastic (*mastix*)
sorrel (*rumex*)

and many others.

SPICES

The word 'spices' calls up visions of journeys on camels or boats to distant lands, while 'herbs' evokes a spade and a watering-can in your own back garden. But the scientific dividing line between herbs and spices is not clear.

For the Romans there was a big difference between products from a Roman province and those from beyond the borders of the Empire. Eastern spices came from countries far outside Roman dominion, and were costly. They were bought from traders in Armenia, Mesopotamia, Syria, Judaea, Arabia and Egypt. Often the Romans did not even know where the spices had originally come from because the traders would not tell them. Romans believed that cinnamon grew in Ethiopia and cardamom in Persia, but both came from much further afield. In general Roman sources were well informed, but not on spices.

Some trade routes were known. The Romans were aware that silk came from China and pepper from India, so they could go and fetch the goods themselves – pepper was much cheaper in Rome than other spices. Fleets of camels laden with gold regularly set off for the Orient:

> By the most modest reckoning our empire pays an annual 100 million HS to India, China and the Arab peninsula. That is the cost of our luxury and our women.*   (Plin. N.H. XII-xli-84)

Cinnamon and Cassia (*cinnamonum* and *casia*)

Both cinnamon and cassia are the bark of Indian trees, related to the laurel family. Initially the Romans were told that the nests of the mythical phoenix were made of cinnamon, and it was dangerous to approach them. All you could do was wait at the foot of the mountain on which the nest was to be found until some cinnamon fell down from it, which would happen when the bird dropped a stolen pig or cow on to it.

* The mention of women refers to the importation not of spices but of silk.

In another story cinnamon was said to grow in inaccessible swamps, where it was protected by giant bats with terrible claws, and by winged snakes. Pliny realized that all this nonsense was invented to push up the price of cinnamon. He thought the Arabs brought cinnamon from Ethiopia, but this was not so. He believed that in Ethiopia cinnamon was dedicated to Jupiter as 'Assabinus' or to the sun. Supposedly cinnamon bark could not be harvested without the agreement of the god, to whom forty-four oxen, goats and rams had to be sacrificed first – all of which hiked up the price. Then a priest halved the supply of cinnamon between the god and the traders. In another version, the harvested cinnamon was divided into three portions and lots were drawn to see which parts should be given to the sun god and which to the traders. Once this was clear, the sun god took his own share by causing the cinnamon to burst spontaneously into flames.

Cinnamon was expensive. The price rose to 4000 HS per pound, or even 6000, when forest fires had destroyed the harvest (a show of greed on the part of the sun god). Most cinnamon was bought up by the affluent perfume industry, but it was much enjoyed in wine (as it is in mulled wine today) and in sweet or savoury dishes (Plin. N.H. XII-xlii).

Cardamom (*cardamomum*)

Although cardamom also came from India, it was considerably cheaper than cinnamon or pepper, at 12 HS per pound. It was thought good for the digestion, and therefore appeared in many dishes. The Romans bought the seeds with the shell still around them, just as we do today, and some recipes mention this. Crack open the shells in the mortar, taking care not to crush them too fine, then separate them from the black seeds. Discard the shells and finely grind the seeds. The taste is penetrating: a mere sprinkling in the belly cavity of a boar endows the whole animal with its flavour.

Ginger (*zingiber*)

The Romans did not know where ginger came from either. Some thought it was the root of the pepper plant, and others said it was nothing of the sort. It was popular and is mentioned among the ingredients of about thirteen of Apicius' recipes. He ate ginger on lamb, meatballs, lettuce, garden beans, peas, bread, in chicken and in stuffed suckling pigs, but not, as in eastern countries, with fish. In Pliny's time it cost 24 HS per pound.

Clove (*syzygium*)

The clove came late to Rome. It made its first appearance on customs lists of imported spices in AD 176. After this it became a favoured ingredient of incense and perfume. It does not appear in classical Roman recipes; neither does nutmeg nor mace.

Pepper (*piper*)

Pepper is the king of all spices, and no other spice is so widely used internationally. Few people have the vaguest notion of what the pepper plant looks like. It is a climber like the vine, but Pliny was confident that the pepper tree looked like our juniper bushes. He knew correctly, however, that green berries ripened to fine black peppercorns, and that white pepper came from the almost ripe red berries, with their outer shell removed.

The Romans were also familiar with 'long pepper' (*piper longum*), another member of the pepper family. Pliny describes it as a kind of pod. Long pepper is no longer popular in the West but is still used widely in the Far East. It was cultivated in northern India, which had been conquered by Alexander the Great, so it has been known for longer than the black or white pepper from southern India. The Romans continued to prefer the long version, as prices reveal.

Long pepper costs 60 HS per pound, white pepper 28 and black pepper 16.* It is curious that pepper should be considered so delicious. Why should that be? Some herbs are valued for their delicious taste, others because they look attractive. But neither the leaves nor the berries of pepper are anything special. The only

* About the price of a *tunica*.

agreeable thing about it is that it is hot. And for that we go and
fetch it from India!   (Plin. N.H. XII-xiv)

Some Romans thought that pepper was made from the berries of
the ginger plant. The confusion arises from an old substitute for pepper
that came from West Africa, known in English as 'grains of paradise'
(*amomum melegueta*). This plant is a member of the ginger family and
also has sharp-tasting berries, which were popular in Europe through
the seventeenth and eighteenth centuries but are now eaten only in the
areas where they grow.

OTHER INGREDIENTS

Olive Oil (*oleum*)

The olive tree was dedicated to Minerva, the goddess of wisdom.
Intellectual achievements were recognized with a wreath of olive twigs
presented to the scholar.

Olive oil was available then as now in various different qualities.
The most expensive was called *omphacium*. It was pressed from unripe
olives, harvested in August, and the oil was light, colourless and delicate. It was used principally in the preparation of perfumes, medicines
and cosmetics. In second place, but also exclusive, came *acerbum*,
pressed from green olives harvested before October. Athletes smeared
themselves with this oil before they began their exertions. After they
had finished they scraped it off, along with the sweat and dirt. Third
was normal green oil: *viridum*. This was made from late-harvested
olives that were turning black. Green oil was divided into three qualities: virgin oil from the first pressing was called *olei flos*, the second
pressing was *oleum sequens*, and the third, the cheap oil made from the
dregs, *oleum cibarium*.

Oil was used in cooking, for baking, roasting and frying; it was
added to sauces and poured over vegetables; it was used in bread and
sweet buns – in fact, in almost every dish. Oil from Venafrus was highly
esteemed on salad, but the most famous oil came from Liburnia in

Dalmatia. The cheapest was African oil, which was used only as fuel for oil lamps (Plin. N.H. XII-lx).

Perfume (*unguentum*)

Perfumes and ointments were based on *omphacium*. Other kinds of oil were also mixed, such as myrtle, mastic, almond, sesame and Egyptian date oils.

Perfume was sometimes coloured with ox-tongue (the plant, not what you buy from the butcher), dragon's blood (red gum), scarlet or saffron. Salt was added as a preservative, and gum or resin to prevent the aromatics evaporating too quickly.

The creation of a fragrance involved the combination of many different ingredients, of which Pliny and Theophrastus mentioned the following, among others: myrrh, myrtle, cardamom, cinnamon, cassia, fenugreek, cyperus, storax, bay, spikenard, oregano, thyme, lemon verbena, mint, balsam, roses, gladioli, lotus, lilies, iris, iris root, pomegranate rind, quince, honey and wine. In early imperial times a combination of myrrh and cinnamon was in vogue.

According to Pliny, the most expensive perfumes cost more than 1600 HS per Roman pound. He thought this was a shocking luxury and, indeed, it is about twenty times as much as perfumes cost today. The wealthy doused themselves in the latest scent. As a result cities flourished and fell into decline as their perfumes went in and out of fashion. Only Athens, the Paris of ancient times, had an unshakeable reputation for elegant fragrances.

Perfume was offered to the gods along with incense, and large quantities of scent were used at cremations, to shield delicate noses from unpleasant odours. And, of course, perfume and incense were offered at the carousal. Sometimes perfume was poured into the wine:

> By Hercules, nowadays they even put perfume in their drink, so that despite its bitter taste, not only the outside but also the inside of the body can enjoy the luxury. (Plin. N.H. XIII-iv-25)

Pliny calls the scenting of wine a novelty, but the Greek Theophrastus had described the practice about three centuries earlier. Perfume was an ingredient of lentil soup too (see page 200):

Odysseus is with us now, so, as the saying goes: the perfume is in the lentil soup so we have nothing to fear.   (Ath. IV-160b)

It was used in cooking until the nineteenth century.

Cheese

Dairy products did not predominate but the Romans ate plenty of cheese. It was the primary way to preserve milk, and was made from the milk of all kinds of animals. According to Pliny, animals with two nipples – goats and sheep – made the best cheese. Milk from animals with more than four nipples, like cats and dogs, was unsuitable. Cheese was made from horse milk and donkey milk. Camel cheese was also highly valued. Milk of the hare and the deer was turned into cheese, and rabbit-milk cheese was supposed to cure diarrhoea. The cow has four nipples; its cheese was therefore inferior but popular nevertheless (*caseus bubulus*), partly because the cow produced great quantities of milk. Cow's-milk cheese was considered nutritious but hard to digest.

Cheeses fell into two major groups: that which would keep, and fresh cheese. Columella described in detail the preparation of a cheese that would keep:

Cheese is made from pure milk, which must be as fresh as possible, because if it is left to stand for a period of time or mixed with water it will quickly sour. Generally speaking it is turned into curd with rennet of lamb or goat,* but it can also be curdled with the flower of the wild thistle, or with saffron seed. A good alternative is the sap of the fig tree, if an incision is made in the bark while it is still green.

The best cheese is made with as little rennet as possible. The smallest quantity needed for a vat of milk weighs 3.5 grams. There is no doubt that cheese curdled with the young shoots of fig trees has a very pleasant taste.

---

* Rennet, or hydrochloric acid, was extracted from the pickled stomachs of these animals, as is still the case today.

The milk-vat must always be kept slightly warm, but not exposed to the fire as some people do. It must be kept at some distance from the flames.

Once the liquid has curdled, the curds must be siphoned as quickly as possible into wicker baskets or cheese-moulds. It is extremely important that the whey should be allowed to drip out as quickly as possible, and separate from the solid parts. For that reason country folk do not allow the whey to drip away, but press it down with weights – as soon as the cheese has been shaped – in order to extract the whey with pressure.

Then the cheese is taken from the moulds or baskets, and placed in the dark to prevent spoiling. Although it is placed on very clean planks, the cheese is scattered with ground salt to draw out some of the sourness. When the cheese has become firm, it is pressed again, with great force, so that it becomes compact. Then it is scattered once again with salt, and pressed under weights once more. When this has been done for nine days, the cheese is washed in fresh water.

The cheeses are placed in rows on wicker in the dark, so that one cheese does not touch another, if a very firm cheese is desired, or close together on different planks for a softer cheese, and not exposed to the wind. Under these circumstances one ends up with a cheese that is not full of holes or too salty or too dry. In the first case the cheese has not been pressed hard enough, in the second case too much salt has been used, and in the third case the cheese has been scorched by the sun. This kind of cheese can be exported.

(Col. R.R. VII-viii)

Romans liked old cheese, *caseus senescentus*. Pliny praises *caseus bithynus*, which was an old cheese:

Among foreign cheeses, the Bythynian is very famous. The meadows there are salty, which you cannot see, but you notice it from the fact that the cheeses turn salty by themselves, as they mature.

(Plin. N.H. XI-xcvii)

Cheeses came to Rome from all of the provinces. Pliny declared that the cheeses from Gaul (France) were the most delicious:

In Rome, where delicacies from all countries are enjoyed, cheese
from the province of Nemausum [Nîmes] are most highly
valued, from the villages of Lesur and Gabalicus [La Lozère
and Gévaudan], although these cheeses can only be recommended
when they are young.*   (Plin. N.H. XI-xcvii)

The Alps also enjoyed a good reputation for cheese, as did the
Apennines and the Dalmation mountains. One large cheese weighing
about 327 kg came from Liguria. A famous cheese produced near Rome
was called *caseus vestinus*. Just as popular, if not more so, was fresh
curd cheese, *caseus recens*. It was white in colour and went off quickly.
The curds were placed in salt or brine then dried for a short time in
the sun. *Recens* was not unlike cottage cheese, ricotta, fromage frais, etc.
Fresh cheese was sold as loose curd or sometimes kneaded into a ball.
This was known as *caseus manu pressus*.

Because fresh cheese had little taste, flavourings were often added
to it. Some people added green fir-cones or pine kernels to the milk
pail; others preferred thyme. In addition, many cheeses, not only fresh
ones, were smoked with apple wood.

Curd cheese was used in many dishes: in pastry (such as *placenta*),
bread dishes (for example, *sala cattabia*) or omelettes (*patinae*). It was
eaten on its own with bread, at breakfast, at lunch and, above all, as a
starter. Athenaeus observed that cheese was also served on the carousal
(Ath. 658d).

Curd cheese was often pounded in the mortar with herbs. This
mixture was called *moretum*, and generally included a great deal of
garlic, but elegant Apicius provides a garlic-free mixture.

Moretum

*Moretaria: mentam, rutam, coriandrum, feniculum, omnia virida,
ligusticum, piper, mel, liquamen, si opus fuerrit, acetum addes.*

Mortar mixture: mint, rue, coriander, fennel, all fresh, lovage,
pepper, honey, *garum*. Add some vinegar, if necessary.   (Ap. 36)

---

* Young cheese: *caseus musteus*.

In this case no garlic and no laser. Apicius does not mention that the pounded herbs had to be stirred into curd cheese – clearly that spoke for itself. It is a simple recipe: put the herbs into the mortar in the order in which Apicius lists them. The salt and lovage seed will help in pulping them. The honey, *garum* and (possibly) vinegar will turn the mixture into a sauce with which you can flavour cottage cheese or ricotta. Scoop it into a mould, leave it to set, then turn it out and serve.

Hypotrimma

Apicius describes another cheese dish that, because of its sweetness, is more suitable as a dessert than as a starter. It is rather like the pashka that Russians eat at Easter:

Hypotrimma: piper, ligusticum, mentam arridam, nucleos pineos, uvam passam, caryotam, caseum dulcem, mel, acetum, liquamen, oleum, vinum, defrutum aut caroenum.

Hypotrimma: pepper, lovage, dried mint, pine kernels, raisins, dates, sweet cheese, honey, vinegar, *garum*, oil, wine, *defrutum* or *caroenum*.   (Ap. 34)

1 kg unsalted curd cheese
200 g white raisins
200 g dates
100 g pine kernels
200 ml white wine
2 tablespoons strong wine vinegar
2 tablespoons virgin olive oil
3 tablespoons dried mint
3 tablespoons honey
1 tablespoon lovage seed
1 tablespoon pepper
garum or salt, to taste

Soak the raisins in the wine overnight. Then pit the dates and chop them finely. Grind the spices and herbs. Knead all the ingredients with the cheese, which Apicius forgets to mention. Press into a greased mould and leave to cool for several hours in the fridge. Turn out the mould on to a board and serve with bread.

PART TWO

V

FROM THE LAND

On Grain, Pulses, Vegetables and Fruit

CEREALS

Men went hunting, women gathered fruits and plants: such was the division of labour in ancient times, so it is not unlikely that women established the first agriculture. They were probably the first to notice that grass seeds can be sown to provide a rich harvest the next year. The ancients attributed this miraculous multiplication to a female deity of fertility, Mother Earth or the Great Mother. The Romans called her Ceres, the patron of agriculture in general and of cereals in particular.

Figure 5.1 – Grain shop

Cereals, the first plants cultivated, keep for a long time, but the production is labour-intensive. The ground has to be ploughed, then the seed is sown, protected against birds, then harvested. Before use the grain has to be separated from the chaff, and often milled.

When Rome was founded, it was specified that women should not have to grind grain. That task went to a slave: the *pistor*. According to Pliny it was 'generally known' that he had to be a chained prisoner-of-war, often a rough foreigner who spoke poor Latin. The *pistor* was given a wooden mortar and a wooden pestle, reinforced with metal.

For the first 300 years in Rome's history the separation of grain and chaff was particularly hard work, given that the Romans were not yet familiar with wheat but relied on 'spelt', a type of grain that closely resembles wheat, but which is not as easily husked (Plin. N.H. XVIII-62). It was backbreaking work for the *pistor*. It must have been a relief when spelt was replaced with wheat.

Where tradition was respected, spelt remained the preferred cereal. The Latin word for spelt is *far*, hence, *farina*, meaning flour. The Latin word for the traditional wedding took its name from spelt, *confarreatio*, because the bride and groom shared a spelt loaf, *farreum*. For the *mola salsa* spelt was still the prescribed cereal. Only the finest grains could be used in it, and for a long time it was customary to assign beggars to seek them out. As a reward they were allowed to eat some of the sacrificial meat. Their name, *parasiti*, later assumed a completely different meaning (see page 61–2).

Spelt grains were generally polished into pearls, called *alica*. They were produced by the same chained *pistor* with his mortar, who either left the pearls intact or broke them down. Broken spelt, rolled spelt (spelt flakes) or the ground kernels were all available as various kinds of *alica*. Bulgur, made of wheat, is a modern version. To make spelt pearls, the grains were rubbed with chalk or sand until they turned white. After this they were washed and the abrasives were sieved away. The washing was done either at home or at the bakery, not always very well – sometimes a little sand was found in cheap *alica* bread. *Alica* was also produced in the provinces, but Romans boasted that they made the whitest *alica* pearls of all.

Alica needs only to be soaked and boiled to make a nourishing porridge, the oldest Roman dish: the famous *puls*.

Puls Punica

Pure *puls* consisted solely of water and cereals, but the oldest recipe comes from Cato the Elder. It is very sweet:

> *Pultem punicam sic coquito. Libram alicae in aquam indito, facito uti bene madeat. Id unfundito in alveum purum, eo casei recentis p. iii, mellis p. s, ovum unum, omnia una permisceto bene. Ita insipito in aulam novam.*

> Punic *puls* is made as follows: soak a pound of *alica* until soft. Transfer it to another dish and add three pounds of curd cheese, half a pound of honey and an egg. Knead this into a mass and pour into a new bowl.   (Cat. N.H. LXXXVI)

The cereal is not boiled, just soaked to soften the grains for several days under running water, to prevent fermentation. Cato used curd cheese; we might try ricotta. Half a pound of honey is rather a lot for modern palates, so add it gradually to taste.

Puls Juliana

A much less primitive *puls*, described by Apicius, indicates that Roman *puls* resembled risotto, its direct descendant. The only difference is that risotto rice is used, rather than spelt, but anyone who has made risotto should have little difficulty in putting a refined *puls* on the table.

According to Vehling, this dish was named after the emperor Julian. Given the large amounts of meat in it, this seems a little wide of the mark: Julian was a vegetarian.

> *Pultes iulianae sic coquuntur, alicam purgatam infundis, coques, facies ut ferveat. Cum ferbuerit, oleum mittis, cum spissa verity, lias diligenter. Acidies cerebella duo cocta et selibram pulpae quasi ad isicia liatae, cum cerebellis teres et in caccabum mittis. Teres piper, ligusticum, feniculi semen, suffundis liquamen et vinum modice, mittis in caccabum supra cerebella et pulpam. Ubi sais ferbuerit, cum*

*iure misces. Ex hoc paulatim alicam condies, et ad trulam permisces
et lias, ut quasi sucus videatur.*

Julian *puls* is cooked as follows: place cleaned *alica* in water. Boil
it. Do this until it is hot. When it is hot, add oil. If it becomes
too thick, dilute it carefully.

    Take two cooked brains and half a pound of meat ground as
for forcemeat. Pound them together and transfer to a different
pot. Grind pepper, lovage and fennel seed. Add *garum* and a small
amount of wine. Pour this into the pot with the brains and the
meat. When it is heated through, mix it with the stock. Add
the meat carefully to the *alica* and stir with a spoon, diluting it
until it has the thickness of a sauce.   (Ap. 186)

1 pair brains
250g pork sausagemeat
1 teaspoon lovage seed
1 tablespoon peppercorns
1 tablespoon fennel seed
600ml meat stock, salted with *garum*
200ml white wine
1 dash olive oil
500g pearled spelt, or more, soaked overnight

Prepare the 'sauce' first. Remove the skins and veins from the brains
and simmer for 20 minutes in salted water, then leave to cool. Take the
sausagemeat and put it into a blender with the brains. Whiz until
smooth.

    Pound the lovage seed in the mortar, then add the pepper and the
fennel seed and grind to a powder. Stir the mixture into the meat. Pour
it into a saucepan and warm it slowly. When it begins to simmer, add
a little of the meat stock with a little of the wine and bring it slowly to
the boil.

    Then prepare the spelt. Take your largest shallow pan. Apicius
boiled the grain before adding the oil, but nowadays (with risotto
and paella) it is more usual to fry it in oil then add stock and wine
gradually until it has all been absorbed. Either can be done. When
the grits are ready, their consistency may be somewhat gluey. Finally,
one spoonful at a time, add the meat sauce to the grain and stir well.
Serve.

Tisana

A less heavy dish in which whole grains were used was a kind of thin vegetable minestrone. The word *tisana* comes from the Greek *ptisánè*, meaning ground barley, which suggests that barley rather than spelt was used in it. However, it is not unlikely that the Romans often put spelt into it: although spelt is almost forgotten now, the Italians still use it in regional minestrones.

Tisanam vel sucum. Tisanam sic facies: tisanam lavando fracas, quam ante diem infundes. Impones supra ignem. Cum bullierit, mittis olei satis et anethi modicum fasciculum, cepam siccam, satureiam et coloefium, ut ibi coquantur propter sucum. Mittes coriandrum viride et salem simul tritium et facies ut ferveat. Cum bene ferbuerit, toles fasciculum et transferes in altrum caccabum tisanam sic, ne fundum tangat propter combusturam. Lias bene et colas in caccabulo super acronem coloefium ut bene tegatur. Teres piper, ligusticum, pulei aridi modicum, liquamen, refundis in caccabum super coloefium acronem. Facies ut ferveat super ignem lentum.

Tisana or *broth*. Tisana is made like this: crush barley grits soaked overnight. Place on the fire [in water]. When boiling, add a generous amount of oil and a modest sprig of dill, dry onion, savory and a taro root. Boil all of this together for a good broth. Add fresh coriander crushed finely with salt and allow it to cook through. When it is boiling remove the sprig of dill and transfer the grits to another pot. Take care not to burn it. Rub them fine and pour them back into the other pan so that the taro root is covered. Crush pepper, lovage, a little dried pennyroyal, cumin and dried fennel. Moisten with honey, vinegar, *defrutum* and *garum* and pour over the taro root. Cook over a low flame.

(Ap. 172)

200g taro root, peeled and diced
2 tablespoons dried onion
200g fresh dill
100g fresh savory
125g bulgar wheat, soaked overnight

1 teaspoon lovage seed
1 teaspoon cumin seed
1 tablespoon dried fennel seed
1 tablespoon dried pennyroyal *or* mint
1 tablespoon peppercorns
1 level tablespoon coarse sea salt
100 g fresh coriander
1 teaspoon honey
garum
defrutum
vinegar

Apicius did not make things easy: 'Take care not to burn it,' he writes. You can either enslave yourself to the pot and stir it continuously for hours or, simply, make a stock from the taro root, dried onion, dill and savory, removing the dill when it's cooked. Cook the bulgar wheat in the stock, then strain, reserving the stock. In a mortar, pound the wheat or break it up with a spoon. A blender will grind the grain too finely.

Meanwhile reduce the stock, letting the taro root cook through. In a mortar, grind the lovage seed to powder, then add the cumin, fennel seed, pennyroyal or mint, peppercorns, salt and coriander, and grind everything into a paste with the honey, a few drops of *garum*, *defrutum* and vinegar. Add this mixture to the soup. Stir in the grain. From this point on, keep stirring to avoid burning at the bottom of the pan.

Amulum

A thickener, needed for sauces, was also made from unmilled grain: *amulum*. Pliny writes:

Amulum is made from all qualities of grain, but the best is made from grain that is three months old. We owe its invention to the island of Chios. The most highly regarded kind still comes from there. The name derives from the fact that it is unmilled. After the *amulum* of three-month-old grain, that made from lighter grains is the best.

The grain is first placed in water in wooden barrels so that it is just immersed. The water is replaced five times a day. It is better that this be done at night, so that it is evenly distributed. Before the soaked grain turns sour, it is filtered in linen or wicker sieves. It is spread out on a tiled floor, with leaven. It is left like this to thicken in the sun.   (Plin. N.H. XVIII-7, 17)

Cato gave another recipe:

Amulum is made like this. Take well-cleaned wheat. Place in a vessel and pour on water twice a day. On the tenth day the water is poured off and the wheat well pressed. It is kneaded well in a clean vessel so that it has the consistency of wine lees. Take a small amount and put it in a new linen bag* and press the mash into a new pan or a mortar. Do this with the entire contents. Then knead again. After this, place it in a pan and leave it in the sun. When it is dry, put it in a new pan and cook it with milk.
                                                    (Cat. R.R. LXXXVII)

Amulum was laborious to prepare, but it was also available ready-made in the market. Since this is no longer the case, most translators of Apicius suggest substituting cornflour, but cornflour is made from maize, which the Romans didn't have. Rice (*oryza*) was used also as a thickener. The Romans were familiar with rice: it had been brought to the West by Alexander the Great in 327 BC. In the following recipe Apicius uses it as a thickener:

Amulatum aliter: ossucla de pullis exbromas. Deinde mittis in caccabum porros, anethum, salem. Cum cocta fuerint, addes piper, apii semen, deinde oryzam infusam teres, addes liquamen et passum vel defritum. Omnia misces et cum isiciis inferes.

Another bound sauce: cook chicken bones and add leek, dill and salt to the pot. When it is boiling, add pepper, celery salt and well-soaked rice. Add this with *garum*, *passum* or *defrutum*. Mix together and serve with meatballs.   (Ap. 51)

---

* Coarse linen to be used as a sieve.

In another recipe Apicius uses the water in which rice has been cooked as an alternative thickener to *amulum*.

Tractum

Another item that featured unmilled grain. *Tractum* was a kind of biscuit or cracker. Crushed, it was also used to thicken sauces. Apicius makes a sauce for roast lamb from milk and crumbled *tracta*, not unlike our bread sauce. Cato the Elder relates how *tractum* is made:

> Take 4 pounds of flour and 2 pounds of the best *alica*. Soak the *alica* in water. When it has become soft, pour off the water and place the *alica* in a clean mortar. Then knead it with the hands. When it has been well kneaded, add the flour bit by bit. The *tracta* are shaped from this dough. Put them on a basket to dry. When they have dried they can be placed side by side. Treat each *tractum* as follows. After they have been kneaded, brush with a cloth that has been soaked in olive oil. Brush both sides like this. These are *tracta*. Heat the oven in which, and the lid beneath which, the *tracta* are to be baked to a high temperature.   (Cat. R.R. LXXVI)

'Shape the *tracta*,' says Cato, without specifying the shape. The *Dictionnaire des Antiquités Romaines* suggests that the *tractum* is actually a roll pulled from a spindle, and that the *tractum* biscuit resembled one of these. If this is correct, it was like a breadstick, and in that case *placenta*, which is prepared with *tracta*, curd cheese and honey, might be the predecessor of tiramisu.

E. Pina Ricotta (*L'Alimentazione nel Mondo Antico*) translates *tractum* into Italian as *galetta*, a flat biscuit. Several other Italians identify it as the ancestor of lasagne and filo pastry.

The word '*tractum*' clearly comes from *trahere*, 'to pull', which points to the French interpretation of *tractum* as a pulled thread, but the Italians point out that when they roll out lasagne they are 'pulling pasta'.

Cato's recipe tends to indicate that *tractum* was a rather tasteless biscuit. According to Athenaeus, flavourings were sometimes added to it. He mentions wine, pepper, milk and a little oil or lard (Ath. 113d).

To make *tracta*, the *alica* must be soaked for a long time under running water, from a few days to a week. Pound the bulgar wheat in a large wooden mortar until you have a wet, stringy dough. Then gradually add twice as much flour, and salt to taste. Moisten the dough with white wine or milk if it seems too dry. It must be rather drier than bread dough, and very well kneaded. Put it through a pasta mill or roll it very thinly with a rolling pin then cut it into pieces. Leave it to dry for a few hours, then set the oven to its highest temperature. Brush the *tracta* on both sides with olive oil and then place side by side on baking parchment. Put them into the oven and bake until crisp.

Sweet Pastries

Tractum formed the basis of various sweet pastries, particularly the oldest kinds, from an era when Roman cookery was still simple and rather coarse. Because Apicius' books about luxury tarts, breads and other sweets have been lost, we have only the recipes of Cato the Elder, who lived at least three hundred years earlier.

Confectioners in imperial Rome made dozens of wonderful delicacies like currant buns, fruit tarts, cracknels, light egg-based brioches and croissants (in the shape of little horns rather than crescent moons), but unfortunately we no longer have precise recipes for these. We do, though, for *placenta* and *libum*, which were comparatively primitive but highly popular. They also had an important religious function as sacrificial cakes.

> I have *libum* coming out of my ears. Like a priest's runaway slave,
> I'd rather have bread than *placenta*.   (Hor. Ep. I-x-10)

Libum

Cato's *libum* was no more than cheese mixed with flour and baked.

> *Libum* is made like this: knead 2 pounds of cheese in the mortar. When it is well kneaded add 1 pound of [white] wheat flour, or if you want it a little lighter, half a pound of flour. Mix this well with the cheese, add an egg and mix again. This makes a bread that can be placed on leaves and slowly baked in an oven, covered with a lid.
>   (Cat. R.R. LXXV)

The cheese to use is ricotta, curd, cottage cheese, etc. The leaves on which the cheesy breads are to be placed are possibly bay. Three quarters of an hour in an oven on 180°C/350°F/Gas 4 should do the trick.

Placenta

Placenta was a little more sophisticated and is frequently mentioned in literature. It was the base for various other kinds of sweetmeat made from the same ingredients – dough, *tracta*, fresh cheese and honey.

> *Placenta* is made like this: take 2 pounds of flour for the crust and make *tracta* with 2 pounds of *alica* and 4 pounds of spelt flour . . . Mix the 2 pounds of flour with water and knead to make a thin base dough. Soak 14 pounds of sheep's cheese, not sour but very fresh, in water. Knead and change the water three times. Take a piece of cheese, squeeze it dry and put it in the mortar. When all the cheese has dried, knead it by hand in the clean mortar, and make it as fine as possible. Then take a clean flour-sieve and press the cheese back into the mortar through the sieve. Add 4 pounds of good honey, and mix it well with the cheese.
>
> Then place the base dough, 1 foot wide, on greased bay-leaves on a clean baking tray. Shape the *placenta* as follows: place a single row of *tracta* biscuits along the whole length of the base dough. This is then covered with the mixture from the mortar. Place another row of *tracta* on top and go on doing so until all the cheese and honey have been used up. Finish with a layer of *tracta*. Fold the base dough as a cover and a decoration over the contents and prick little air holes. Then place the *placenta* in the oven and put a preheated lid on top of it. Place hot ashes around and on top of it. Remove the lid two or three times to ensure that everything is going well. When ready, honey is poured over the *placenta*. That is how one makes a 4.3 litre *placenta*.*
>
> (Cat. R.R. LXXVI)

---

* A 'semi-modius', Cato writes, which seems very small, given quantities like 14 pounds of cheese, and 4 pounds of honey. These quantities were probably for making several *placentas* of 4.3 litres.

Placenta, then, was made of layers of sheep's cheese alternating with layers of thin *tracta*. The whole thing was baked in pastry dough. The dish looks like the predecessor of modern baklava, except that nowadays the sheep's cheese would be replaced with nuts.

The Greeks and the Turks still argue over which dishes were originally Greek and which Turkish. Baklava, for example, is claimed by both countries. Greek and Turkish cuisine both built upon the cookery of the Byzantine Empire, which was a continuation of the cooking of the Roman Empire. Roman cuisine had borrowed a great deal from the ancient Greeks, but *placenta* (and hence baklava) had a Latin, not a Greek, origin – please note that the conservative, anti-Greek Cato left us this recipe. Also, *placenta* played a traditional role in ancient Roman religion.

Take the quantities and ingredients listed by Cato. The pounds are Roman pounds (= 330g), but any pound will do.

    4 lb wheat flour, for the *tracta*
    2 lb spelt grits, for the *tracta*
    14 lb sheep's curd cheese, or ricotta
    4½ lb best honey
    2 lb wheat flour, for the crust
    olive oil
    a bed of fresh bay leaves

Make the *tracta* (see page 182–3) and roll out as you would very thin lasagne. Then take the cheese and crumble it into a bowl. Cover it with water and change the water several times until it remains clear. Then pour it off and leave the cheese in a sieve to drain. The result is a little like cottage cheese. Mash it finely, then mix it with the honey reserving a little for glazing.

Make a pastry dough with the wheat flour and some olive oil and roll out into a long sheet 30 cm across. Preheat the oven to 180°C/350°F/Gas 4.

Line the inside of a wide rectangular baking tin, large enough for the *tracta*, with greaseproof paper. Then lay the pastry in the tin, so that all the sides are covered with dough, with more hanging over the sides.

Place a single layer of *tracta* on the pastry and cover it with a thick layer of the sweet cheese. Then add another layer of *tracta* and another layer of cheese. When the baking tray is full, fold the flaps of pastry dough over the filling and put it into the oven for 30 minutes.

Then take it out and snip off the greaseproof paper that is sticking out over the edges. Take an ovenproof serving dish and cover it with fresh bay leaves. Put the tin upside down on it so that the *placenta* settles on the leaves. Remove the baking tin and the paper. If the paper sticks, put the *placenta* back into the oven until the paper dries out and will peel off. When the paper has been removed, glaze with some more honey so it covers all of the sides. Turn the oven up to 220°C/425°F/Gas 7. Put the *placenta* back in and bake it for another 15 minutes and serve in slices, hot or cold.

Variations

Cato gives a number of variations on *placenta*:

> *scribilita* – savoury *placenta* without honey
> *spira* – *placenta* in the form of a roll
> *erneum* – *placenta* cooked in a bain-marie
> *spaerita* – roll-shaped *placenta* the size of a fist.

Globus

Globi are a kind of tortellini, filled with cheese, not boiled but fried in hot lard.

> *Globos sic facito. Caseum cum alica ad eunem modum misceto. Inde quantos voles facere facito. In ahenum caldum unguen inddito, singulos aut binos coquito versatoque crebro duabus rudibus, coctos eximito eos melle unguito, papaver infriato, ita ponito.*

Globi are made like this: mix the cheese and the *alica* in the same way, in the same quantities. Melt fat in a copper pot and fry the *globi*, one or two at a time, regularly turning with the help of *rudices* [sticks]. Take them out when they are finished, pour honey over them, sprinkle with poppy seed and serve.

(Cat. R. R. lXXIX)

Cato made a dough of flour and water, to which you would add salt to taste. Knead it and roll it out on a table dusted with flour. Cut the pastry into squares.

Mix ricotta with honey and place a dollop of cheese on each square. Fold the pastries tight, and brush the joins with egg white so that they stick. Leave the *globi* to dry for several hours, turning them every now and then. Heat some lard in a frying-pan and fry the *globi* until they are golden. Drizzle them with honey, sprinkle over some poppy seed and serve.

Mills

Most grain was not kneaded into *tractum* or *amulum*, or cooked to a porridge, but milled to make flour, originally by hand, between flat round stones. Later the Romans developed hourglass-shaped mills in which one heavy stone rotated on another, the grain between them.

The milling of flour cost a great deal of blood, sweat and tears: the stones were turned not by wind-power but by a donkey or slave.

Figure 5.2 – Milling grain

Apart from handmills, the Romans also improved watermills and adopted them on a large scale. Windmills did not appear until the Middle Ages.

Varieties of Flour

The Romans primarily used flour made of spelt, wheat (*triticum*) and rye (*secale*). Millet (*millium*) was used in southern Italy.

> Millet flourishes in Campania,* where it is used to prepare a very white *puls*. An excellent bread is also made from it. The Sarmartians† live primarily on millet porridge, and even eat the flour raw. They mix it with horse's milk and with blood from the veins in a horse's leg.   (Plin. XVIII-xxiv)

The Romans inherited barley (*hordeum*) from the Greeks. Ground barley was called *polenta*, seen as the Greek equivalent of Roman *alica* and *puls*. Oats (*avena*) were viewed as a weed, but given how well they grew in cold climates, they were popular among the Germans and Celts.

Milled grain was sieved and sometimes milled twice to create white flour (*siligo*, made from wheat), fine flour (*fior* or *pollen*, from all types of grain), or it was left coarse and used as wholemeal flour (such as spelt, *farina*).

BREAD (*panis*)

To a great extent we owe the art of breadmaking to the Romans. In the early years of Rome bread was not especially impressive. Yeast was still unknown, so 'bread' was unleavened crust. Cato calls this 'kneaded bread' (*panis depicius*):

> Kneaded bread is made as follows: the flour* is placed in a baking-trough, and some water is poured over it. Knead. When the dough

* Southern Italy.
† A people on the Black Sea.

has been kneaded roll it out and bake it beneath a cover.

(Cat. R.R. LXXIV)

It looks like modern pitta and is an ancestor of the pizza. Another form of unleavened bread was 'quick bread' (*panis strepticius*), which was rolled into wafer-thin sheets then baked quickly, probably on hot stone or against the wall of the oven.

Yeast

Yeast made its debut in the days of the Republic. Conservatives resisted the temptation to eat the light bread as it was thought unhealthy. However, there was no stopping its invasion. Pliny describes six different kinds of yeast culture (Plin. N.H. XVIII-xxvi):

1. Millet kneaded with must. It should keep for a year.

2 Wheat bran soaked for three days in the must for white wine, then kneaded into rolls, soaked in water, heated and kneaded again with flour. This sort of yeast was supposed to produce high quality bread, but was not thought to keep well. It was made in the autumn when fresh must was available.

3. Dough balls of barley and water, baked brown in the ashes then kept until they fermented. They were dissolved in water before use.

4. Barley bread required a yeast culture made from chickpea flour, or from vetch.

5. In Pliny's time the commonest yeast was sourdough, prepared by boiling unsalted flour with water to a porridge and leaving it to ferment. Then it was used as yeast.

6. Another common form of leavening was simply to keep part of the previous day's risen dough and mix it with fresh dough.

The introduction of yeast almost coincided with the arrival of baking as a specialist occupation. Until this point bread was made in the

---

* *Farina*, which is wholemeal spelt flour

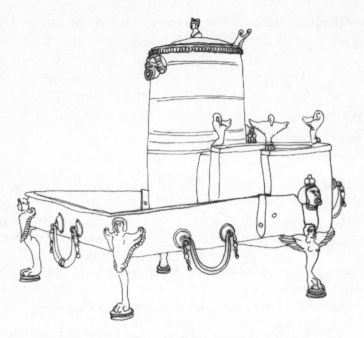

Figure 5.3 – Bronze oven with hot water pot

home. According to Pliny, yeast arrived with the outbreak of the Third Macedonian War (171–168 BC). The word *pistor* now began to mean 'baker', and bread began to take over from *puls* as a national staple. The people demanded 'bread and circuses', rather than '*puls* and circuses'.

Many people ate bread at every meal, with every course and between courses. It was used as an item of cutlery, almost like a spoon, as a plate (as in the Middle Ages) and even as a napkin for wiping the hands.

Types of Bread

Bread was made from all kinds of cereal, and even from ground pulses or rice. The dough was sometimes mixed with oil or bacon fat, which meant it kept fresh for longer. Pliny records that in the provinces bread was 'even' made with butter. Sometimes grape juice was mixed into the dough, as were wine, milk or eggs. Spices, such as cumin, pepper, caraway, fennel, sesame and poppy seed, were also used as flavourings.

Bread was baked in a stone oven (*fornax*), or in a small bronze oven (*clibanus*). Flat breads were baked over hot coals, in hot ashes or on a spit (Ath. 113). According to Pliny, you could not begin to name all the types of bread, but here are a few examples:

Panis mustaceus – bread baked in a ring with a laurel wreath on top (see page 194). Cato gives the ingredients: 660g fat, 330g fresh cheese, 8.7 litres *farina*, anis, cumin and must, which gives the bread its name (Cat. R.R. CXXI). It was eaten at wedding feasts, hence the large quantities. Reduce them in the same proportions.

Panis farreus – bread made of coarse spelt flour, to be broken and shared by the bride and groom on their wedding night.

Panis adipatus – a kind of pizza containing pieces of bacon and bacon fat.

Panis militaris – soldiers' bread, which came in two varieties, camp bread, *castrensis,* and marching bread, *mundus.* Both were a kind of dry biscuit that had to be soaked in water before eating, like Italian *friselle* (see Plin. N.H. XVIII-68).

Panis nauticus – probably resembled soldiers' breads, or ship's biscuits (Plin. N.H. XXII, 138).

Panis picentino – also comparable to *friselle,* in that it had to be soaked before eating, in this case in milk or *mulsum.* It was a luxury bread, made from *alica,* which was soaked for nine days then kneaded with raisin juice (*uvae passae suco,* the sweet juice of dried grapes). It was shaped into a long roll, placed in a clay pot and baked in the oven until the pot burst (Plin. N.H. XVIII-106).

Panis quadratus – despite its name this bread is not square but circular. It owes its name to the incisions in the dough that divided the bread into chunks (Ath. 114e).

Panis boletus – bread that had risen in the shape of a mushroom. It was placed in the mould covered with poppy seeds to ensure that it did not stick. It was the colour of smoked cheese (Ath. 113c).

Panis alexandrinus – a popular and frequently mentioned bread. We do not know exactly how it was made, except that it contained Egyptian cumin, hence the name, and probably honey.

Panis cappadocianus – this 'Turkish' bread was made from a wet dough of flour and milk with large quantities of salt. It was not baked for long so it had a soft crust (Ath. 113b).

Panis lomentus – bread made from the flour of dried and ground broad beans (Plin. N.H. XVIII-117).

Panis secundarius – originally white bread was a luxury, but by the time of the Empire it was eaten by the common people. Brown bread was older, heavier and considered healthier, which is why many such as Emperor Augustus preferred it. White bread was supposed to cause constipation (Suet. Aug. 76).

Orindes – bread made from rice (Ath. 110e).

Cybus – cube-shaped bread, with aniseed, fresh sheep's cheese and olive oil (Ath. 114a).

Mazas – barley biscuits (Ath. 114e).

Cribana – bread containing curd cheese, in the shape of a woman's breast (Ath. 114f).

General Recipe for Bread

Breadmaking is so simple yet so specific that no two bakers produce identical loaves. All bread is based on flour and liquid, usually water. The purest bread consists solely of water and flour. Bread without salt is unusual, but is still made in Tuscany. When Pliny describes how to make leaven, he recommends that salt should not be added before the bread itself is made. It is the only instance that we have from antiquity in which salt is mentioned as an ingredient of bread – it was taken for granted.

Don't use too much yeast: it leaves an aftertaste. A small amount of yeast and a long rising time leads to a better result. The proportion of yeast to flour depends on the kind of yeast. Take approximately 10g of fresh baker's yeast, and 300 ml water to 1 kg flour.

A sourdough starter is a mixture of half water and half flour that has been left to ferment. Yeast organisms thrive on this, and it is easy to start a culture with some fresh yeast. The older the sourdough starter, the stronger the taste. Sourdough takes longer to rise than dough made with yeast.

Warm 30 ml of water to body temperature – no hotter or you will kill the bacteria. Dissolve the yeast in the water. Mix the liquid with some flour into a paste. Leave it to stand for 10 minutes until it starts bubbling gently. Mix in the flour gradually, then add 1 tablespoon of salt. Knead the dough for at least 15 minutes, but longer if possible. Then leave it to rise, away from draughts, under a damp cloth or plastic sheet so that it does not dry out. Throughout Europe, bread is left to rise in two stages: first, to three-quarters of its final size, after which it is briefly kneaded again, and second, the 'proving', 2–3 hours, depending on the weather.

Light the wood stove. When it has reached a temperature of 250°C/500°F/Gas 9 pizzas and similar varieties of thin bread can be cooked in it. Leave the door open while baking. When the oven has cooled to 140°C/275°F/Gas 1, put in the round loaves. It takes a certain skill to get the loaves into the right place, and once they are in do not move them again. Close the oven tightly, so that it cools slowly. The loaves can generally be taken out after 60–90 minutes.

Brush a loaf straight from the oven with water for a gleaming crust. Otherwise, sprinkle it with flour or glaze it before baking with egg, beaten white for a colourless glaze, yolk for golden-yellow, mixed with water and/or honey, as you wish.

Sala Cattabia

There are many uses for stale bread. For example, you can soak it and stir in herbs, tomatoes or cheese. If you have no stale bread, break fresh bread into pieces and dry it in a warm oven.

Aliter sala cattabia: panem alexandrinum excavabis, in posca macerabis. Adicies in mortarium piper, mel, mentam, alium, coriandrum viride, caseum bubulum sale conditum, aquam, oleum. Insuper nivem et inferes.

Another s*ala cattabia*: take an Alexandrian bread and soak it in *posca*. Add pepper, honey, mint, garlic, green coriander, salted

cow's-milk cheese, water and oil to the mortar. Place in snow and
serve.   (Ap. 116)

1 cumin loaf
500 g flour
300 ml *posca* (spiced vinegar with water)
½ head garlic, peeled and crushed
200 g salted cow's milk cheese (such as *provolone*), crushed
2 tablespoons fresh coriander
2 tablespoons fresh mint
1 teaspoon honey
4 tablespoons olive oil
100 ml cold white wine

Bake a cumin loaf with honey in a rectangular mould. Remove the
crust and cut the crumb when cooled into cubes and soak these in
the *posca*. Mix together all the ingredients with the bread cubes. Put
it into the refrigerator to chill and serve on a hot summer day.

French Toast

*Aliter dulcia: muteos afros optimos rades et in lacte infundis. Cum
biberint, in furnum mittis, ne arescant, modice. Eximes eos calidos,
melle perfundis, compungis ut bibant. Piper asperges et inferes.*

Another sweet dish: cut the crust from the best African *mustaceum*
bread and soak it in milk. When it is saturated bake it in the oven,
but not for too long to avoid drying it out. Remove the bread
when it is hot, and pour honey over it. Prick holes in it so that it
absorbs the honey. Sprinkle with pepper and serve.   (Ap. 301)

This isn't real French toast because it has no egg in it. Also, this
recipe is more laborious than the modern variant, because the bread
has to be specially baked. Make it with a little fresh yeast dissolved in
honey-water, 500 g flour, 2 teaspoons crushed aniseed and 2 teaspoons
crushed cumin. Use white wine and white grape juice to moisten the
dough. Knead the dough, leave it to rest then bake it for 30 minutes.
The crust should not be too firm. As soon as the bread has cooled,

remove the crust and cut the crumb into slices or cubes. Soak them in creamy milk until soft, and bake at 180°C/350°F/Gas 4. Take them out, drench them in honey, sprinkle with pepper and serve.

Pastry Dough

Roman pastry dough was made with lard or olive oil rather than butter. Use double the weight of the fat in flour. Spelt flour needs rather less fat than wheat flour. Rub the fat into the flour until it resembles breadcrumbs. Pour in a little salted water and press the crumbs into a ball. Leave it in a cool place for several hours. Then roll it into a sheet on a marble surface dusted with flour, and use as the recipe requires.

PULSES

Cereal plants might have been the first to be cultivated, but pulses came a pretty close second. Cereals and pulses can be dried, and were both listed by Pliny and Columella as large-scale agricultural products. The Romans did not see pulses as vegetables to be grown in the garden: like grain, pulses were a bulk crop for mass consumption.

The Romans were keen on their pulses. Various noble families owned their names to the products grown by their ancestors. Thus the Cicero family took its name from the *cicer* (the chickpea), the Lentula family from the *lens* (lentil) and the famous Fabii owed their name to the bean (*faba*).

BROAD BEAN (*faba*)

'The highest place among the pulses is occupied by the broad bean,' writes Pliny (Plin. N.H. XVIII-xxx). He gives two reasons for this. First, flour was ground from broad beans, *lomentum*, which was made into biscuits and bread. Second, the beans had a religious status, although he did not know why. Pliny mentions that *puls fabata*, a broad bean soup, was sacred and offered to the gods.

Pythagoras forbade his followers to eat broad beans. According to Pliny, this was because broad beans were thought to be soporific. Others thought that Pythagoras believed the human soul resided in the bean – he spoke of a kind of reincarnation in which the soul did not always dwell in a human but sometimes in an animal or a plant.

Lemuria

An ancient Roman ritual linked the broad bean and the soul. It was performed at the Lemuria, on the nights of 9, 11 and 13 May. That was when ground spirits, *lemures* (see page 55), were believed to come above ground.

During the Lemuria the master of the house had to get out of bed each night at midnight to banish the ghosts. He walked through the house barefoot, washed his hands and stuck his thumb between his second and third fingers (nowadays an obscene gesture). Then he took nine black broad beans, and threw them away from him one by one, without looking where they fell. Each time he threw one he said, '*Haec ego mitto his, redimo meque meosque fabis.*' ('This I throw. With these beans I redeem myself and my family.')

As the master walked on, the beans mysteriously disappeared. Then, nine times, he asked the ghosts to leave: '*Manes exite paterni.*' ('Ghosts of my fathers, be off!') Only then could he look around to be sure that the house was free of ghosts (Ov. Fasti V-435).

Living Broad Bean

One reason for belief in the 'living broad bean' might lie in its shape. Take a fresh pod and remove the beans. On each bean there is a gash that looks a little like a vagina. Now remove the waxy peel, leaving the heart, which looks like a belly with male sexual parts. The broad bean seems thus to represent both sexes.

From the culinary point of view it is important that the broad bean is edible both in female form (with peel) and in male form (without). In female form it can be eaten only when the beans are young.

In all other cases it is better to remove the skins, although this is hard work.

The Romans served skinned beans raw in a salad, mixed with herbs and often fresh cheese. Unskinned beans are always cooked, as are dried beans.

Broad Beans Vitellius

Pisam vitellianam sive fabam: pisam coques, lias. Teres piper, ligusticum, zingiber et super condimenta mittis vitella ovorum, quae dura coxeris, mellis unc. iii, liquamen, vinum et acetum. Haec omnia mittis in caccabum et condimenta quae trivisti. Adiecti oleo ponis ut ferveat. condies pisam, lias, si aspera fuerit. Mel mittis et inferes.

Peas or broad beans à la Vitellius: cook the peas, stir. Crush pepper, lovage, ginger, and to these add hard-boiled egg yolks, 81g honey, wine and vinegar. Put this into a pot with the crushed spices. Add oil and bring to the boil. Season the peas as necessary. Add honey and serve.

(Ap. 197)

500g dried broad beans, soaked and peeled
2 tablespoons salt or *garum* to taste
½ teaspoon lovage seed
1 teaspoon peppercorns
2 tablespoons freshly grated ginger
2 tablespoons honey
3 tablespoons vinegar
6 tablespoons virgin olive oil
4 hard-boiled egg yolks
100 ml white wine
50g (a sprig) of fresh coriander

Wash the beans in several changes of water, then leave them to soak overnight. Then put them into a saucepan and bring them to the boil. Do not add salt, because, Pliny writes,

'In seawater or salt water they will not cook through.'

(Plin. N.H. XVIII-xxx)

And he is right. Salt extracts moisture and helps fresh vegetables to cook, but dried pulses toughen. Seasonings are added only when the beans are soft. During cooking skim off any scum that rises. The beans will be ready after about 20 minutes.

Now make the sauce. Grind the lovage to fine powder, then grind in the peppercorns. Mix the ginger with the honey, pepper and lovage, the vinegar and oil. Then add the egg yolks, mash them in, and stir in the wine. Add this mixture to the beans, stir and leave to stand for a few hours so that the flavours combine. This dish is lovely served cold, but it can also be warmed in the oven, or, as Apicius suggests, fried with olive oil. The coriander should be added just before serving.

Broad Beans with Meatballs

Aliter pisam sive faban: ubil despuma verity, teres mel, liquamen, caroenum, cuminum, rutam, apii semen, oleum et vinum. Tudiclabis. Cum pipere trito et cum isicis inferes.

Another recipe for peas or broad beans: once the beans have foamed, grind honey, caroenum, cumin, rue, celery seed, oil and wine. Mix together. Serve with ground pepper and meatballs.

(Ap. 198)

500g dried broad beans or split peas
500g meatballs (see page 260)
1 teaspoon cumin
1 teaspoon peppercorns
1 teaspoon celery seed
1 teaspoon honey
1 small sprig rue
100ml *caroenum* (reduced red wine)
100ml *garum*
300ml white wine

Soak the beans, then cook them shimming off the foaming scum, until they are almost soft in unsalted water. Drain, then mix them with the meatballs. Pound the rest of the ingredients except the white wine in the mortar. Stir in the white wine and add the mixture to the beans and meatballs. Bring to the boil and leave to bubble until the meatballs are hot and the beans tender.

Lentils

Lentils with Coriander

Aliter lenticulam: coquis. Cum despumaverit porrum et coriandrum viride supermittis. (Teres) coriandri semen, puleium, laseris radicem, semen mentae et rutae, suffundis acetum, adicies mel, liquamine, aceto, defrito temperabis, adicies oleum, agitabis, si quid opus fuerit, mittis. Amulo obligas, insuper oleum viride mittis, piper aspargis et inferes.

Another lentil recipe. Boil them. When they have foamed, add leeks and green coriander. [Crush] coriander seed, pennyroyal, laser root, mint seed and rue seed. Moisten with vinegar, add honey, *garum*, vinegar, mix in a little *defrutum*, add oil and stir. Add extra as required. Bind with *amulum*, drizzle with green oil and sprinkle with pepper. Serve.   (Ap. 192)

250g lentils
2 litres water
1 leek, trimmed, washed and finely chopped
75g fresh coriander
5g coriander seed
3g peppercorns, plus extra for finishing the dish
3g mint seed
3g rue seed
75g fresh pennyroyal, or mint
10ml *garum*
10ml vinegar
5ml honey
olive oil

Wash the lentils and put them into a saucepan with 2 litres of cold water. Bring to the boil, and skim off the scum. When the water has cleared, add the leek and half of the fresh coriander. Grind the spices and the other herbs, and add them with the *garum*, vinegar and *defrutum* to the pan. Let the lentils simmer until they are almost cooked. Check the pan every now and then to ensure that the water has not evaporated. At the last minute add the olive oil, the freshly ground pepper and the remainder of the chopped coriander.

Lentil Soup

There were endless variations on lentil soup, which was eaten in all countries around the Mediterranean. It is even mentioned in the Bible.

> And Jacob made pottage: and Esau came in from the field, and he was faint. And Esau said to Jacob, Feed me, I pray thee, with that same red pottage, for I am faint. [. . .] And Jacob said, Sell me this day thy birthright. And Esau said, Behold, I am at the point to die, and what profit shall this birthright do to me? And Jacob said, Swear to me this day; and he sware unto him: and he sold his birthright unto Jacob. Then Jacob gave Esau bread and pottage of lentils.   (Genesis 25: 29–34)

It is not clear why this famous plate of lentil soup should have been red. Certainly, Egyptian lentils are red when dry, but they turn yellow when cooked. Perhaps there was some sort of dye in Jacob's soup. Athenaeus, for example, refers to perfumed lentil soup (see page 167–8), and some perfumes contained red dye. By coincidence, Judaea and the surrounding area exported large amounts of perfume during the Roman era.

Make perfumed and dyed lentil soup by soaking lentils and boiling them until they fall apart. Then add salt, wine, ground cinnamon, red food dye and a few drops of oil of myrrh. (This can be bought in shops selling incense and oils for religious purposes.) Don't use cheap substitutes, and look out for additives, especially since perfumes are no longer produced for eating. Allow the soup to cook through and serve it.

Variations listed by Athenaeus include 'lentil soup with coriander seed', for which you should use one part coriander seed to twelve parts lentil, and 'lentil soup with bulbs (or onions)', a typical winter dish. Another alternative is lentils with *asafoetida*, or garlic (Ath. IV-158 vv).

PEAS

Peas with Basil

Pisa: pisam coques. Cum despuma verity, porrum, coriandrum et cuminum supra mittis. Teres piper, liguisticum, careum, anethum, ocimum viride, suffundis liquamen, vino et liquamine temperabis, facies ut ferveat. Cum ferbuerit agitabis. Si quid defuerit, mittis et inferes.

Cook the peas. Add the leek when it has foamed, along with the coriander and the cumin. Grind pepper, lovage, caraway, dill, fresh basil, moisten with *garum*, mix with wine and *garum* and bring to the boil. Stir while cooking. If anything is missing, add it and serve.   (Ap. 193)

500g dried peas
1 leek, trimmed, washed and cut into rings
1 sprig fresh coriander
1 sprig fresh cumin
1 good sprig fresh basil
1 teaspoon fresh lovage seed
1 teaspoon pepper
2 teaspoons caraway seed
2 teaspoons dill seed
200ml white wine
100ml *garum*

Soak the peas overnight, then boil for 15 minutes in unsalted water. Skim of any scum and add the leek with the coriander and cumin. Grind the spices. Strain the peas, then stir in the spices, the wine and the *garum*. Bring it to the boil until heated through. Add the chopped basil just before serving.

De Luxe Stuffed Peas

Pisam farsilem: coques. Cui oleum mittis, abdomen et mittis in cac-
cabum liquamen et porrum capitum, coriandrum viride. Imponeis
ut coquatur. Isicia minuta facies quadrata et coques simul turdos vel
aucellas vel de pullo concisa et cerebella prope cocta cum iuscello
coques. Lucanicas assas, petasonem elixas, porros ex aqua coques,
nucleorum heminam frigis, lias. Angularem accipies, qui versari
potest. et omentis tegis. Oleo perfundis deinde nucleos aspargis et supra
pisam mittis ut tegas fundum angulis et sic componis supra petasto-
nis pulpa, porros, lucanicas concisas, iterum pisam supermittis. Item
alternis aptabis obsonia, quousque impleat angulis. Novissime pisam
mittis, ut intus omnia contineat. Coques in furno vel lento igni
imponis, ut ducat ad se deorsum. Ova dura facies, vitella eicies, in
mortario mittis cum pipere albo, nucleis, melle, vino candido et
liquamine modico. Teres et mittis in vas ut ferveat. Cum ferbuerit,
pisam mittis in lancem et hoc iure perfundis. Hoc ius candidum
appelatur.

Stuffed peas. Boil. Then add oil. Put the bacon in a pot with
the *garum* and leek including its head, and fresh coriander. Cook
on the fire. Dice the meat and bake it with pigeon or another
bird, or pieces of chicken, and with brains cooked in the stock.
Roast Lucanian sausages. Boil shoulder-ham with leek. Roast
300g pine nuts. Crush pepper, lovage, oregano and ginger.
Add bacon stock and stir. Take a rectangular baking-tin that
can be inverted, and line it with pork caul. Pour in oil, sprinkle
in pine nuts and then some of the peas to cover the base. On
this place pieces of ham, the leek and the chopped Lucanian
sausages, then another layer of peas. Fill the baking-tin with the
ingredients in layers after this fashion. End with a layer of peas.
Cook in the oven on a low flame until everything is cooked
together. Take hard-boiled eggs, remove the yolks and grind the
white in the mortar, with white pepper, pine nuts, honey, white
wine and a little *garum*. Turn the pea-tart out on a serving bowl
and pour the sauce over as soon as it boils. It is called white
sauce.   (Ap. 194)

Not a simple plate of peas, but certainly worth the trouble.

500g dried peas
200g bacon
200g Lucanian sausages
500g shoulder ham
300g small meatballs
500 pigeons and poultry
1 leek
200g pine nuts
1 pair lamb's brains
pork caul (see page 257)
olive oil
200g pine nuts

for sauce 1
2 teaspoons peppercorns
1 tablespoon oregano
1 tablespoon freshly grated ginger
1 tablespoon freshly chopped lovage

for sauce 2
6 boiled eggs
200g pine nuts
100ml white wine
garum

Soak the dried peas overnight in fresh water, then boil them for 25 minutes. Preheat the oven to 180°C/350°C/Gas 4. Cut up the meat (apart from the brains), the poultry and the leek and fry everything in a pan with some olive oil. Then add water and simmer for an hour. Clean the brains and cook, until most of the moisture has evaporated. Strain the liquid from the meat pan into another saucepan, when there is about 400ml over. Allow the meat and the brains to cool, then finely chop the brains.

Grind together the ingredients for sauce 1. Stir the paste into the cooking liquid from the meat. Taste, and add salt if necessary.

Line a large baking tin with greaseproof paper, then with pork caul. Pour over some olive oil, then cover it with some of the pine nuts and peas. Place some of the meat on top and moisten it with sauce 1. Repeat, until everything has been used up. Fold the caul over the top. Seal the baking tin with silver foil and bake at least 1 hour.

Meanwhile put the ingredients for sauce 2 into a blender and whiz to a smooth sauce. Pour it into a bowl, set the bowl over a saucepan of simmering water and let it heat through. The caul should have melted or turned golden in colour. If not, return the tart to the oven. To serve, turn out the tart on to a serving plate and pour over sauce 2.

CHICKPEAS (*cicer*)

Chickpeas were boiled then seasoned like other pulses, but also soaked, roasted in the oven, salted and eaten like peanuts – as they still are in Turkey and southern Italy. Apiciuis has a variation on this:

> *Aliter faseolus sive cicer: frictos oenogaro et pipere.*

> Another way of preparing *faseolus** or chickpea: eat them baked with *oenogarum* and pepper.   (Ap. 212)

Soak some chickpeas, bake them in the olive oil and serve with pepper, white wine and anchovy paste.

LUPIN (*lupinus*)

Lupins are familiar as a garden flower but, like all members of the papilionaceous family, they produce pods. The beans in the pods of the *Lupinus albus graecus* are edible. The Romans and Greeks grew lupins because they enrich impoverished soil.

> They [the beans] are . . . suitable for human consumption once they have been soaked in hot water. For cattle, one bulb per animal is enough to make them strong. They are even used as a medicine against stomach pains in children.
>
>   (Plin. N.H. XVIII-xxxvi)

Lupin beans are still popular in Italy where they are salted. Before being eaten they are rinsed under running water and skinned.

Figure 5.4

Conchicla

With many pulses, like peas and broad beans, it was not only the beans themselves that were eaten but also the pods when they were young and tender, just as we eat sugarsnaps, mange-touts and French beans. Dishes of pea- or bean-pods were called '*conchicla*' and B. Flower and E. Rosenbaum in *The Roman Cookery Book* suggest that *conchicla* were served on a scallop-shaped dish. According to these authors, *conchicla* recipes were prepared with dried peas, but they were named after the serving dish, just as *patina* dishes are named after a pan. The recipes call for skimming, which is not usually necessary with fresh pods. Apicius writes in the recipe below, 'Take a *conchiclarem*', which, indeed, seems to indicate a bowl. He also mentions 'peas that are cooked but not yet seasoned', which suggest dried peas.

On the other hand most Italian historians claim that *conchicla* means 'fresh young beans in the pod'. Here is an example of this much-debated dish:

* *Faseolus* is sometimes translated as French bean, although that seems unlikely in here.

Aliter conchiclam sic facies: concidis pullum minutatim, liquamine, oleo et vino ferveat. Concidis cepam, coriandrum minutum, cerebella enervate, mittis in eundem pullum. Com coctus fuerit, levas et exossas. Concides minutatim cepam et coriandrum, colas ibi pisam coctam non conditam. Accipies conchiclarem pro modo. Componis varie. Deinde teres piper, cuminum, suffundis ius de suo sibi. Item in mortario ova duo dissolves, temperas. Ius de suo sibi suffundis pisae integre elixae, vel nucleis adornabis, et lento igni fervere facies et inferes.

Another *conchicla* recipe is made as follows: cut a chicken into small pieces and cook in *garum*, oil and wine. Finely slice an onion and [fresh] coriander and peeled brains, and add these to the chicken. When it is cooked take the chicken out of the liquid. Remove the bones. Finely chop an onion and coriander, rinse with cooked beans that have not yet been seasoned. Take a suitable *conchiclarem* and put the various ingredients into it. Then grind pepper and cumin and add some of the chicken stock. Also break two eggs above the mortar and mix with the rest. Pour the remainder of the chicken stock over the whole cooked peas, decorate with pine nuts if you wish. Heat over a low flame and serve.   (Ap. 206)

Prepare this dish however you like with pulses, French beans, sugar-snaps or dried peas. Cook and serve in a scallop-shaped dish with pieces of chicken, brains, onion and fresh coriander in a strong chicken stock flavoured with cumin, pepper and *garum* and enriched in two beaten eggs.

VEGETABLES

Grain and pulses are grown in the field, vegetables in the garden. Romans distinguished sharply between agriculture and horticulture:

In our laws, the word 'farm' is never used, only ever the word 'garden'. And that is what it means.   (Plin. N.H. XIX-xix)

Agriculture was mass production out in the field, and the Romans put it out to contract. Rome's overseas provinces, like Sicily and Africa, became the imperial breadbasket. Egypt almost went bankrupt as a result of the grain-based monoculture imposed on it. However, the Romans preferred to do their own gardening:

Even the kings of Rome did their gardening with their own hands.

(Plin. N.H. XIX-xix)

HORTUS

The word for garden, *hortus*, was elastic. Originally it referred to an inner courtyard with herbs, vegetables and fruit trees. It was surrounded by a wall or a thorn hedge, to keep out wild animals and apple-thieves, and keep in the insect-eating fowl and the children. It featured fountains and ponds, which not only served a practical purpose in watering plants and animals but also turned the garden into a playground. Temples, waterfalls, *triclinia*, decorative flowers, colourful birds and statues were introduced.

In every garden there was at least one statue of Priapus, the god of gardens (see also page 82). He had a beard, and his face was red. We often see him wearing a red Phrygian cap, which makes him look rather like the garden gnomes of today of which he is clearly an ancestor. Priapus differed from the gnome in one crucial respect: 'In the garden, seek no statue of Daedalus or Polyclitus . . . for there in the middle stands Priapus, frightening children with his enormous member and chasing off intruders with his sickle' (Col. R.R. X 34). Given the many statues of him, he must have been popular, despite his appearance.

A town house originally had a courtyard, rather than a garden, surrounded on all sides by a gallery of columns, the *peristylum*, where only some potted herbs and vegetables were grown for domestic use. The covered cloister could be used for storing tools, and protecting herbs when the sun was too hot. Over time these courtyards and the gardens became bigger until they eventually resembled country estates.

Nowadays, under the name *hortus*, people own whole farms in the middle of the city. This was first done in Athens, by the expert in

luxury comforts: Epicurus. Prior to this, the custom of having
country houses in town had not existed. In Rome the *hortus* had
always been a simple man's farm. The lower classes normally
fetched their food from the garden. Ah, how innocent life was
back in those days!   (Plin. N.H. XIX-xix)

Cultivation

A Roman patrician's pride and joy were his vegetables. Earning money
from trade was considered vulgar, fishing was for decadent Greeks, and
the herding of cattle was left to barbarians. Vegetable-growing, though,
was perfectly acceptable.

Learned men took agriculture and horticulture seriously, and
accumulated considerable knowledge on the subjects. They became
masters of irrigation, manure, grafting, pruning and crop rotation.

Figure 5.5 – Greengrocer

Agriculture and horticulture were environmentally sound: the Romans knew exactly which plants should and should not be placed adjacent to one another, to avoid disease and insects. If an insecticide was required, wild cucumbers were soaked in water, which was poured over the offenders (Varr. RR. I-ii), or insect-eating birds were introduced.

The Romans did not think of vegetables as side dishes. They merited a place of honour at the table – the gourmet knew his onions. The Romans took wild, sometimes unpalatable plants and developed them into vegetables that are now common: cabbage and other brassicas like kale, cauliflower, sprouts, broccoli, as well as lettuce, endive, onions, leek, asparagus, French beans, courgettes, artichoke, radishes and cucumber.

Pliny thought the mania for vegetables was going too far. They should, he thought, remain cheap and available to all.

> The ordinary people complain that there are vegetables that are not meant for them. Even kale is so fertilized that it assumes enormous dimensions for which there is no longer any room on poor people's tables. Asparagus grows wild in nature. Anyone can go and pick it. But behold, now it's being cultivated and in Ravenna they weigh 100g apiece. Oh, the horrors of greed. We would think it odd for our cattle to eat thistles, but nowadays there are thistles* beyond the pocket of the plebeians.
>
> (Plin. N.H. XIX 54)

Pliny was an advocate of peasant simplicity and may have found asparagus and artichoke a little too dainty, but he was even less impressed by other delicacies:

> Does it give more pleasure to dive to the depths of the sea in search of a certain kind of oyster and run the risk of shipwreck? Or to go beyond the river Phasis to catch birds that not even legendary horror stories can protect? They are in fact prized all the more highly because of those stories! Or going hunting for birds in Numibia, or among the graveyards of Ethiopia? Or to chase wild

---

* Artichokes and cardoons.

beasts and thus, while looking for something to devour, ending up being devoured oneself?

I have only one thing to say: how cheap, delicious and healthy vegetables are for everyone.   (Plin. N.H. XIX-xix)

Turnips (*rapum*)

The turnip was seen as simple fare. The plant is native to Europe, nutritious, easily cultivated and therefore cheap. Opinions differed about how healthy it was. The great doctor Democritus rejected turnips, believing they made people feel bloated. Other doctors saw the turnip in a more positive light:

Diocles praises the turnip plant, declaring that it stimulates the amorous propensities. So too does Dionysius, who adds that its effects are even stronger if eaten with rocket.   (Plin. N.H. XX-viii)

Healthy or not, the turnip had many devotees, of whom Emperor Claudius was one. When he died, it was announced that he was to be deified so there would be someone in heaven who could eat turnip with Rome's founding father, Romulus (Sen. Apoc. 9).

Martial wrote an *apophoreta* on the subject of this winter vegetables:

Turnip I give, to bring you some cheer in the frost of the shortest day, while Romulus – no less – is eating the same in heaven.

(Mart. XIII 16)

Boiled Turnip

Apicius gives two sauces for boiled turnip. One consists only of olive oil and 'if you wish' a little vinegar. The other is more complex:

Elixates, exprimes, deinde teres cuminunum plurimum, rutam minus, laster particum, mel, acetum, liquamen, defritum, et oleum modice. Fervere facies et inferes.

Boil [the turnip] and allow it to drain. Then grind more cumin and less rue, *asafoetida*, honey, *liquamen*, *defrutum*, and a little oil. Boil and serve.

This sauce is easy to make if you have the ingredients. Otherwise it can be quite laborious. If you have no *defrutum* in the house, make some (see page 148). Put about a glass of it into a pan with two glasses of stock, salted with anchovies or a salty *garum*. Flavour with a tablespoon of honey, a few tablespoons of vinegar and a dash of olive oil. Crush a tablespoon of toasted cumin seeds and a smaller amount of rue seeds and stir them into the sauce. Add a tiny pinch of *asafoetida*, diluted in a spoonful of liquid. Bring the sauce to the boil. Then add the pre-cooked turnips, cut into bite-sized pieces, so that they can absorb the sauce.

Preserved Turnip

Turnips keep well in a dark space in their natural state, but they were also preserved as a luxury item. In modern France grated turnip is pickled, with salt and juniper berries, like sauerkraut – *choucroûte de navets*. The Romans tended to leave the turnips whole, just scored them. Here is a recipe from Apicius:

> *Rapae ut diu serventur: ante accuratas et compositas asperges myrtae bacis cum melle et aceto. Aliter: sinapi tempera melle, aceto, sale, et super composites rapas infundes.*

> To preserve turnips: first clean them and put them into a pot. Sprinkle myrtle berries over them with honey and vinegar. Otherwise mix mustard and honey, vinegar and salt and pour this over the potted turnips.   (Ap. 24)

Apicius' recipe is, as usual, incomplete – there's no salt. Fortunately Columella has also left detailed instructions for preserving turnips:

> Take the roundest turnips you can find and scrape them clean if they are dirty. Peel them with a sharp knife. Then, with an iron sickle, make an incision in the shape of an X, as picklers

do, but be careful not to cut all the way through. Then sprinkle the incisions with salt, not especially fine. Place the turnips on a basket or in a trough, with a little extra salt, and allow the moisture to dry out for three days. After three days a piece from the inside of one turnip should be tasted, to tell whether the salt has penetrated through. If it has been absorbed, remove the turnips and wash them in their own moisture. If not enough moisture has been secreted, add some salt liquor and wash them in that.

Then place them in a square wicker basket, not too tightly woven, but strongly made with thick wicker. Then place a board on the turnips that can be pressed down within the opening of the basket if necessary. When the board is in place, put heavy weights on it and leave the turnips to dry overnight. Then place them in a jug treated with resin, or in a glazed pot, and pour vinegar with mustard over it, so that they are submerged. You can use them after thirteen days.   (Col. R.R. XII-1vi)

If only Apicius were as precise and detailed in his recipes! To this last description we need only add that about 1 tablespoon of mustard should be used for every 5 turnips, and that it is well worth taking the trouble to preserve some. The turnips assume a flavour reminiscent of horseradish. Cut them into thin slices before serving.

BEETROOT

Beetroot with Mustard

Beetroot leaves were eaten as well as the roots. They were served together, possibly with the leaf still attached to the root, as they are often shown in pictures. Beetroot can be boiled, with leaves and stalks above the water where they steam lightly.

Betas elixas: ex sinapi, oleo modico, et aceto bene inferuntur.

Boiled beet: served with mustard, a little oil and vinegar they are very good.   (Ap. 92)

Boil 4 small red beetroot, leave to cool, then peel. Cut them into slices. Make a vinaigrette of 50 ml oil, 50 ml vinegar and 3 tablespoons of mustard. Pour this over the beetroot and serve.

Roman *Borshch*

Beetroot soup was already in vogue.

Aliter betacios varroni. Varro: 'betacios, sed nigros, quorum detersas radices et mulsa decoctas cum sale modico et oleo vel sale, aqua et oleo in se coctas iusculum facere et potari, melius etiam si in eo pulus sit decoctus.'

Another beetroot recipe from Varro: 'Take red beet, scrape the beets clean and boil in *mulsum* with a little salt and oil, or make a soup from them with salt, water and oil. It is drunk like this. It is better if a chicken is cooked in it.'
(Ap. 64)

Make a stock of water, sweet white wine, salt and a skinny old chicken. Then peel 4 beetroot and add them to the stock. Remove the chicken. When the soup is dark red and tasty, strain it and pour it back into the pan. Leave it to cool. If preferred remove some of the chicken fat and replace it with a dash of olive oil. The Russians often use fermented beetroot juice in borscht. In all likelihood the Romans also discovered that the soup tastes better after a few days. Bring it to the boil every 12 hours to prevent it spoiling. Add pieces of chopped beetroot before serving.

RADISH

Radishes with Pepper

Rafanos cum piperato, ita ut piper cum liquamine teras.

Radishes with pepper: grind pepper with *garum* and use to season the radishes.
(Ap. 30)

Carrot (*caroeta*)

Roman carrots were yellower and tougher than ours.

Caroetae frictae: oenogaro inferuntur.

Fried carrots: served with *oenogarum*.   (Ap. 113)

The recipe is rather abrupt and somewhat incomplete. Raw carrots are not easy to fry, and this would have been even more true of the woody Roman variety. The Turks still use a recipe for fried carrots in which the carrots are first blanched in slices or strips, then coated with seasoned flour. To stay close to Apicius, omit the flour.

Fry the carrots in very hot olive oil until they are brown and leave them to drain on a piece of bread. Serve immediately with a pot of *oenogarum* as a dipping sauce. In Turkey caraway seed is sprinkled on the carrots.

Parsnip (*pastinaca*)

Apicius equates the parsnip with the carrot, and the recipes for each vegetable are interchangeable. Apart from the above recipe for fried carrot he also suggests that carrots can be eaten with oil, vinegar and salt, possibly referring to a salad of raw carrots. A third recipe is a little sharper.

Aliter: caroetas elixas concissas in cuminatuo oleo modico coques et inferes. Cuminatum coliculorum facies.

Alternative: cut the boiled carrots into small pieces and boil in cumin sauce with a little oil. Serve. Use the cumin sauce for cabbage.   (Ap. 113)

Peel the carrots or parsnips and parboil them in salt water. Then dice them. The cumin sauce for cabbage is not very different from the cumin sauce for turnips (see page 210–11):

Cuminum, salem, vinum vetus, et oleum. Si voles addes piper et ligusticum, mentam, rutam, coriandrum.

Cumin, salt, old wine and oil. If you wish, add pepper, lovage, mint, rue and coriander.   (Ap. 81)

Once again Apicius leaves some options open, but cumin should obviously remain the principal flavour.

½ tablespoon cumin seed
1 teaspoon peppercorns
3 glasses old red wine
1 teaspoon lovage seed
1 teaspoon rue seed
1 teaspoon coriander seed
1 tablespoon chopped or dried mint

Crush the spices and leave them to soak in the wine for a day. Strain the liquid, then reduce it to two-thirds of its volume over low heat, without boiling. Then put in the parboiled parsnips, and cook until tender, when it will have coloured, and absorbed the flavours of the spices. Serve.

Taro (*colocasia*)

The Romans brought taro from Africa, but it is more widely known under its Indian name, dasheen. Peel the taro, cut it up and boil it like a potato. Apicius suggests the following sauce.

In colocasio: piper, cuminum, rutam, mel, liquamen, olei modicum. Cum ferbuerit, amulo obligas.

For taro: pepper, cumin, honey, *garum* and a little honey. When it is boiling, bind with *amulum*.   (Ap. 325)

Grind the spices, mix them with *garum* then bind the mixture together with *amulum*, as Apicius says, or substitute another binding agent such as taro flour. Serve with taro.

GARLIC (*alium*)

'When taking an oath, the Egyptians swear by garlic and onions as though they were gods,' wrote Pliny (Plin. N.H. XIX-xxxii). Magical and curative powers have always been attributed to garlic. It was considered a panacea for all ills. Garlic was eaten by workmen, soldiers, galley slaves and anyone who had to perform heavy labour. Workers ate crushed garlic for breakfast and had a typically pungent breath. Pliny had a remedy:

> To prevent these plants from stinking, they should be planted when the moon is below the horizon. They must be harvested when the moon is in coitus [?]. Also, the Greek Menander writes, the stench that comes from eating garlic can be neutralized by eating beets that have been roasted over hot coals.   (Plin. N.H. XIX-xxxiv)

Pliny also mentions one of the curious properties of garlic:

> There is a kind of garlic that grows in the field, called *alium*. Boil this to prevent it growing again, then scatter it as a protection against the ravages of seed-eating birds. When the birds eat it, they fall rigid. If you wait, these tranquillized birds can be picked up by hand.
> (Plin. N.H. XIX-xxxiv)

The more elegant classes did not each much garlic, partly for fear of bad breath, but also because it tasted like medicine. A medicinal taste is not what a great cook strives for. The only two garlic dishes mentioned by Apicius are the peasant *Sala Cattabia* (see page 193–4) and a healthy starter:

Garlic Digestive

Aliter salsum sine salso: cumini tantum quantum quinque digitis tollis, piperis ad diminium eius et unam spican alei purgatam teres. Liquamen superfundes, oleum modice superstillabis. Hoc aegrum stomacum valde et digestionme facit.

Another substitute for salted fish: take as much cumin as one can hold between five fingers and half that quantity of pepper. Take a clove of garlic. Pour *garum* over this and drizzle a little oil. This will settle a sick stomach, and is good for the digestions.

(Ap. 443)

'As much cumin as you can hold between five fingers' does not mean a fistful, but a good pinch. The quantities are small, which contributes to the medicinal character of this recipe. Eat it on bread, as Apicius suggests.

Aïoli

Mashed garlic, the breakfast of farm workers and galley slaves, resembles *aïoli*.

2 bulbs fresh garlic
1 pinch coarse salt or *garum*
1 tablespoon vinegar
150 ml olive oil

Crush the garlic in the mortar with coarse salt. Grind it to a smooth paste and slowly add the oil. Modern *aïoli* is bound with egg yolk, but here the quantity of garlic acts as a thickener. In some countries breadcrumbs are added to soften the taste. Eat on brown bread or as a side dish.

ONION (*cepa*)

Homer sang of raw onions as a snack with wine (*Iliad,* XXIII-323). A surprising snack – raw onion is somewhat overpowering. Three hundred years after Homer, Xenophon writes:

Homer says somewhere: 'An onion, a snack to eat with drink.'
So if someone brings us an onion we can do as he says and thus enjoy more of our drink.

'Gentlemen,' said Charmides, 'Niceratus wants to go home stinking of onions so that his wife will think absolutely no one would kiss him.'

'No doubt,' said Socrates. 'If we don't live up to our reputation we will be ridiculed. The onion is the best side-dish, given that not only food becomes more tasty, but drink does as well. If, on the other hand, we do not only eat onions with our meal, but also with the carousal, people will understand that we have really only been at Callias' house to fill our stomachs.'*

'Please don't,' came the reply. 'I admit that someone looking for a fight must gnaw on an onion, just as fighting cocks are given garlic. But we don't plan to fight tonight. Rather we hope to get a kiss.'   (Xen. Simp. IV-8)

Pliny describes a selection of onions and shallots – big ones, small ones, red and white ones – from all corners of the world. '*Omnibus odor lacrimosus,*' he writes. 'They all have an aroma that brings tears to the eyes' (Plin. N.H. XIX-xxxii). Onions were salted and pickled, but it is not certain that they were eaten as a vegetable. Apicius refers to onion as a herb. However, he gives a number of recipes for *bulbi*, bulbs, which includes onions.

FLOWER BULB (*bulbus*)

The Dutch, who remember eating flower bulbs during the winter of starvation in 1944–5, have bad memories of the experience. The whole nation knows that flower bulbs are edible but taste horrible. The Romans, however, ate flower bulbs because they liked them.

There is no agreement about the kind of flower bulbs that were eaten. Some historians name narcissi and irises. For the sake of ease, others translate the word 'bulb' as 'onion'. The onion is a flower, related to the lily and the hyacinth, but not all flower bulbs are onions, and the Romans ate various different kinds.

It is possible that the 'bulbs' mentioned in Apicius are the bulbs of the grape hyacinth, which are still eaten in Italy. They are rather like shallots, with a similar texture but a bitter taste. They require lengthy preparation.

* And not for any amorous purposes.

In Italy the bulbs are first peeled then soaked in running water either overnight or for 2–3 days, according to local tradition. Then they are boiled, the water changed 2–3 times to remove the bulbs' bitterness. They are served with salt and pepper. Apicius flavoured them with a vinaigrette oil, vinegar, *garum* and cumin.

Once boiled they can also be fried, stuffed or pickled. In the last alternative they are rather like pickled onions. Street vendors sold this kind of marinated bulb around the bathhouses of ancient Rome. Apicius described flower bulbs under the heading *polyteles* delicacies:

Bulbus tundes* atque ex aqua coques, deinde oleo frigis, ius sic facies: thymum, puleium, piper, origanum, mel, acetum modice et si placet et modice liquamen. Piper aspergis et inferes.

Soak the flower bulbs and boil them in water. Then fry in oil. Make the sauce like this: thyme, leek, pepper, oregano, honey, a little vinegar and if you wish a little *garum.* Sprinkle with pepper and serve.

(Ap. 309)

The soaking and cooking of flower bulbs has not changed much over the centuries. In Puglia the bulbs are first stuffed with goat's cheese, breadcrumbs and parsley, then dredged in a flour and egg mixture, before being plunged into hot olive oil.

for the sauce
1 teaspoon dried thyme
1 teaspoon peppercorns
1 tablespoon chopped fresh leek or mint
1 teaspoon honey
1 tablespoon wine vinegar
1 tablespoon *garum*

Mix the ingredients and spoon over the bulbs.

---

* This word should probably have been 'fundis'.

It is not easy to make a tasty dish of flower bulbs, but it is worth trying: apart from their unusual flavour they were believed to have an aphrodisiac effect.

> *Varro: 'si quid de bulbus dixi: in aqua, qui veneris ostium quaerunt, deinde ut legitims nuptiis in cena ponuntur, sed et cum nucleis pipeis aut eraucae succo et pipere.'*

> Varro said: 'If you ask about flower bulbs, I reply: [They must be prepared] in water before you seek in them the gateway to Venus, as they are served at official wedding banquets, but [they are also tasty] with pine nuts or with a sauce of rocket and pepper.'
>
> (Ap. 310)

The hyacinth, however, retards sexual development: 'The hyacinth grows principally in Gaul . . . The root is a bulb well known to slave-traders. This bulb has the effect, when soaked in sweet wine, of deferring the onset of puberty' (Plin. N.H. XXI-xcvii).

Fried Bulbs

> *Bulbos frictos: oenogaro inferes.*

> Fried flower bulbs: serve with *oenogarum*.   (Ap. 312)

Slice the edible flower bulbs or onions into rings and fry them over a low heat in olive oil until crisp. Sprinkle with *oenogarum* or a mixture of vinegar and anchovies.

ASPARAGUS (*asparagis*)

Both wild and cultivated, green and white asparagus were popular. The Romans had discovered that asparagus could be kept white by constantly covering the growing shoots with soil. They were eaten on their own with a vinaigrette dressing. Apicius gives two *patina* recipes for them.

Asparagus *Patina*

Aliter patina de asparagus: adicies in mortario asparagorum prae-cisuras, quae proiuntur, teres, suffundies vinum, colas. Teres piper, ligusticum, coriandrum viride, satureiam, cepam, vinum, liquamen et oleum. Sucum transferes in patellam perunctam, et, si volueris, ova dissolves ad ignem, ut obliget. Piper minutum asperges.

An asparagus *patina*: put protruding asparagus tips* into the mortar. Crush, add wine and drain. Grind pepper, lovage, fresh coriander, savory, onion, wine, *garum* and oil. Add the mixture to a greased *patina* pan and break eggs over it if you wish. Put on the flame until it sets. Sprinkle with ground pepper.   (Ap. 126)

500g green and purple asparagus tips
50g green and purple asparagus tips
50g fresh coriander
50g fresh savory
1 teaspoon pepper
1 teaspoon lovage seed
2 tablespoons olive oil
100ml white wine
3 small eggs
garum, or salt to taste

Preheat the oven to 220°C/425°F/Gas 7.

Crush the asparagus tips with the other ingredients in a mortar or blender. Oil an oven dish and tip the mixture into it. Cover the *patina* with a lid and put it into the oven for 30 minutes or until it has set. Serve hot or cold, sprinkled with freshly ground pepper.

Apicius' second asparagus *patina* is almost the same as the previous: the only difference is that he places small *ficedulas* on top of the asparagus dish.

---

* Green or purple asparagus tips protruding just above the ground.

Cardoon and Artichoke

Cardoon and artichoke are botanically related. They were prized by the Romans, the artichoke for its large flower bud with the tender heart, the cardoon for its bitter stem.

Cardoon or Artichoke with Egg

Carduous: liquamine, oleo et ovis concisis.

Cardoons: *garum*, oil and chopped egg.   (Ap. 106)

This dish is not unlike a popular modern way of eating asparagus, with butter, salt and a mashed hard-boiled egg. Apicius' combination of egg, *garum* and oil would enhance either artichokes or cardoons. To prepare cardoons remove the strings from the stems, and boil them in salted water until tender. For artichokes, cut the stalks level with the base, and cook as for cardoons.

Cardoon Salad with Fennel

Aliter carduous: rutam, mentam, coriandrum, feniculum, omnia viridia teres. Addes piperlicusticum, mel, liquamen et oleum.

Another cardoon recipe: grind rue, coriander, and fennel, all green. Add pepper, lovage, honey, *garum* and oil.   (Ap. 106)

A word of warning: cardoon and rue are both bitter. Cardoon is made palatable by blanching the stems as for asparagus or celery. Prepare the cardoons as above and boil in salted water until they are tender, approximately 30 minutes. Let them cool. Then slice them. Chop the herbs and put them into a bowl with the cardoon slices. Stir together the rest of the ingredients and pour the dressing into the bowl. Stir well and serve.

100g fresh fennel (leaves)
25g fresh mint
10g fresh coriander
10g fresh rue
50ml *garum*
50ml virgin olive oil
1 teaspoon finely ground lovage seed
1 teaspoon honey

LEEKS

Leek Vinaigrette

Porros maturos fieri: pugnum salis, aquam et oleum mixtum et ibi coques et eximes. Cum oleo, liquamine, mero infres.

Fully grown leeks: boil the leek with water, oil and a fistful of salt. Remove. Serve with oil, *liquamen* and undiluted wine.   (Ap. 87)

Cut the leeks lengthwise, trim them and wash them. Boil them in water with plenty of salt until they are tender, then leave them to drain. Make a vinaigrette of oil, *garum* and wine or vinegar. Lay the leeks in a serving dish, pour over the vinaigrette and serve at room temperature.

Leek with Olives

Aliter porros: in baca coctos ut supra inferes.

Another leek recipe: boil the leek with [olive] berries and serve as above.   (Ap. 89)

100ml water
100ml oil
1 large leek, trimmed, washed and sliced into rings
200g green olives
100ml strong white wine
garum or salt

Bring the water and oil to the boil in a saucepan, put in the leek and
let it stew. Stone the olives and chop them roughly into quarters then
add them to the leek when the water has evaporated. Leave to stew
in the oil. Remove the olives and leek from the oil and place them in
a heated serving dish. Stir in the wine and *garum* or salt, and serve.

Roast Leek and Cabbage Rolls

*Aliter porros: opertos foliis cauliculorum in prunes coques, ut supra
inferes.*

Another leek recipe: wrap the leek in cabbage leaves and roast on
hot coals; serve as above.   (Ap. 87)

2 large leeks
9 cabbage leaves
olive oil

Cut the leeks lengthwise, trim, wash and cut them into 10-cm lengths.
Boil them in salted water for 5 minutes.

Blanch the cabbage leaves in boiling water for 1 minute. Remove
the thick veins, so that each leaf is of an even thickness. Then wrap the
slivers of leek, with salt and pepper, in the cabbage leaves to make nine
parcels. Brush the parcels with oil and roast on a grill over hot ashes or
in the oven. Turn every 10 minutes, until the cabbage leaves are dry
and crunchy. Place the parcels in a preheated dish, pour over a little
wine and *garum*, and serve.

PUMPKINS, GOURDS, COURGETTES and CUCUMBERS (*cucurbita*)

The gourd, squash or pumpkin family (of the genus *cucurbita*) includes
many different varieties. In Italy the courgette is called *zucchino*, which
means 'little pumpkin' (from *zucca*, pumpkin). Martial wrote about
pumpkins:

Caecilius is the Atreus of pumpkins. He lacerates them into a
thousand pieces, as though they were the sons of Thyestes. [At his

house] you'll eat them as a starter. Then he serves them with the
first and second course. You'll have them in front of you once
again for pudding, and he makes them into a late supper snack.
His baker makes pumpkins into tasteless *placentas*, building all
manner of assemblages. His cook uses them for various fricassées,
so you would think you were eating beans and lentils. He
makes pumpkins into imitation mushrooms and black pudding,
or tunny-tails or little *mendoles*. The confectioner displays his
expertise by marinating Capellian sweetmeats with leaves of rue
to change their flavour. In this way he fills his dishes and plates,
his gleaming tureens and trays. He calls that 'refined'. He thinks
it amusing to make so many courses at such little expense.

(Mart. XI-xxxi)

Pliny has another use for pumpkins.

Pumpkins have recently come into use as vases in bath-houses, but
previously they were even used as wine-vessels.

(Plin. N.H. XIX: xxiv)

It was, of course, sturdy gourds or big winter pumpkins that were used
as vessels, not courgettes. Pliny also describes courgette-like pumpkins:

The rind of the pumpkin is green and tender, but is still removed
if the vegetable is to be eaten.   (Plin. N.H. XIX: xxiv)

Fried Courgettes

Cucurbitas frictas: oenogaro simplici et pipere.

Fried courgette: simply *oenogarum* and pepper.   (Ap. 71)

Fried courgette is still a popular starter; the vegetable is sliced, fried in
oil with chopped garlic, then marinated for a few hours in a little
vinegar. Otherwise, use a little of the best *garum* mixed with white
wine. Sprinkle with pepper.

Courgettes with Cumin Sauce

Patina de cucurbitis: cucurbitas elixas et fricas in patina compones, cuminatum superfundes, modico oleo super adiecto. Fervere facias et inferes.

Courgette *patina*: boil the courgette and fry it. Place in a *patina* pan. Pour over some cumin sauce with a little oil. Heat and serve.

(Ap. 130)

Cut the courgettes into 1-cm slices and blanch them for a few minutes in water with plenty of salt. Drain, then leave the courgettes to cool. Press out the moisture, dry the courgettes on kitchen paper and fry them in olive oil. Spread a little cumin sauce (see page 210–11) on each slice and serve.

Alexandrian Pumpkin

Cucurbitas more alexandrine: elixatas cucurbitas exprimis, sale asperges, in patina compones. Teres piper, cuminum, coriandri semen, mentam viridem, laseris radicem, suffundis acetum, adicies caryotam, nucleum, teres, melle, aceto, liquamine, defrito, et oleo temperabis, et cucurbitas perfundes. Cum ferbuerint, piper asparges et inferes.

Pumpkin in the Alexandrian style: press out the moisture from the pumpkin, sprinkle salt over it and place it in a *patina*. Grind pepper, cumin, coriander seed, fresh mint and *asafoetida*, pour vinegar over it, add dates and pine nuts, grind. Bring honey, vinegar, *garum, defrutum* and oil to the boil and add the pumpkin. Sprinkle with pepper when hot, and serve. (Ap. 75)

1 kg courgettes
salt
1 tablespoon cumin
1 tablespoon coriander seed
1 tablespoon peppercorns, plus extra to finish the dish

5 tablespoons pine nuts
1 pitted date
4 tablespoons chopped fresh mint
2 tablespoons vinegar
4 tablespoons *garum*
5 tablespoons white *defrutum*
1 teaspoon honey
olive oil

Dice the courgettes. Salt and steam them for 10 minutes until they are tender, or boil them in salted water. Drain them, leave to cool, then press out the moisture. In a mortar, crush the cumin and coriander seed to a powder. Sieve it if you see flakes of husk. Grind the pepper into the powdered spices, then the pine nuts, the date flesh and the mint, until you have a smooth paste. This will thicken the sauce. Add the vinegar, *garum*, *defrutum* and honey. Mix well then pour in a dash of oil.

Place the courgette slices in an oiled flameproof dish and pour over the sauce. Put it over a medium heat until it is very hot. Grind over some pepper and serve.

Cucumber Salad

Cucumeres rasos: sive ex liquamine, sive ex oenogaro: sine ructu et gravitudine teneriores senties.

Peeled cucumber: either with *garum* or with *oenogarum*. This makes them more tender and less bad for the stomach.   (Ap. 76)

Peel the cucumber, halve it lengthwise and remove the seeds. Slice it thinly and salt it with *garum*. Leave it to marinate for 30 minutes. Then press the cucumber to remove some of the moisture and put it into a serving dish. Mix it with wine or vinegar to taste and serve.

Cucumber Salad with Mint

Aliter cucumeres: piper, puleium, mel vel passum, liquamen et acetum. Interdum et silfi accedit.

Another way of serving cucumbers: pepper, pennyroyal, honey or *passum, garum* and vinegar. Sometimes *laserpithium* is added.

(Ap. 78)

1 cucumber
50g pennyroyal or fresh mint
1 teaspoon honey
1 teaspoon pepper
1 tablespoon vinegar
1 small clove crushed garlic and a pinch of *asafoetida*

Peel, slice and salt the cucumber as above. Mix together the dressing ingredients, pour over the cucumber and serve.

LETTUCE (*lactuca*)

Nothing is more typically Roman than lettuce and salads. Here is Pliny, again, writing about the good old days:

> Of all the things that come out of the garden, the most greatly favoured were those that needed no fire for cooking, and saved on firewood, which were always ready to eat. Hence their name, salads [*acetaria*]. Easily digested and not heavy on the stomach.

(Plin. N.H. XIX-xix)

Salad was eaten just as it is today, with vinegar, oil and salt (or *garum*). The Romans considered vinegar the most important ingredient in the dressing. Their word for salad was *acetarium*, from *acetum*, vinegar. Our 'salad' comes from *sal*, salt.

Columella Salad

Columella's writings suggest that Roman salads were a match for our own in richness and imagination:

> *Addito in mortarium satureiam, mentam, rutam, coriandrum, apium, porrum sectivum, aut si non erit viridem cepam, folia*

*latucae, folia erucae, thymum viride, vel nepetam, tum etiam viride
puleium, et caseum recentem et salsum: ea omnia partier conterito,
acetique piperati exiguum, permisceto. Hanc mixturam cum in catillo
composurris, oleum superfundito.*

Put savory in the mortar with mint, rue, coriander, parsley, sliced
leek, or, if it is not available, onion, lettuce and rocket leaves,
green thyme, or catmint. Also pennyroyal and salted fresh cheese.
This is all crushed together. Stir in a little peppered vinegar. Put
this mixture on a plate and pour oil over it.   (Col. R.R. XII-lix)

A wonderful salad, unusual for the lack of salt (perhaps the cheese
was salty enough), and that Columella crushes the ingredients in the
mortar.

100g fresh mint (and/or pennyroyal)
50g fresh coriander
50g fresh parsley
1 small leek
a sprig of fresh thyme
200g salted fresh cheese
vinegar
pepper
olive oil

Follow Columella's method for this salad using the ingredients listed.
    In other salad recipes Columella adds nuts, which might not be a
bad idea with this one.
    Apart from lettuce and rocket many plants were eaten raw –
watercress, mallow, sorrel, goosefoot, purslane, chicory, chervil, beet
greens, celery, basil and many other herbs.

Purée of Boiled Lettuce

*Aliter holus molle ex foliis lactucarum cum cepis: coques ex aqua
nitrata, expressum concides minutatim, in mortario teres piper,
ligustcum, apii semen, mentam siccam, cepam, liquamen, oleum et
vinum.*

Another vegetable purée of lettuce leaves and onion: boil in soda water, press dry and cut into small pieces. In the mortar, grind pepper, lovage, celery seed, dried mint, an onion, *garum*, oil and wine.   (Ap. 99)

1 Roman (kos) lettuce
1 tablespoon bicarbonate soda
1 teaspoon peppercorns
1 teaspoon celery seed
1 teaspoon lovage seed
1 tablespoon dried oregano
1 tablespoon dried mint
100 ml white wine
2 tablespoons olive oil
1 tablespoon *garum*

Boil the lettuce leaves in the water with the bicarbonate of soda for 7 minutes. Drain, then cut the ribs from the leaves and chop finely. Grind the peppercorns with celery seed, lovage seed, oregano and mint, then add the spring onion and pound to a smooth paste. Stir in the wine with the olive oil and serve. Put the lettuce into a bowl, pour on the dressing, toss well and serve.

Apicius gives recipes for another two vegetables purées. One is for celery, for which the recipe is the same, except that it contains no celery seed. The other is for alexanders in which he uses dried rather than fresh onion, with savory, lovage seed, pepper, oil, wine and *garum*.

Patina of Stinging Nettles

Use only the light green shoots that grow in the spring, and later in the year after the plant has been cut back. Apicius wrote:

Pluck the wild stinging nettle when the sun is in the sign of the ram and use against sickness, as you wish.   (Ap. 102)

He also gives a recipe:

Patina urticarum calida et frigida: urticam accipies, lavas, colas per colum, exsiccabis in tabula, eam concides. Teres piperis scripulos x, suffundes liquamen, fricabis. Postea adicies liquaminis cyathos ii, olei unicias vi. Caccabus ferveat. Cum ferbuerit, coctum tolles ut refrigescat. Postea patinam mundam pergunes, franges ova viii et agitabis. Perfundes, subtus supra cincerem calidam hebeat. Cocta, piper minutum asparges et inferes.

Warm or cold *patina* of stinging nettle: take the stinging nettles, wash them, allow to drain and leave to dry on a board. Chop finely.

Grind 6.8 g pepper, moisten with *garum* and stir. Add 90 ml *garum* and 164 ml oil. Bring to the boil in a pot. Once it has boiled, remove from the pot and leave to cool.

Then oil a *patina* pan. Break 8 eggs and beat them. Put everything in the *patina* pan and place in hot ashes so that it is heated both above and below. When it is cooked, sprinkle ground pepper over it and serve.

What a shame that Apicius left out the quantity of nettles required for this amount of dressing!

500 g fresh nettle leaves
7.8 g peppercorns
90 ml *garum*
150 ml olive oil
8 small eggs

Preheat the oven to 180°C/350°F/Gas 4.

Wash the nettles, dry them, then chop them finely. Grind the pepper with a little *garum*, then mix it in a pan with the olive oil and the rest of the *garum*. Put in the nettles and stir them through the sauce. Pour a little water into the pan to prevent the bottom drying out. Cover the pan with its lid and stew the nettles over a low heat for 10 minutes. Remove them from the pan and leave them to cool.

Oil a shallow oven dish. Beat the eggs, stir them into the nettles, then pour the mixture into the dish. Cover it and place it into the oven for about 15 minutes or until the egg has set. Serve hot or cold as a starter.

Brassica

Cato was a great lover of cabbage:

> The cabbage beats all other vegetables. It can be eaten raw or
> cooked. If you eat it raw it must be dipped in vinegar. It is good
> for the digestion and has a laxative effect. The urine is good for
> all sorts of things. If you are going to drink heavily at a feast, eat
> as much raw cabbage with vinegar as you can beforehand, and
> another six leaves after dinner. You should feel as though you have
> not had dinner, and you can drink as much as you like.
>
> (Cat. R.R. CLVI)

Here, he elaborates on cabbage urine:

> If you keep the urine of someone who eats a great deal of cabbage
> and warm it up and bathe a patient in it, he is certain to recover.
> This has been proven. Babies are also fortified by urine baths. An
> eyebath with urine helps people with poor eyesight. Headaches
> and neck pain are cured with warmed urine. A woman who
> warms up her sexual parts with this fluid will have no further
> pain. Warm up as follows: when the urine is boiling, put it under
> a stool with holes. The woman sits on this and is covered up.
> Make sure she is fully wrapped in cloths.   (Cat. R.R. CLVII)

The miracles performed with cabbage are almost endless. Other
authors also describe it at length, but no one is so in awe of it as Cato,
who ate his cabbage raw. Pliny is a little more succinct: 'One sort of
cabbage with wide leaves and a fat stem,* another with crinkled leaves,†
a third has little stalks,‡ light and tender, but otherwise nothing special'
(Plin. N.H. XIX-xli).

The existence of cauliflower and broccoli in Rome is confirmed by
illustrations in reliefs.

---

* Green cabbage.
† Kale.
‡ Broccoli (or cauliflower).

Boiled (Green) Cabbage

Apicius was also economical in his cabbage recipe:

Folia cauliculorum: liquamen, vinum, oleum.

Cabbage leaves: *garum*, wine, oil.   (Ap. 81)

Fortunately Pliny gives a little more information:

While cooking, the addition of soda to the water preserves the
colour of the cabbage, as in Apicius' recipe in which the cabbage
is marinated in salt and oil even before cooking.
                                             (Plin. N.H. XIX-xli)

So the days of raw cabbage with vinegar were over. Take the cabbage
leaves and marinate them overnight in oil and salt. Then boil them in
soda water, slice them finely and serve with *garum*, oil and wine or,
in honour of Cato, with vinegar.

OTHER VEGETABLES

Broccoli with Olives

*Aliter: cauliculos condies ut supra, admisces olivas virides et simul
ferveant.*

Alternative: flavour the broccoli as above, but add fresh olives and
cook them along with it.   (Ap. 85)

A comparable dish is eaten today in southern Italy: cut the broccoli
into florets and fry them in oil with garlic. Add some black olives, put
the lid on the pan and stew everything in the juices until the broccoli
is tender.

Cauliflower with Cumin

*Aliter: cauliculi elixatie in patina composite condiuntur liquamine,
oleo mero cumino. Piper asparges, porrum. Cuminum, coriandrum
viride super concides.*

Alternatively, boiled cabbages are placed in a *patina* and flavoured
with *garum*, oil, undiluted wine and cumin. Sprinkle with pepper.
Add leek, cumin and green coriander.   (Ap. 83)

Slice a small tender leek thinly and wash. Separate some broccoli or
cauliflower into florets. Make a vinaigrette of equal parts of oil, *garum*
and white wine, then stir in some ground pepper and cumin. Toss the
vegetables with the sauce and serve.

Brussels Sprouts with Herbs

Brussels sprouts were known as *cyma* by the Romans:

This is a sprout that grows off the cabbage stalk, more tender and
delicate than the cabbage itself, although the luxurious Apicius
disliked it.   (Plin. N.H. XIX-xli)

*Cymas: cuminum, salem, vinum vetus et oleum. Si voles, addes piper
et ligusticum, mentam, rutam, coriandrum.*

Sprouts: cumin, salt, old wine and oil. If you like you can add
pepper, lovage, mint, rue or coriander.   (Ap. 81)

Remove the outermost leaves from 500g Brussels sprouts, then boil
them for 15 minutes in water with salt and bicarbonate of soda. Drain
and rinse them in cold water. Grind together 1 teaspoon each of
cumin and peppercorns. Stir this with olive oil, white wine, and plenty
of salt. Add the sprouts and toss them with the dressing, then leave to
marinate for a few hours. Chop a large bunch of herbs, scatter over the
sprouts, stir again and serve.

Pickled Vegetables

Columella gives a long list of vegetables that can be pickled:

> When the vinegar and brine are ready, around midsummer it
> will be time to pickle the following vegetables for later use:
> sprouts, cabbage stalks, capers, parsley stalks, rue, unopened buds
> of alexanders, the unopened flower of fennel and its stalk, the
> unopened flower of wild turnip, both wild and cultivated, bryony
> flower, asparagus . . . leek, pennyroyal, catmint, wild thyme,
> mustard, samphire . . . and the tender stalks of fennel. All of these
> herbs can be easily pickled in a combination of two parts vinegar
> to one part brine. Only bryony, black bryony, asparagus, turnips,
> calamint and samphire need to be first laid out separately on
> baskets.
> (Col. R.R. XII-vii)

Many other vegetables can be pickled too, like roots, onions, garlic,
artichoke hearts, all varieties of cabbage but particularly cauliflower,
and so on. Don't boil them before you pickle them. Place them in an
airtight jar in a mixture of brine and vinegar, or salt them, then put
them in vinegar. The art of pickling has been somewhat lost since the
invention of the deep freeze, but pickled vegetables deserve a special
place on the table. Their sharp freshness makes an excellent foil to
heavy dishes with complex sauces.

Figure 5.6

Mushrooms

Mushrooms were not cultivated but gathered in the forest. Their harvest could be just as dangerous as hunting wild animals:

> Mushrooms grow on the ground and some are edible. Most of
> them cause death by asphyxiation.   Ath. II-60e)

Experiences of this kind led the Celts and Germans to attribute dark powers to the mushroom. However, the Romans were so familiar with them that they attributed mushroom poisoning to stupidity or trickery. Poisoners were keen on mushrooms: Agrippina murdered the Emperor Claudius with them, and Nero subsequently became emperor:

> Nero made a witty observation about Claudius. At a banquet
> mushrooms were brought in. Someone said that mushrooms were
> the food of the gods, whereupon Nero added: 'That's right. It was
> from eating a mushroom that my father became a god.'
> *(Cassius Dio. LXI. 35)*

Mushrooms were feared and loved, and we can assume that the Romans were familiar with the same varieties as ourselves. On frescoes in Pompeii there are mushrooms that look like ceps, chanterelles and truffles. In all likelihood they also knew field mushrooms, morels and horns-of-plenty, although we cannot be sure of this. The names that the ancient Romans gave to mushrooms are not necessarily the same Latin names that more contemporary biologists have given them.

Ceps with Coriander

*Boletos fungos: caroenum, fasciculum coriandri viridis. Ubi fer-
buerint, exempto fasciculo inferes.*

Ceps: *caroenum*, a bunch of fresh coriander. When it is ready,
remove the coriander and serve.   (Ap. 316)

Ceps – or *porcini*, as the Italians call them – can be gathered free in forests or bought at a high price. Stew them in their own juices, or roast them on the barbecue, flavoured with reduced wine and a bunch of coriander. Remove the coriander before serving.

Roast Ceps

Boletos aliter: caliculos eorum liquamine vel sale aspersos inferunt.

Another cep recipe: serve the caps with *garum* or sprinkled with salt.   (Ap. 317)

Preheat the oven to 200°C/400°F/Gas 6.

Take fresh ceps gathered on a dry day. (Apicius does not specify whether they should be boiled or fried, but they could also be barbecued.) Grease the grill with olive oil, place the mushroom caps on it. Halfway through roasting, sprinkle with salt, unless you have first-class *garum* at your disposal. This is an excellent way of cooking ceps, but it can also be used for other mushrooms.

Chopped Mushroom Stems

Boletos aliter: thyrsos eorum concisos in patellam novam perfundis, addito pipere, ligustico, modico melle. Liquamine temperabis. Oleum modice.

Another cep recipe: finely chop the stems and place in a shallow pan. Add pepper, lovage and a little honey. Mix with *garum* and a small amount of oil.   (Ap. 318)

The stems were not as highly esteemed as the caps, hence the rougher treatment. You can use any mushroom stems for this recipe.

1 teaspoon lovage seed
1 teaspoon peppercorns
500g chopped mushroom stems
1 teaspoon honey

50 ml *garum*
20 ml olive oil

Grind together the lovage and the peppercorns, then put all the ingredients together in a pan over a low heat and cook until the moisture has evaporated from the mushrooms. Serve with bread.

Chanterelles with Pepper

Fungi farnei: elixir, calidi, exsiccate in garo piperato accipiuntur, ita ut piper cum liquamine teras.

Chanterelles: boiled and then dried, served with pepper sauce of ground pepper and *garum*.   (Ap. 313)

We do not know for sure whether *farnei* are chanterelles, but Pliny tells us that they grow on wood, like a variety of chanterelle.

Chanterelle Salad

In fungis farneis: piper, caroenum, acetum et oleum.

Chanterelles: pepper, *caroenum*, vinegar and oil.   (Ap. 314)

Preheat the oven to 200°C/400°F/Gas 6.
    Clean the mushrooms and remove the stems. Sprinkle with salt and leave to dry out in the oven for 15 minutes. Then mix the mushrooms with a vinaigrette made with olive oil, vinegar and reduced wine. Sprinkle with pepper and serve.

Roast Truffles

Aliter tubera: elixas et, asperse sale, in surculis adfigis et subassas, et mittis in caccabum, liquamen, oleum viride, caroenum, vinum modice et piper confractum et mellis modicum, et ferveat. Cum ferbuerit, amulo obliges, et tubera compunges, ut combibant illud.

Exonas. Cum bene sorbuerint, inferes. Si volueris, eadem tubera omento porcino involves et assabis et sic inferes.

A truffle recipe: boil, sprinkle with salt and impale on skewers. Roast them. Put oil in the pot, with *garum*, virgin oil, *caroenum*, a little wine, crushed pepper and a little honey. Bring to the boil. Bind with *amulum*. Prick the truffles so that they absorb the sauce. Remove from the skewer. When they have absorbed everything, serve them. If you wish, each truffle can be wrapped in pork caul and roasted.

(Ap. 320)

And why not roast truffles by the kilo as though they were potatoes? At Roman markets there were whole jars of truffles, which would suggest that they were not as rare as they are nowadays.

FRUIT AND NUTS

If mushrooms were dangerous, the same could not be said of the cherries, blackberries, currants, elderberries, dates, pomegranates, peaches, apricots, quinces, melons, plums, damsons, figs, and the dozens of varieties of apples and pears that grew in the garden. The grape flourished in the orchard, with pistachio, walnut, almond, hazel, pine and chestnut trees for company. Pliny wrote that the gods had lived in the trees since the earliest times, and that no sculpture in god or ivory was superior to a tree. The only sound in the orchard came from the bees, which flew back and forth between hive and blossom. This was a peaceful place.

Grapes, fruit, nuts and honey, the gifts of Priapus and Liber, belonged together at dinner: they formed the dessert. Peace-loving Romans preferred raw fruits to spectacular meat or fish dishes:

Even now fruit is served as *mensa secunda*, while nowadays it must hold its own against game that has been acquired with great difficulty, or a particular carrion-feeding fish that happens to be in fashion at the moment.*

* The moray eel.

Fruit, displayed elegantly around a statue of a phallus, or in the lap of Priapus (see page 82) retained its popularity, not least because it was served during the *mensa secunda* when the wine was poured. We don't have many dessert recipes because, sadly, a substantial chapter is missing from Apicius' work.

Dates with Almond and Honey

Dulcia domestica: palmulas vel dactyllos exepto semine, nuce vel nuclei vel pipere trito infercies, sale foris contingis, frigis in melle cocto et inferes.

Pudding for the home: take one kind of date or another and remove the stone. Stuff in a nut, or pine nuts or ground pepper. Salt on the outside, bake in boiled honey and serve.   (Ap. 300)

This is a splendid yet curious dish, splendid in that it brings together the products of the orchard – honey, fruit and nuts – and because a nut replaces the stone, as though the cook was merely making a small alteration to nature. It also provides a typical Roman joke: when diners bit on the almond, they nearly had a fit, fearing to break their teeth. It was a relief to discover that the 'stone' was an edible almond.

Take dried dates, not fresh or candied ones. Remove the stone and stuff in a boiled, peeled almond or some chopped nuts. Close the date. Bring some honey to the boil and let it reduce as far as possible. Then pour it over the dates. Serve, once the caramelized honey has cooled.

Nut Tart

Patina versatilis vice dulcis: nucleos pineos, nuces fractas et purgatas, attorrebis eas, teres cum melle, pipere, liquamine, lacte, ovis, modico mero et oleo, versas in discum.

Try *patina* as dessert: roast pine nuts, peeled and chopped nuts. Add honey, pepper, *garum*, milk, eggs, a little undiluted wine and oil. Pour on to a plate.   (Ap. 136)

400g crushed nuts – almonds, walnuts or pistachios
200g pine nuts
100g honey
100ml dessert wine
4 eggs
100ml full-fat sheep's milk
1 teaspoon salt or *garum*
pepper

Preheat the oven to 240°C/475°F/Gas 9.

Place the chopped nuts and the whole pine nuts in an oven dish and roast until they have turned golden. Reduce the oven temperature to 200°C/400°F/Gas 6. Mix the honey and the wine in a pan and bring to the boil, then cook until the wine has evaporated. Add the nuts and pine nuts to the honey and leave it to cool. Beat the eggs with the milk, salt or *garum* and pepper. Then stir the honey and nut mixture into the eggs. Oil an oven dish and pour in the nut mixture. Seal the tin with silver foil and place it in roasting tin filled about a third deep with water. Bake for about 25 minutes until the pudding is firm. Take it out and when it is cold put it into the fridge to chill. To serve, tip the tart on to a plate and pour over some boiled honey.

Elderberry Custard

Patina de sambuco calida et frigida: accipies semen de sambuco, purgabis ex aqua decoques, paulum exsiccabis, patinam perunges et in patinam compones ad surcellum. Adicies piperis scripulos vi, sufundes liquamen, postea adicies liquaminis cyathum unum, vini cyathum, passi cyathum, teres, tandem in patinam mittes olei unc. iv, pones in thermospodio et facies ut ferveat. Cum ferbuerit, franges postea ova vi, agitabis et patinam sic obligabis. Cum obligaveris, piper asperges et inferes.

Hot or cold elderberry *patina*: take elderberries, clean and boil in water. Allow to dry a little. Grease a *patina* pan and push the elder-berries into the pan with a twig. Add 7g pepper, pour in a little *garum* followed by 45ml *garum*, 45ml wine, 45ml *passum*. Grind. Finally add 27g oil to the pan and place in a bain-marie until it boils. When it is boiling, break 6 eggs over it, and beat while the *patina* binds. When it has bound, sprinkle with ground pepper and serve.   (Ap. 128)

About 1 kg of elderberries should be enough for the quantities above. Cook the elderberries with the *garum*, *passum*, (red) wine, oil and pepper in a bowl set over a saucepan of boiling water until they begin to fall apart. Beat the eggs and add them to the elderberries. Stir until the custard has thickened, then serve, warm or cold.

Peach with Cumin Sauce

Patina de persicis: persica duriora purgabis, frustatim concides, elixas in patina compones, olei modicum superstillabis et cum cuminatuo inferes.

Peach *patina*: peel some firm peaches, cut into pieces and cook. Place in a *patina* pan and drizzle with oil. Serve with cumin sauce.
                                                          (Ap. 167)

Apicius mentions many cumin sauces in his books (see also boiled turnips page 210–11). This one, for example:

Aliter cuminatum: piper, ligusticum, petroselinum, mentam siccam, cuminum, plusculum, mel, acetum, liquamen.

Another cumin sauce: pepper, lovage, dried mint, a large amount of cumin, honey, vinegar, *liquamen*.   (Ap. 30)

This is a curious recipe. Boiled peaches in perfumed olive oil sounds fine – but with cumin sauce? A challenge to the chef.

Quince Jam

Patina de cydoneis: mala cydonia cum porris, melle, liquamine, oleo, defrito coques et inferes, vel elixa ex melle.

Quince *patina*: boil quinces with leek, honey, *garum* and oil in
defrutum and serve. Or boil quinces in honey.   (Ap. 170)

1 kg quinces
1 small leek, white part only
500 ml *defrutum*, not too thick, or reduced grape juice with wine
300 g honey
salt or *garum*
a dash of oil

Peel and stone the quinces. Cut them up and put them into a pan, with
the stones, the finely chopped leek, the *defrutum*, honey, *garum* and oil.
Put the lid on the pan and cook slowly until the quinces are tender.
Remove the stones. Leave to cool and serve with bread.

VI

FROM THE FIRE

Concerning Meat from the Sacrificial Altar,
The Butcher's Shop and the Hunt

EATING MEAT

Originally Romans ate little meat. They were reluctant to slaughter their cattle, since farm animals fulfilled all kinds of practical functions. Sheep were kept for their wool. Goats gave their milk. Geese and chickens laid eggs and supplied down. The bullock, which grew into a sturdy ox, pulled the plough or the cart. Some farmers also had a donkey, a mule or a horse, all of which worked for a living and were allowed to reach old age. The meat from beasts of burden was nearly too tough to eat. The only animal that had no other use than for the pot was the pig. Pork was succulent, luxurious meat. Only the pig lives to be eaten.

According to Athenaeus, civilization began with the slaughter of animals, and he attributes this quantum leap to a cook:

A: Didn't you know that the cook has contributed more to religion than anyone else?
B: Is that so?
A: Certainly, you foolish barbarian. His art is the one that freed us from a bestial and lawless existence. He it was who led us away from the most frightful cannibalism to civilization, and introduced us to the life we know now.
B: How is that?
A: Pay attention and I will tell you. In a time when cannibalism and all kinds of evil still existed, a very intelligent man arose, the first to sacrifice an animal and roast its flesh.   (Ath. 661f)

Plutarch, however, was of the opposite opinion. He claimed that man was vegetarian by nature, and only took up meat-eating to protect his vegetables:

> From the words and religious customs of our distant ancestors we may conclude that he could not bear to eat, or even to kill, an innocent creature.
>
> But wild animals reproduced until they became over-populated, whereupon the oracle of Delphi (according to the story) asserted that agricultural products needed protecting, and that offerings of meat had to be made. In those days people still considered sacrifice unpleasant and sinister, and said: 'I'll go and do one [sacrifice].'
>
> They considered making a sacrifice a serious matter, just as nowadays we take care not to kill an animal before libations have been poured over it, and the animal has nodded its agreement.
>
> Apart from that, if mankind were to eat no more chickens, or, for example, hares, their numbers would become so great within the shortest time that it would no longer be possible to maintain cities or even to fetch in a harvest. That is how they started, simply out of necessity. But pleasure makes it very difficult for us to relinquish our carnivorous habit.   (Plut. VIII 8-792f)

This is a curious hypothesis. Man has been eating meat for much longer than he has been practising agriculture. Neanderthals didn't run after bison to chase them out of their strawberry patches and the Romans must have understood this, because Varro wrote, about 150 years before Plutarch, that there were three stages in mankind's development (Varr. R.R. II-I-4). In the first we lived on wild fruits like animals. In the second we wandered around with flocks as herdsmen, eating meat with some berries. In the third we made the transition to agriculture.

Plutarch wrote that man began by sacrificing wild animals, but it is unclear how he came by that idea. Wild-animal sacrifice had been sporadic and among Romans it was prohibited – only domesticated animals were fit for sacrifice. A devout man had to offer something from his own livestock; a wild animal belonged to the gods. For the farmer, sacrifice was an expensive business; he could lose a producer of milk, wool, eggs or a beast of burden. Animals were not killed outside religious festivals.

SACRIFICE

Death establishes contact between men and the gods, as though the soul, rising to heaven, is bringing with it a report from the world below.

Nowadays we declare someone dead if brain activity has ceased, but for the Romans, the moment at which the last breath was exhaled was the crucial moment between life and death. The 'life-breath' (*anima*) was identified with the soul (see page 250). People sat attentively by the deathbeds of their parents or loved ones so that, when the last moment came, they could place their mouth over the mouth of the dying person to try to inhale their final breath, and thus to absorb their soul into their own body.

When animals died their souls returned to the intangible world of gods and spirits. In the Christian era people have questioned whether animals have souls, but the ancient Romans had little doubt of this. *Animal* means 'with *anima*'. Gods were *anima*.

When the priest killed an animal in sacrifice, the deity absorbed the liberated *anima* and was strengthened by it. That was the essence of the sacrifice. The meat of the sacrificial animal was eaten by all those in attendance on the occasion.

Preparation

A lot of work went into readying a sacrifice and, to ensure that the deity did not refuse it, the preparations had to be made to perfection. The slightest mistake could make an entire ritual invalid.

The priest was responsible for the strict performance of the rituals. Within the family and on the farm the head of the household took on the role of the priest, dressed in a toga which he drew respectfully over his head. Senior politicians had the same function in the cities.

The Sacrificial Animal

It was the priest's duty to select the sacrificial animal and subject it to a thorough investigation. The criteria for this were established in law

Figure 6.1 – Suovetaurilia

and varied from one god to another. In general, male animals were sacrificed to gods and female animals to goddesses. Black animals were for the gods of the underworld, while sacrifices to heavenly gods like Jupiter and Juno had to be completely white. If the priest found the tiniest patch of black on a white bull, the feast was called off. The animal had to be healthy and uninjured, and it had to go along willingly to the sacrifice. According to Plutarch, it even had to nod in agreement. If an animal resisted, the sacrifice was invalidated. If an animal objected, the sacrifice was cancelled: the gods were making it clear through the beast that they didn't approve of the sacrifice.

Specific animals were dedicated to each deity. Freud called this totemism: deities were identified with animals that were both holy and ritually slaughtered on special occasions. This kind of totemism existed among both the ancient Egyptians and the Romans. To Priapus, for example, the Romans sacrificed the highly sexed donkey; to Faunus, the god of herdsmen, they offered mountain goats and a dog; to Mars, god of war, a horse; to Hercules, the fighting hero-god, a cock. Nox, goddess of the night, also got a cock, in her case because of its early-morning crowing. Diana, goddess of hunting, received a doe. And two pregnant cows were offered to Mother Earth.

This is not to say that the gods accepted only one kind of animal. Many accepted a variety of sacrifices, depending on the occasion. Lists of all possible sacrifices hung in the temples. The best-known sacrifice, suitable to many gods and events, was the *suovetaurilia*, a combination of a pig (*sus*), a ram (*ovis*) and a bull (*taurus*). Sometimes they had to be full-grown animals; on other occasions a piglet and lamb and a calf would suffice. A piglet could be sacrificed at few days old, a lamb at a week and a calf at a month.

The Ritual

Once a suitable animal had been earmarked, the temple was booked and a flautist hired, along with other temple staff, before the ceremonies could begin. Friends and family were required to be present at the festivities, but enemies were banned. Women and slaves were not allowed to attend certain rituals.

The sacrificial animal was decorated with garlands, banners and wreaths of flowers that were woven between the horns, if the animal had them, and around the tail. Those with enough money gilded the horns.

1. The animal was led to the altar. The more willingly it walked, the better the omen. Juvenal brags, for example, that his bull pulled on the rope to get to the altar.

2. When the animal reached the altar (which stood outside the temple), the fire was stoked up. The priest called, '*Procul, procul este profani.*' ('Be off, profane ones.') After this only those who had been invited, who had taken a bath and were wearing clean clothes were allowed to stay. Then the priest demanded silence: '*Favete linguis.*' ('Hold your tongues'.) Only the flautist could still be heard.

3.   The priest and the other participants covered their heads with their togas, and the priest picked up a wooden plate holding the *mola salsa* (see page 176). He sprinkled this between the horns of the animal, and on the sacrificial knife.

4.   The next step was libation. Beside the altar stood a tripod holding wine in a flask. The priest poured some into a deep bowl (*patera*). He held it in his right hand then poured it over the sacrificial animal.

5. The garland was removed from the animal, and the 'knife holder' (*cultrarius*) ran the blade symbolically along the length of the animal. Sometimes he would cut off some hair, and this would be thrown on to the altar.

6. Prayers were said by the priest, or by those people at whose expense the sacrifice was being performed and who wanted something from the deity. The speaker turned to face the statue of the god.

Most prayers were uttered according to a fixed pattern. First an appeal was made to the god, which could cause problems: important gods had many names and different manifestations, so care had to be taken not to select the wrong one. If necessary they were all named in a litany, or something was said along the lines of 'O Jupiter, or by whatever name it please thee to be addressed . . .' Often they added, 'And all other gods and goddesses.'

Then a compliment was paid to the god, thanks given for his support in suffering, and a request made for renewed assistance. At the same time the sacrificial animal was brought into view in the spirit of give and take: '*Do ut des*.' ('I give that thou mayst give.') All of this was expressed in fixed formulae, which had to be uttered without hesitation or error, or the whole ceremony would have to start again.

7.   When all this had been done properly, the big moment came. The object of devotion became the sacrificial animal. A servant with a hammer (the *popa*) asked if he might strike: '*Agone?*' When the priest replied, '*Age!*' ('Strike!') he raised his hammer and brought it down hard on the animal's head. The animal collapsed and the *cultrarius* picked up his knife. He held up the animal's head (or held it down, for underworld gods), and sliced its throat.

8.   The animal had to die as peacefully as possible. The horror of violent resistance was seen as a bad omen. An animal that ran away, for example, presaged the most terrible adversity (and this once happened to Caesar). When the animal had breathed its last, the climax was past. The sacrifice had been made, and a reply from the gods hung in the air. This was the right moment to start looking for signs.

9.   The animal was turned on its back and its belly was cut open. The priest had to establish that the animal was as intact and perfect inside as it appeared on the outside. If its entrails were imperfect, it was such a bad omen that making another sacrifice would have been superfluous. The gods had spoken clearly. Emperor Caligula once sacrificed an animal whose liver appeared to be missing. And, sure enough, that year he was murdered with his wife and child.

Since ancient times the studying of entrails had been as an important form of prophecy. The Etruscans were skilled in it, hence its Latin name *Etrusca Disciplina* (Etruscan science). The office of the priests specializing in this art was hereditary, and the sole preserve of one aristocratic Etruscan family. The Romans had the deepest respect for

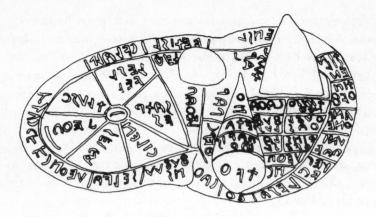

Figure 6.2 – Bronze Etruscan liver with inscriptions

these priests (*haruspices*), and consulted them so frequently that the Etrusca Disciplina became a normal part of Roman religion.

Exactly how the Etrusca Disciplina worked is not known, but it is clear that the liver played an important part in it. In depictions of sacrifices, *haruspices* are often shown with a liver in their hands. Bronze livers have been excavated, bearing Etruscan inscriptions with the magical significance of all parts of the liver. Just as many modern people know something about astrology, most Romans had some knowledge of the Etrusca Disciplina. Caligula wouldn't have needed a *haruspex* to understand that the absence of the liver meant there was trouble ahead.

Caligula's successor, Claudius, decided to deprive the Etruscans of their exclusive ownership of this practice, which became the common property of all Roman priests.

10.   After the reading of the entrails (*exta*), a portion was chopped into small pieces, *prosecta*, then wrapped in a piece of fat and thrown into the flames on the altar to feed the deity.

One might be tempted to think that the burning of the *prosceta* was the actual sacrifice but the real gift to the gods was the life-breath, the *anima*, of the beast.

There is a widespread misunderstanding that the Romans gave the offal to the gods and kept the tastiest cuts for themselves. In fact, the meat they kept was much tougher than the tender steaks available to us and offal was considered superior. There were three reasons for this:

(a) The organs are vitally important: a pig can live without one of its hams, but not without its liver.

(b) An animal has proportionally much more flesh than it has organs. Anything that was scarce was expensive, and anything expensive was delicious.

(c) On the day of the sacrifice, the meat was fresh and therefore tough. Nowadays we hang beef for weeks to become tender before we eat it. On feast days everyone wanted the offal. Offal was party food.

In his sausages, ragoûts and other dishes the elegant Apicius preferred to use minced offal. Poor people probably used mincemeat. So, in giving offal to the gods, the Romans were offering them the best they had, and only the very best was suitable (Ath. III-94c and III-100e).

11. As soon as the gods had received their delicious *prosceta*, the *cultrarius* cut the rest of the meat into pieces. In a tub the meat was lightly coated with the holy *mola salsa* with which the living animal had been dusted. It was then distributed among those present. The priest and his attendants were given a fixed portion, set out in the regulations.

Beef might have been tough for immediate consumption, but Plutarch knew that fresh sacrificial poultry could be made tender by salting and hanging on a fig-tree for a few hours. In fact, he believed the scent of the fig was strong enough on its own to make the bird tender (Plut. VI-10).

Preparations for the feast were made near the temple. Often kitchens had been included in the temple complex, and permanent *triclinia* were raised in front of it.

Anyone who had sacrificed such a large quantity of meat that it could not all be eaten on the spot was permitted to take the rest to market. Sacrificial meat was considered especially healthy-giving because of its holiness and was highly esteemed. The Christians, however, were horrified by it: sacrificial meat was imbued with the power of idols. To avoid demonic contamination many abstained from meat altogether.

A worshipper who could not afford to hire a *triclinum* near the temple could take the meat home and have a little feast on his own. In some cases, however, the meat had to be eaten on the spot, as in the rites for Silvanus and Hercules. But the participants always tried to make the occasion festive and jolly: conviviality was pleasing to the gods.

MEAT DISTRIBUTION (*visceratii*)

Over time, sacrificial duties came to focus more on festivities and less on religion. Originally a devout man was called a *polyteles*, 'one who sacrifices often'. During the Empire, the word came to mean 'glutton'. Similarly, many people nowadays celebrate Christmas with a festive meal and have little time for the religious side of the occasion.

By the imperial age little remained of the frugal, almost vegetarian diet of the early Romans. Meat had slowly become one of the most important items on the menu. The poor had always been wooed with free grain, but now they were given meat, called *visceratii*.

In 328 BC a certain Marcus Flavius distributed meat to the poor on the occasion of his mother's funeral (Cic. De Off. II-55), and others followed suit. Caesar, for example, organized meat distributions at his triumphal processions. During the rule of Emperor Aurelian the state distributed 50 g of meat per head of population. In AD 369 200,000 Romans who depended on the state for support received 1360 g of food per day, including oil, bread and meat, but no vegetables (J. André, *L'alimentation . . .*).

ANIMAL SUFFERING

Sacrifice may have been peaceful and holy, but the increase in meat consumption was bad news for the animals. The Romans were not squeamish – hard on themselves and hard on others – and they treated animals roughly. In the Latin novel *The Golden Ass*, by Apuleius, the main character turns into a donkey, and the narrative continues from the animal's perspective. The donkey is beaten so often and so hard that it is almost unbearable for the reader, but the beast accepts the punishment with good humour. The author, who empathized with a donkey, seemed not to find such thrashings objectionable.

However, Plutarch expresses his disgust at the production of various delicacies:

Animals must be killed with pity and sorrow, and should not be teased and tortured as happens a great deal at present. Some people stick glowing red spits into the throats of pigs, so that the blood will thicken and run smoothly through the veins, making the meat tender and delicate.

Others jump on the udders of a sow that is about to give birth, to mix blood and dirt together and at the same time to kill the unborn piglets at the moment of their birth. And all this in order to eat the swollen sow's udders.

Others still sew shut the eyes of cranes and swans, and lock them up in the dark to stuff them fat with curious concoctions and spiced morsels. (Plut. II-996f)

This quotation comes from an article promoting vegetarianism, but Plutarch might not have been exaggerating. Pliny, however, Pliny was enthusiastic about the invention of *foie gras*:

Our fellow countrymen are more sensible [than the Egyptians, who maintained that geese could fall in love with human beings]: we value the goose for the tastiness of its liver. Force feeding with food makes it very large. When it is then marinated in wine with milk it becomes even bigger. A good reason to wonder who its inventor was. Was it Scipio Metellus, the consul, or his contemporary Marcus Seius, king of Rome?

However that may be, it is clear that Messalinus Cotta, the son of the orator Messala, invented a dish for which goose legs are roasted and cooked to perfection in a *patina* with the combs of tame cocks. With utter conviction I award the palm to both culinary achievements. (Plin. N.H. X-xxvii)

Geese are still force-fed to enlarge and improve their liver. Pliny described a method for achieving a similar result with pig's liver:

There is a method, invented by Marcus Apicius, for treating the liver of a sow in a similar manner to that of the goose. It is force-fed with dried figs and, after enough mead has been drunk, suddenly slaughtered. (Plin. N.H. VIII-1xxvii)

A liver obtained in this way was called *ficatum*, fig-liver. Apicius gives two recipes for it. But people called any old liver *ficatum*. The Latin word for liver is *iecur*, but the Italian word is *fegato*, derived from *ficatum*.

The use of alcohol during slaughter was normal. Small mammals and long-necked birds were simply drowned in wine. The Romans thought that this was an honour for the animals and good for their flavour. They also watered their vegetables with wine.

Castration and sterilization were also methods of fattening poultry and pigs:

> Sows are sterilized in the same way as camels, by hanging them up by the forefeet after starving them for two days, then cutting out their wombs. This fattens them quicker. (Plin. N.H. VIII-1xxvii)

Cows were washed with warm water to fatten them. Some people pricked holes in their hides to blow air between the muscles with a reed, perhaps a trick to make them look fatter for the market.

However hideous these practices were, cruelty to animals in antiquity was not comparable with the misery inflicted on animals today. Pigs suffered sterilization or slaughter, but they spent most of their lives snuffling around in the woods eating acorns. The celebrations for Caligula's enthronement included what was probably the closest thing to the modern scale of slaughter:

> So great was the joy of the people that within three months more than 160,000 sacrificial animals had been slaughtered.
>
> (Suet. Caius IV-1)

That makes about 1,775 slaughters a day. The blood must have been gushing down the temple steps in torrents. In these conditions it is unlikely that animals would have tripped willingly to the altar as the rules decreed.

PORK (*sus*)

Pigs are native to Europe and have been raised for consumption for some nine thousand years. In Roman times domesticated pigs looked more like wild boar than like little pink piglets and had a shaggy coat of bristles. According to Pliny, the interbreeding of wild boar and domesticated pigs did not create problems. As the only animal raised purely for consumption, the pig enjoyed such popularity that Apicius writes 'meat' when he means 'pork'.

> No other animal produces so much material for cooking: the pig has about fifty different flavours, which is why the sumptuary laws prohibit pigs' chitterlings, sweetbreads, testicles, womb or cheek from being served at dinner.   (Plin. N.H. VIII-1xxvii)

Figure 6.3 – Graffiti showing ready-made snacks

Pliny's fifty flavours sound like a lot, but today we treat boiled ham, prosciutto and bacon as different products. The Romans ate every bit of the pig, apart from the bones and the eyes; the ears, the cheek, the jaw, snout and tongue were all considered delicacies. These cuts were called 'boiled meat', because they were boiled for a long time and some-times served in soup, which contained so much gelatine from the bones that when it cooled it set to a stiff jelly. It was eaten cold in slices. Apicius devoted a whole chapter to 'boiled meat and slices' (*In Elixam et Copadia*). '*Elixam*' corresponds more or less to present-day cold cuts. '*Copadia*' includes chops and escalopes.

Egg and leek sauce (for tongue or pig's ears)

Ius on copadiis: ova dura concidis, piper, cuminu, petroselinum, porrum coctum, myrtae bacas, plusculum mel, acetum, oleum.

Sauce for slices of meat: crushed hard-boiled eggs, pepper, cumin, boiled leek, myrtle berries, plenty of honey, vinegar, *garum* and oil.   (Ap. 286)

This sauce goes well with sliced pork, lamb, ox tongue and boiled ham. It is still eaten with pig's ears.

Take a small leek, trim and wash it, then slice into thin rings. Steam or blanch the leek for 5 minutes. Peel 3 hard-boiled eggs and chop finely.

Make a vinaigrette with equal amounts of vinegar, *garum* and olive oil, flavoured with a teaspoon of honey, a teaspoon of ground cumin, a slightly larger amount of myrtle berries (remove the seeds), and 2–3 tablespoons of freshly chopped parsley. Mix the vinaigrette with the egg and leek and serve with the meat.

Or salt pig's ears and leave them overnight. Then wash and cook them for at least 3 hours. Cut them into very thin strips and marinate overnight in the egg and leek mixture.

Cold Dill Sauce for Sausages

In elixam anethum crudum: piper, anethi semen, mentam siccam, laseris radicem, suffundis acetum, adicies caryotam, mel, liquamen, sinapis modicum, defrito, et oleo temperabis. Et in collari porcino.

Cold dill sauce for boiled meat: pepper, dill seed, dry mint, *asafoetida*. Pour on vinegar, a date, honey, *garum*, a little mustard and *defrutum* and oil to taste. This is also good with shoulder of pork.

(Ap. 287)

This sauce is really vinaigrette with added spices. Mix 50 ml vinegar with 50 ml olive oil, then beat in a tablespoon of mustard. Add a teaspoon of honey, a piece of finely chopped date, a teaspoon of *defrutum*, and a shot of *garum*. Season with pepper, a tiny quantity of *asafoetida* or garlic, a teaspoon of dried mint and 2 teaspoons of finely crushed dill seed. Beat well and serve the result with slices of cold meat or sausage.

Pork Caul (*omentum*)

Caul is a cooking aid. It consists of the firm net of fat that holds the intestines together. Caul can be taken from various animals, but usually the pig. It is available, usually frozen. Sometimes it is salted, in which case it must be soaked and washed before use.

Pork caul is wrapped around tender meats, like liver, kidneys, sweetbread and brains, if they are to be roasted on an open fire. It keeps the meat from falling apart and drying out. The Romans also wrapped poultry, rabbit and truffles in pork caul. They made many different kinds of sausage or minced-meat dishes with pork caul: *omentata*.

Intestine (*intestinum*)

Pork intestine was a dish in its own right. The large intestine, well cleaned and boiled, was considered a delicacy, just as it is today in China, although Apicius gives no recipe for it – the only intestine he mentions is the small intestine, which he uses for making sausages. It is still used as sausage skin, so it can be bought at the butcher's. Wash it under the tap before filling it. The Romans probably used their fingers to stuff sausages, as was usual until the nineteenth century, but nowadays machinery is available to help you. A simple funnel also does the trick. Pack tightly, squeezing out any air, and twisting off the sausages at regular intervals.

Fig-fed Liver (*ficatum*)

Ficatum praechidis ad cannam, infundis in liquamine, piper, ligusticum, bacas lauri duas. Involves in omento et in craticula assas et inferes.

With a reed, make incisions in the fig-liver and marinate in *garum*, pepper, lovage and two bay berries. Wrap the liver in pork caul, roast on a grill and serve.   (Ap. 263)

This is a recipe for the notorious *ficatum* (see page 254), which is no longer available. Instead we have the equally notorious calf's liver, which can be a substitute.

Take a calf's liver that weighs about 1 kilogram. Remove its outer skin and make some small incisions in it. Cover the liver with a mixture of ground lovage seed, crushed pepper, *garum* and 2 bay berries. Leave the liver to stand for a few hours, then wipe it clean. Sprinkle again with salt and pepper and wrap in pork caul.

Roast the liver for 10 minutes on one side on the barbecue, then 10 minutes on the other side. It should now feel firm. Remove it from the heat, but allow it to rest for another 10 minutes in a warm place. Then cut it into pieces and serve with the following sauce.

Sauce for Fig Liver

In ficato oenogarum: piper, thymum, liguscum, liquamen, vinum, oleum.

Wine and *garum* sauce for fig-liver: pepper, thyme, lovage, wine, oil.   (Ap. 261)

This is a salty vinaigrette. Take 100 ml of the best *garum*, 100 ml sweet white wine and 100 ml best olive oil. Add pepper to taste, a teaspoon of fresh thyme and a tablespoon of ground lovage seed.

Liver Sausage

Omentata ita fiunt: assas ieucr porcinum et enervas. Ante tamen teres piper, rutam, liquamen, et sic superinmittis iecur et teres et misces sicut pulpa omentata, et singular involvuntur lauri, et ad fumum suspendundtur quamdiu voles. Cum manducare voleris, tolles de fumo et denuo assas.

Make pork caul sausages as follows: roast pork liver and remove the veins. Grind pepper, rue and *garum*. Then add the liver, crush and mix together. Shape into caul sausages. Wrap each caul sausage in a bay leaf and hang in the chimney for as long as you wish. When you want to eat it, bring it down and roast it again.

(Ap. 40)

Put a pig's liver weighing 1 kg in salted water for a few hours to remove the blood. Wash it and brush it with olive oil. Roast for 20 minutes in a moderately hot oven until the liver is firm, but still pink inside, and leave to cool. Then chop it as finely as possible. Crush 2 teaspoons of pepper in the mortar and add to the chopped liver, along with some ground rue seed and 6 teaspoons of *garum*.

Mix to an even mass and shape into small balls. Spread out a piece of pork caul and lay young, pale green bay leaves on it in a row. Place a ball of liver on each bay leaf then roll up the pork caul. Separate each ball from the next by tying a knot between them, as with sausages, without cutting through the caul. Then hang this in the chimney above the hearth, or smoke it for several hours in a smoker. Fry briefly in olive oil before serving.

In Corsica they make a smoked liver sausage that resembles the Roman version and is called *figatello*. *Figatelli* are tiny and flavoured with bay leaf, pork fat and garlic. They can be eaten cold or hot.

Meatballs

Isicia omentata: pulpam concisam teres cum medulla siligine in vino infusi. Piper, liquamen, si velis, et bacam myrtae exenteratam simul conteres. Pusilla formabis, intus nucleis et pipere posiis. Involuta omento subassabis cum caroeno.

Meatballs in pork caul: chop boneless meat finely and grind it with bread that has had its crust removed and that has been soaked in wine. At the same time grind pepper, *garum* and, if you wish, myrtle berries (seeds removed). Shape these into little balls, and press pine kernels and whole peppercorns into them. Wrap in pork caul and fry with *caroenum*.   (Ap. 43)

Meatballs keep their shape perfectly well without pork caul, but here the caul is required to prevent the pine kernels and peppercorns falling out, as the meat shrinks.

Take 1 kg of mince and knead it with 2–3 slices of crustless bread, which have been soaked in sweet white wine. Add a good grinding of pepper and 6 tablespons of *garum*, or anchovies or salt to taste. Myrtle berries are difficult to find and laborious to seed, but they do provide a distinctive flavour.

Make small meatballs, about 2.5 cm across, press in a few pine kernels and wrap them in pork caul. Heat olive oil in a pan and fry the meatballs until they are golden brown. Then add 250 ml *caroenum*, or fill the pan with equal quantities of red wine and grape juice, and a spoonful of honey. Reduce slowly until the liquid has the thickness of a sauce and serve.

Black Pudding

Botellum sic facies: sex ovi vitellis coctis, nucleis pineis concisis cepam, porrum concisum, ius crudum misces, piper minutum et sic intestinum farcies. Adidies liquamen et vinum et sic coques.

Blood sausage is made as follows: 6 hard-boiled egg yolks, finely chopped pine kernels mixed with onion, finely sliced leek. Mix

raw blood with finely ground pepper and fill a pig's intestine with
this. Add wine and *liquamen* and cook.   (Ap. 55)

Take 1 litre of blood, 6 hard-boiled egg yolks, 1 small leek, 1 onion,
200g pine kernels and 3 teaspoons of finely ground pepper. Season
the blood with salt. Chop the onion and the leek finely in a food-
processor. Add the mashed egg yolks, then the blood, and mix thoroughly. Funnel the mixture with the coarsely chopped pine kernels
into a pig's intestine, then twist it into sausages.

Put the sausages into cold white wine with *garum* and bring it
slowly to the boil. Simmer until they are cooked.

Lucanian Sausages

Lucanicas similer ut supra scriptum est: teritur piper, cuminum,
satueia, ruta, petroselinum, condimentum, bacae, lauri, liquamen,
et admiscetur pulpa bene tunas, ita ut denuo bene cum ispo subtrito
fricetur. Cum liquamine admixto, pipere integro et abundanti
pinguedine et nucleis inicies in intestinum perquam tenuatim
productum, et sic at fumum suspenditur.

Lucanian sausages are made in the same way as above.* Grind
pepper, cumin, savory, rue, parsley, condiment,† bay berries and
garum. Mix this with well-minced pork. Then knead the mince
again to the same consistenty. Mix with *garum*, whole peppercorns, a good deal of fat and pine kernels. Stuff into a pig's
intestine and pull this thin. Hang in the chimney like this.

(Ap. 56)

Lucanian sausages are mentioned often in Latin literature, and crop
up in some of Apicius' other recipes. They are the ancestors of Italian
salame and other kinds of dried pork sausage with whole peppercorns and herbs. Salami de Strasbourg is stretched thin, like Lucanian sausages. Some salami are flavoured with fennel seed, but Lucanian
sausages contain cumin.

---

* Like blood sausage in a pig's intestine.
† An unspecified mixture of dried herbs and spices.

1 tablespoon cumin
1 tablespoon bay berries
1 tablespoon peppercorns
5 little green bay shoots
1 small bunch fresh parsley
2 stalks fresh rue
2 stalks fresh savory
2 tablespoons dried herbs
1 kg minced pork
200 g diced bacon fat
200 g pine kernels
6 tablespoons *garum*

Grind the cumin, bay berries and 1 teaspoon of the peppercorns to powder. Remove the stalks from the herbs and finely chop the leaves. Then mix all the ingredients together and knead to remove all air bubbles. Press the mixture into a pig's intestine and ensure again that there are no air bubbles. Tie off the sausages and hang them somewhere not too hot above the fireplace to dry slowly in the smoke, or put them into a smoker.

Brain Pâté

Isicium: adicies in mortarium piper, ligusticum, origanum, fricabis, suffundes liquamen, adicies cerebella cocta, teres diligenter, ne assulas habeat. Adicies ova quinque et dissolves diligenter, ut unum corpus efficias. Liquamine temperas et in patella aena exinanies, coques. Cum coctum fuerit, versas in tabula munda, tesselas concides. Adicies in mortarium piper, ligusticum, origanum, fricabis. In se commisces, suffundes liquamen, vinum. Mittis in caccabum, facies ut ferveat. Cum ferbuerit tractum confringes, obliges, coagitabis et exinanies in boletari. Piper asperges et appones.

Pâté: put pepper, lovage and oregano into the mortar and pound. Pour in *garum* and boiled brains. Grind thoroughly to remove lumps. Add 5 eggs and stir thoroughly again until it forms a mass. Add *liquamen*. Pour everything into a bronze *patina* and boil. Turn out the dish on to a clean plate when cooked. Slice into blocks.

Pound pepper, lovage and oregano in the mortar. Stir and pound again. Pour in *garum* and wine. Put in a pot and bring to the boil. Crumble *tracta* over it as it cooks. Stir and pour the sauce into a *boletarium*. Grind pepper over it and serve.   (Ap. 41)

calf's brains, or 2 sheep's brains
1 teaspoon ground lovage seed
15 salted anchovies
1 tablespoon peppercorns
1 tablespoon dry oregano
3 eggs

for the sauce
200 ml sweet white wine (or Madeira)
1 tablespoon anchovy paste
1 teaspoon lovage seed or freshly chopped lovage
1 teaspoon peppercorns
1 teaspoon oregano
tractum or dried breadcrumbs

By Roman standards this is a delicate dish, in which the only discernible flavourings are wine, oregano and lovage. The subtle taste of the brains is not overwhelmed.

Wash the brains under cold running water. Remove the veins and the membrane, then leave to soak in cold water for an hour. Wash again. Poach the brains in salted water for 15 minutes. Preheat the oven to 180°C/350°F/Gas 4. Remove them from the liquid and whiz until smooth in a blender. Pound the lovage seed to powder in the mortar, then pound in the anchovies and peppercorns to form a paste. Grind in the oregano and add the eggs. Add this mixture to the brains in the blender and whiz until it is well combined.

Line a baking tin with greaseproof paper. Pour in the pâté mixture. Cover with aluminium foil and seal. Half-fill a roasting tin with water, place the baking tin in it and put it into the oven for 45 minutes. Take it out and leave to cool.

Heat the wine to just below boiling point and beat in the anchovy paste. Grind the lovage seed to powder, then add the peppercorn and grind again. Stir this into the wine. Stir in the *tracta* or breadcrumbs.

Leave it to stand until the crumbs have absorbed the sauce. Serve the pâté sliced with the sauce.

Pig on a Spit

The pig on a spit has always been a symbol of great feasts, but only mentions roasts and fried meats, and occasionally specifies an oven.

The Romans had enormous cooking pots in which pigs were precooked before roasting whole and this was often done, but few modern kitchens have such gigantic cauldrons. The Romans also had slaves prepared to hold a pig in hot steam, which we don't. However, modern restaurants have large steam ovens, which speed up the process of roasting a whole pig. If you don't have such an oven don't despair: a pig spit-roasted in the open air is very tasty.

The Roman spit consisted of an iron rod with a ring at each end. It is worth taking the trouble to bore little holes in the spit so as to be able to tie the pig's trotters tightly with wire. The day before roasting, marinate the pig inside and out with coarse salt, olive oil and spices (pepper and fennel seed are nice, but pepper and cumin seem to have been more commonly used). Impale the pig on the spit from mouth to rectum and tie it on tightly. This is where the rings come in handy.

The animal must hang 60–80 cm above the embers. Make sure there are no large flames directly beneath it. Build a flaming fire of good-quality logs – from fruit-trees if possible, next to the pig. It will provide embers you can rake beneath it. Hard wood is more suitable than soft wood; pine burns too quickly and imparts a resinous taste to the meat.

Piglets (up to 7 kg) are cooked within 3 hours. Add 1 extra hour for each additional 7 kg. Check whether the meat is ready by poking a stick into a fatty part and feeling with your finger whether the meat is hot inside. For the meat to be evenly roasted, the spit should be turned often, at least every 20 minutes. After turning, baste the outside of the pig with olive oil and herbs, or with the roasting juices.

The skin should be crisp and reddish golden all over. If it seems in danger of burning, protect it with greased aluminium foil. (The Romans used papyrus for the same purpose.) Always cover the delicate ears, nose and cheeks. When the pig is cooked, take it off the fire

Figure 6.4

and remove the spit. Leave it to rest for 20 minutes. Stick an apple in its mouth, olives in its eyes, decorate with garlands of flowers and whatever else you can come up with. Serve with ceremony.

Sauce for Suckling Pig or Spit-roasted Pig

Porcellum assume: teres piper, rutam, satureiam, cepam, ovorum coctorum media, liquamen, vinum, oleum, conditum. Bulliat. Conditura in boletari perfundes et inferes.

Roast pig on a spit: grind pepper, rue, savory, onion, boiled egg-yolk, *garum*, wine, mixed herbs. Boil this, pour into a bowl and serve. (Ap. 383)

2 teaspoons rue seed
2 tablespoons herbs to taste
2 tablespoons peppercorns

salt, anchovies or *garum*
50 g savory
8 hard-boiled egg yolks
30 ml olive oil
1 onion

Pound the rue seed and the other herbs to a powder in the mortar. Add the pepper and the salt, anchovies or *garum*, and the savory, and mix to a paste. Pound in the egg yolks and add a dash of olive oil. In a blender, whiz the onion. Add the mixture from the mortar and whiz again. Stir in some dessert wine and serve.

Stuffed Suckling Pig

Porcellum hortolanum: porcellus hortolanus exossatur per gulam in modum utris. Mittitur in eo pullus isiciatus particullatim concisus, turdi, ficedulae, isicia de pulpa sua, lucanicae, dactyli exossati, fabriles bulbi, coclea exemptae, malvae, betae, porri, apium, cauliculi elixi, coriandrum, piper integrum, nuclei, ova xv superinfunduntur, liquamen piperatum. Et consuitur, et praeduratur. In furno assatur. Deinde a dorso scinditur, et iure hoc perfunditur. Piper teritur, ruta, liquamen, passum, mel, oleum modicum. Cum bullierit, amulum mittitur.

Bone a suckling pig via the throat, so that the animal becomes a kind of bag. Fill it with pieces of chicken (roasted whole), thrushes, figpeckers, pork sausages, Lucanian sausages, pitted dates, dried flower bulbs, snails removed from their shells, mallow, beetroot, leek, celery, boiled sprouts, coriander, peppercorns and pine kernels. Finally add 15 eggs and *garum* with ground pepper.

Sew shut and brown the meat. Then go on roasting in the oven. When the animal is cooked, cut open the back and pour in a sauce of pepper, rue, *garum*, *passum*, honey and a little oil.

(Ap. 384)

It is not easy to bone a pig 'via the throat', so you may choose to bone it in the usual manner or ask the butcher to do it for you. A pig is usually boned via the belly; cut out the ribs one by one. Many butchers leave the spine in place, but saw it through at the head and tail. For this dish it is best to remove the spine. Work a long, thin filleting knife around the bones – detach the meat. Cut through the joints with kitchen or garden shears. Bone the legs down to the knees, leaving the trotter intact. You should be left with the feet and head still attached to the boned carcass. Sprinkle it with salt and, perhaps, cumin, pepper and garlic, smear it with honey, and leave the pig to marinate overnight at room temperature. The following day, wipe it dry.

Then make the stuffing. Apicius gives a long list of poultry, vegetables and other delicacies. Take your lead from him. The ingredients for the stuffing must be cooked beforehand. Small garden birds, such as thrushes and nightingales, can be roasted on the barbecue and added whole to the stuffing; chicken should be cooked then boned. Sausage must be removed from its skin. Spread out the carcass with the meat upwards. Pile the filling on top.

Mix – don't beat – 15 eggs with 150ml *garum* and a tablespoon of crushed pepper. It is important not to beat the eggs or the air bubbles may cause the stuffing to burst out of the pig during cooking. Pour the egg mixture over the rest of the filling and stir it in.

Then close the pig with metal skewers securing the skin, then stitch it up with string. Wrap string around the skewers, like the strings of a corset, to tighten.

Now the pig should have regained its natural shape. If it is still slack and there is not enough stuffing in it, push in more. Do not stuff it tightly: the pig will shrink and the stuffing expand during cooking. Now take a sharp knife and make tiny incisions in the skin to prevent it tearing and also to allow some of the fat to escape during roasting. Preheat the oven to 180°C/250°F/Gas 4.

Lay the pig in a big roasting tin, brush it with olive oil and scatter over some salt. Place it in the oven. Allow 13 minutes' roasting time for each 500g, including the stuffing. Baste every half-hour. When the pig is ready the skin will be brown and crisp.

Now make the sauce. If you haven't any *amulum*, make a béchamel of 100ml oil, 2 tablespoons of flour and 7ml of *passum* (or dessert wine, or white wine with 4 tablespoons of honey). Add *garum* or anchovy paste and rue to taste, cook over a low heat until it has thickened.

When the pig is ready, remove the skewers and string. Pour over the sauce and serve the pig whole, decorated with flowers and fruit.

Ham and Fig Pie

Pernam, ubi eam cum caricis plurimis elixa veris et tribus lauri foliis, detracta cute tessellatim incidis et melle complebis. Deinde farinam oleo subactam contexes et ei corium reddis et cum farina cocta fuerit, eximas furno ut est et inferes.

Boil the ham with a large number of dried figs and 3 bay leaves. Remove the skin and make diagonal incisions into the meat. Pour in honey. Then make a dough of oil and flour and wrap the ham in it. Take it out of the oven when the dough is cooked and serve.

(Ap. 293)

Immediately after this Apicius gives a recipe for ham cooked in the same way with figs, but served diced with croûtons or *mustaceum* bread. The pastry, however, allows a better opportunity for spectacular presentation.

Cover the base of a pan, large enough to take the ham, with figs and lay the ham, stuffed with figs, on top. Fill the pan with water, and add 3 bay leaves. Cover, and boil the ham for 1 hour over a low heat. In the meantime make the pastry (see page 195). When the ham is cooked, dry it well and make incisions all over the flesh. Baste it with honey while it cools. Then wrap it in the dough and decorate it. Preheat the oven to 200°C/400°F/Gas 6, and bake for 30 minutes until the crust is golden. Leave to cool.

Fricassée of Shoulder of Ham with Apricots

Minutal ex praecoquis: addicies in caccabum oleum, liquamen, vinum, concides cepam ascaloniam aridam, spatulam porcinam coctam tessellatim concides. His omnibus coctis terres piper, cuminum, mentam siccam. Anethum, suffundis mel, liquamen, passum, acetum modice, ius de suo sibi, temperabis. Praecoqua enucleata mittis. Facies ut ferveant, donec percoquantur. Tractam confringes ex ea obligas. Piper asperges et inferes.

Apricot fricassée: put oil, *garum* and wine in a pot. Finely slice a dried shallot and chop a cooked shoulder of ham into small pieces. Grind in pepper, cumin and dried mint when it is all cooked. Add honey, *garum*, *passum*, a little vinegar and a bit of stock. Mix together. Add pitted, precooked apricots and bring everything to the boil. Crumble *tracta* and bind. Sprinkle with pepper and serve.   (Ap. 176)

1 kg ham shoulder
2 tablespoons honey
2 tablespoons vinegar
100 ml *passum*
400 ml white wine
1 teaspoon cumin
1 teaspoon peppercorns
1 tablespoon dried mint
1 dried shallot
500 g apricots

Chop the ham into small pieces and place it in a pan with all the liquids. Bring it to the boil. Finely grind the cumin, add the peppercorns, and mint and shallot and grind again. Put them into the pot with the ham. Simmer for 30 minutes. Remove the ham and add the apricots. Leave to cook for 5–10 minutes. Then take out the apricots, reserve them and reduce the liquid. Taste, and adjust seasoning. Replace the ham and apricots in the pot and serve.

Womb

The sow was valued for two delicacies she produced: the womb and the udder. Some authors prefer a virgin womb, but not Pliny:

> The womb is better if there has been a miscarriage than if a normal birth has taken place. The first of these wombs is called *ejectitia*, the second *porcaria*. It is best after the second pregnancy and least tasty when the womb has been weakened by numerous births. After the sow has given birth the womb becomes pale and thin, unless the sow is slaughtered within a day. The wombs of sows

that are too young are not so highly valued unless they have had one pregnancy. Those from slightly older sows are better, at least if they have not been completely cleaned and if they have not been slaughtered two days before or after giving birth, or on the same day. After a womb that has had a miscarriage, one from a day after the birth is the tastiest.

The udder is also at its most delicious when the piglets have not yet drunk from it. On the other hand the udder of a sow that has had a miscarriage is the least good.   (Plin. N.H. XI-LXXXXIV)

Depending on the age and breeding experience of the sow, the womb can be tough, and has to be simmered with spices for a long time.

The Chinese, who are familiar with this delicacy, serve sow's womb cut into thin slices, along with roasting juices. Apicius preferred to serve it with subtle sauces, containing pepper, *garum* and *laser*.

Stuffed Womb

Vulvulae isiciatae sic fiunt: piper tritum et cuminum, capita porro-rum brevia duo ad molle purgata, ruta, liquamen. admiscenteur pulpae bene tunsae et fricat denuo, ipso subtrito ita ut commisceri possint, mittas piperis grana et nucleos, et calcabis in materia bene lota. Et sic ocquuntur ex aqua oleo liquamine, fasciculo porrorum et anetho.

Womb stuffed with mince is made as follows: grind pepper, cumin and the heads of two leeks, washed to the white, with rue and *garum*. Add fine mince and grind again so that everything is mixed well together. Add pine kernels and peppercorns and stuff the mixture into a well-washed womb. The dish is cooked like this with oil, *garum*, a bundle of leeks and dill.   (Ap. 54)

Use a non-virgin womb for this dish. Remove the ovaries and soak the womb in salt water. Wash it and stuff it with the ingredients indicated by Apicius. Sew it up tightly. Cook with a little leek and a lot of dill, in water, *garum* and olive oil, over a low heat. Take out the womb, then strain the cooking liquid and reduce it to a sauce.

Sow's Nipples

Sumen elixas, de cannis surclas sale aspargis et in furnum mittis vel in craticulam. Subassas. Teres piper, ligusticum, liquamen, mero, et passo, amulo obliges et sumen perfundis.

Boil the udder and stick together with skewers. Sprinkle with pepper and place in an oven or on the barbecue. Roast. Grind pepper, lovage, *garum*, undiluted wine and *passum*, bind with *amulum* and pour this over the udder. (Ap. 261)

Remove any unwanted fat from the udder and sprinkle with coarse sea salt and pepper. Leave it overnight. Sow's udder is long, so it can be rolled up like a roulade, with the nipples outward. Boil this for a few hours, on a low fire, so they retain their shape. Then cut up the roulade into single or double breasts and roast these on the barbecue. Alternatively wash the salted udder, skewer up like Apicius suggests and roast in an oven for a very long time. Wrapping the breasts in tin foil can help to avoid the skin getting too tough.

Make a sauce out of *amulum* or a little rice flour, olive oil and dry white wine, and flavour with *garum*, pepper and lovage. Before serving, add a dash of *passum* (*vino santo*).

THE SACRED BULL

The bull was originally sacred. In the first few centuries of the Republic, it was forbidden to slaughter cattle because oxen were too useful in agriculture. But during the Republic it became normal to sacrifice them. During the Empire, Emperor Domintianus breathed new life into the old taboos, and forbade the sacrifice of bulls (Suet. Dom. 9).

Figure 6.5 – Cretan bull

Veal

The Romans were keener on bulls than they were on cows. Bulls made themselves useful as beasts of burden. Cows just gave milk, which the Romans didn't care for, considering it inferior to the milk of other animals. They readily sacrificed cows to Ceres, the goddess of agriculture:

> The good Ceres is satisfied with little, as long as it is clean. Half-naked servants, keep your knives far from the ox. Let the ox go to plough. Offer up the idle cow. Do not touch the neck that is made for the yoke. Let the ox live, and work the hard earth.
>
> (Ov. FAstii 12 Apr.)

They could choose to offer cow or bull – which meant either the male or female calf. The meat of full-grown animals was too tough to eat. The chapter about beef in Apicius says, '*bubula sive vitellina*', cow or female calf. He says nothing about eating male cattle, and gives only four recipes, three of which are for veal.

Fried Veal Escalope with Raisins

Vitella fricta: piper, ligusticum, apii semen, cuminum, origanum, cepam siccam, uvam passam, mel, acetum, vinum, liquamen, oleum, defritum.

Fried veal: pepper, lovage, celery seed, cumin, oregano, dried onion, raisins, honey, vinegar, wine, *garum*, oil, *defrutum*.

(Ap. 335)

for the sauce

¼ teaspoon cumin
½ teaspoon celery seed
1 teaspoon peppercorns
½ teaspoon dried oregano
1 tablespoon lovage
1 tablespoon dried onion
1 teaspoon *defrutum*
1 teaspoon honey
2 tablespoons white raisins
300 ml dry white wine
1 dash vinegar
1 dash *garum*

Pound the cumin and the celery seed in powder, then grind the peppercorns. Mix all the ingredients together and leave the raisins to macerate for at least a few hours and up to a day. Beat the veal fillets with a rolling-pin or meat-tenderizer, until they are flattened. For Roman authenticity, the escalopes should be cut into small pieces or strips after frying – they didn't use knives at table. Sprinkle with salt and pepper, then fry briefly on both sides in a hot pan with a little olive oil. Remove the veal from the pan. Put in the sauce mixture, let it reduce, then pour it over veal and serve immediately.

Veal Ragôut

*In vitulinam elixam: teres piper, ligusticum, careum, apiii semene,
suffundes mel, acetum, liquamen, oleum. Calefacies, amulo obligas
et carnem perfundes.*

For boiled veal: grind pepper, lovage, caraway, celery seed, pour
on honey, vinegar, *garum* and oil. Mix this, bind with *amulum*
and pour over the meat.   (Ap. 357)

Take about 1 kg of veal, chop it into bite-sized pieces and sauté
them in olive oil. Pour over enough salted water to cover and bring
it to a simmer. Grind together, 1 teaspoon lovage seed, 1 teaspoon of
peppercorns, 1 teaspoon caraway seed, 1 teaspoon celery seed, then
moisten it with 2 teaspoons honey, a dash of vinegar and another
of *garum*. Stir this into the veal and leave it to simmer for an hour or
so. Stir in a little rice flour or *taro* flour, and let it bubble for a few
minutes until the sauce thickens. Serve.

Veal with Pine Kernel Sauce

*Aliter in vitulina elixa: piper, ligusticum, feniculi semen, origanum,
nucleos, caryotam, mel, acetum, liquamen, sinapi et oleum.*

Another sauce for boiled veal: pepper, lovage, fennel seed,
oregano, pine kernels, date, vinegar, *garum*, mustard and oil.

(Ap. 358)

This is a more elegant version of the preceding veal ragôut, because the
alumum is replaced with pine kernels. The quantity of sauce is enough
for 1 kg of veal.

250 g pine kernels
1 date, pitted
1 dash vinegar
1 dash *garum*
1 teaspoon peppercorns

1 teaspoon fresh lovage seed
2 teaspoons fennel seed
1 teaspoon oregano
2 tablespoons mustard

Whiz the pine kernels, with the date, vinegar and *garum* in the blender.
Pound the spices one by one in a mortar, then sieve if necessary. Stir
together all the sauce ingredients and heat up the sauce with slices of
veal that have been boiled in stock for over an hour.

Beef or Veal with Leek, or Quince, or Onion, or Taro

Vitulina sive bubulam cum porris vel cydoneis vel cepis vel colocasiis;
liquamen, piper, laser, et olei modicum.

Cow or calf with leek, or quince, or onion, or *taro: garum,* pepper,
laser and a little oil.   (Ap. 356)

What Apicius probably had in mind was a decent-sized piece of
braising steak, sautéd then stewed with one of the above. Use garlic
instead of laser.

SHEEP AND GOAT

Sheep and goats had been herded by the Romans since time immemor-
ial, and Varro writes that sheep were the first animals to be eaten. The
ancient Romans referred to them as *pecus,* and measured their wealth
according to the size of their flocks, trading them as a currency. Their
later word for 'money' was *pecunia.*

Apicius gives only recipes for lamb and kid.

Roast Lamb or Goat

Haedus sive agnus crudus: oleo, pipere fricabis et asparges foris salem purum multo cum coriandri semine. In furnum mittis, assatum inferes.

Untreated young goat or lamb: rub the animal with oil and pepper. Sprinkle it with pure, fine salt and a great deal of coriander seed. Place in the oven and serve roasted.   (Ap. 366)

Preheat the oven to 240°C/475°F/Gas 9.

Wash the lamb and make incisions in the skin so that the flavours can penetrate it. Rub it with olive oil then sprinkle it inside and out with a large amount of ground coriander seed, pepper and salt. Then wrap it in pork caul.

Place the lamb in a greased roasting tin, or skewer it on a spit, and put it into the oven to brown. Baste from time to time with lard or olive oil. Turn down the oven temperature to 200°C/400°F/Gas 6, and continue to roast for 1 hour per kg. Baste regularly with the roasting juices. When it is done, remove it from the oven and leave the meat to rest for 15 minutes. Carve in the dining room.

Variation. Dice the lamb and leave it to marinate for a few hours in white wine. Skewer it, sprinkle it with olive oil, salt, pepper and ground coriander, and grill on the barbecue.

Lamb with Green Beans and Croûtons

Copadia haedina sive agnina: pipere, liquamine coques, cum faseolis faratariis, liquamine, pipere, lasere. Cum inbracto, buccellas panis et oleo modico.

Pieces of meat from young goat or lamb: boil with pepper and *garum*. Serve with fresh green beans, *garum*, pepper and *laser*. Accompany with pieces of bread and a little oil.   (Ap. 359)

1 kg lamb, diced
salt

pepper
olive oil
500 ml stock with *garum*
6 cloves garlic, peeled and crushed
500 g green beans, topped and tailed
1 loaf of bread, crusts discarded, cubed

Sprinkle the meat with salt and a lot of coarsely ground pepper. Then brown it in the olive oil. Add the stock and allow the meat to simmer for an hour until it is cooked. Towards the end of cooking add the garlic.

Cut the beans in half, then blanch them. Refresh them in cold water.

Fry the bread until it is golden brown, then sprinkle it with salt. Put the beans and the meat into a serving bowl, scatter over the croûtons and serve.

Lamb Hash

Aliter haedinam sive agninam ex caldatam: mittes in caccabum copadia. Cepam, coriandrum minutatim sucides, teres piper, ligusticum, cuminium, liquamen, oleum, vinum. Coques, exinanies, in patina, amulo obligas. Angina a crudo trituram mortario accipere debet, caprina autem cum coquitur accipit trituram.

Another recipe for stewed kid or lamb: put the pieces of meat into the pot. Finely chop onion and coriander, grind pepper, lovage, cumin, *garum*, oil and wine. Boil, transfer to a *patina* and thicken with *amulum*. If using lamb, add the contents of the mortar while the meat is still raw, and if using goat meat add during the cooking.   (Ap. 360, 361)

2 large onions, finely chopped
olive oil
1 kg lamb, diced
1 bottle white wine
1 teaspoon lovage seed
2 teaspoons cumin

2 teaspoons peppercorns
anchovies, or salt or *garum*
1 tablespoon flour or *amulum*
100 g fresh coriander, chopped

Fry the onions lightly in the olive oil. Then take them out and put
them into a large saucepan. Sprinkle the meat with salt and pepper
and brown it in the pan. Then put it into the saucepan with the onion
and pour in the wine. Grind the lovage seed, then add the cumin and
grind it, then the peppercorns with the anchovies, salt or *garum*. Add
this mixture to the saucepan. Place over a low heat and cook until the
liquid has reduced by half. Strain off the stock.

Take another saucepan, and heat the flour in some olive oil. Pour
in the lamb stock and stir continuously until the sauce is smooth.
Then put in the meat and the onions and cook until the sauce is
thick. Just before serving, scatter over the coriander.

DOG

Dogs were faithful domestic animals, kept for hunting and protecting the farm. They were not generally eaten. However, there were the
exceptions:

> The habits of our ancestors lead me to say something else about
> dogs. The meat of nursing puppies was considered such a pure
> foodstuff that it was used to appease enemy gods more than any
> other sacrificial offering. Genita Mana* was honoured with a dog
> sacrifice, and puppy meat is, even today, served at meals in honour
> of the deity. We know from the plays of Plautus that it was eaten
> a great deal in former times.   (Plin. N.H. XXIX-xiv)

---

* Goddess of childbirth.

GAME

Hunting

There are two kinds of hunting: noisy and silent – à la Romulus and à la Remus. Remus was a herdsman who lived with the animals in the open countryside. He hunted alone. He followed a trail and listened carefully, keeping himself silent and small. He tried to stay out of the wind. If it pleased Diana, the goddess of hunting, he found his prey. He leaped out and fired an arrow, hit or miss. The silence was broken. Sadly Remus was murdered, and the herdsman's style of hunting died with him.

Soldiers like Romulus hunted in a different way: they tramped through the woods in gangs, making as much noise as possible to flush out the game. They drove the animals towards a central point where officers were sitting on horseback. A battle follows. Officers always came out on top, of course, but sometimes they liked to make things harder by allowing themselves to be enclosed with panicking animals. They had to put up a real fight against the tusks of wild boars, and could thus prove the extent of their courage.

Figure 6.6

Reserves

The Romans were so busy planting the country and sectioning it off into farms and estates that there was hardly any untamed countryside left for hunting. When they realized this, they established hunting reserves, *vivaria*. Large areas of forest, full of game, were walled in and guarded.

> Fulvius Lippinus was the first toga-wearer to hit on the idea of setting up a hunting reserve for wild boar and other forest animals. He introduced the keeping of game to Tarquinia. He had no lack of emulators, like Quintus Hortensius and Lucius Lucullus.
>
> (Plin. N.H. VIII-1xxviii)

Apicius must have been partial to game because in his chapter on quadrupeds (*tetrapus*) he gave thirty-eight recipes for wild boar, wild sheep, deer and hare, and only thirty recipes for domesticated pigs, lamb and goat. Varro mentions hunters too:

> I saw more when I was on the land of Q. Hortensius near Laurentum. He had a wood there, which he said covered more than twelve hectares. It was surrounded by a wall. He didn't call it a rabbit-run, but a game farm.
>
> A *triclinium* was installed on a hill. Orpheus was conjured up. When he appeared, with his cloak and harp, he was told to sing. Instead he blew on a hunting horn. After that deer, wild boar and other quadrupeds came running around us. I found the spectacle no more magnificent than when the aediel holds games with local animals in the Circus Maximus. (Varr. R.R. III-xiii-2)

The Circus

Varro compared the spectacle of the hunt to the circus, which was actually built for horse races, but hunting parties (compare greyhound races) also appeared there: *venationes*. Hunting parties and horse races kept soldiers busy during peacetime.

As football supporters wear the colours of their teams today, the Romans wore the colours of their favourite chariot. And they would fight each other over it then, too, as football supporters still do today. The origin of the horse races, however, was religious. It was a sacred duty to attend the *ludi circenses*. Some circus games were cruel: during the Ceralia, foxes were captured and burning torches tied to their tails; at the Floralia, rabbits and hares were hunted.

The majority of the population thought this was all tremendous fun so, in order to boost their popularity, politicians staged many such events and made them ever more sensational. Rhinoceroses and bulls stormed down the circus track, spurred on by red fabric dolls tied to their backs, and votes were won.

Similar to the circus was the *amphitheatrum*, where games were held on a central stage, the *arena*. Circus buildings were long oblong constructions, but the amphitheatre was 'theatre in the round'. Gladiatorial combat which dated back to Etruscan days when gladiators became the human sacrifice at the funeral of an important person, were held there. They were popular and took on some of the absurdities of the circus.

Traditionally gladiators fought each other in uneven formations: the *retiarius* in heavy armour, fought the *cetarius*, dressed like a fisherman and armed with trident and net. Other combinations included: a wolf against a hippopotamus; a rhinoceros against a giraffe; a panther against an ostrich; an Ethiopian against an elephant; a German against a bear; a woman against a dwarf; a Christian against a lion. These were always fights to the death. It was not always a foregone conclusion that the human won, and certainly not if he or she was tied up or otherwise handicapped. The Colosseum in Rome has become a sacred monument to the Catholic Church because so many Christian martyrs died there.

However cruel the popular entertainments of the circus and the amphitheatre, it was not only the pagan Romans who enjoyed watching them. Many generations of pious Christians witnessed public beheadings, hangings and burnings. It was a day out for the whole-family. Modern man isn't much better. Children of today watch more murders on television every week than a Roman child would have seen in the circus.

Jews and early Christians were among the few to boycott the circus games, principally because the games were dedicated to the pagan gods. For other Romans, their presence at the games was a religious obligation: the games were a kind of offering.

Figure 6.7

Just as sacrificial meat from the altar was in demand, the meat from circus sacrifices fetched a good price, because it was meat from a holy sacrifice; because it was game – often exotic – that the Romans enjoyed; because it was supposed to contain substances that fortified them and because it was scarce. There was nowhere near enough to go round the tens of thousands of greedy spectators. Even today, the meat from bulls of the Spanish arenas is in demand although it's very tough.

The Romans relished animals that had died by the sword or spear, but the greatest delicacy of all was a creature that had been killed by another animal. The teeth of a wild animal were thought to radiate a certain energy that tenderized the meat:

> After this conversation we talked about sheep that had been bitten by wolves: these actually have sweeter flesh . . . A relative of mine, Patrocleas, had a good explanation for this, namely that the bites of the animal make the flesh more tender. In fact the temperament of the wolf is so hot and fiery that even the hardest bones melt and are digested in its stomach. As a result the meat of sheep that have been bitten by wolves has already been partially broken down. (Plut. II-9)

Martial, too, praises a meal at which he is served a kid 'taken from the claws of a wolf' (Mart. X-48). Few lambs are retrieved from wolves these days, so it's hard to check the accuracy of the theory.

WILD BOAR (*aper*)

At the end of the Republic it became customary to serve a boar whole but, according to Pliny, the animal had previously been divided into three parts, and only the middle, the 'saddle', was thought suitable for the table (Plin. N.H. VIII-lxxviii).

The meat of a wild boar is often tough and dry. For that reason it was sometimes salted to break down the sinews and intensify the flavour. When the day came to roast the boar, it was boiled first to get rid of the salt, then roasted in the oven.

Roast Wild Boar

Aper ita conditur: spogiatur, et sic aspergitur ei sal et cuminum frictum, et sic manet. Alia die mittitur in furnum. Cum coctus fuerit perfundutur piper tritum, condimentum aprunum, mel, liquamen, caroenum et passum.

Boar is cooked like this: sponge it clean and sprinkle with salt and roast cumin. Leave to stand. The following day, roast it in the oven. When it is done, scatter with ground pepper and pour on the juice of the boar, honey, *liquamen, caroenum* and *passum*.

(Ap. 330)

For this you would need a very large oven, or a very small boar, but the recipe is equally successful with the boar jointed. Remove the bristles and skin, then scatter over it plenty of sea salt, crushed pepper and coarsely ground roasted cumin. Leave it in the refrigerator for 2–3 days, turning it occasionally.

Wild boar can be dry, so wrap it in slices of bacon before you roast it. At the very least wrap it in pork caul. Then put it into the oven at its highest setting and allow it to brown for 10 minutes. Reduce the oven temperature to 180°C/350°F/Gas 4, and continue to roast for 2 hours per kg, basting regularly.

Meanwhile prepare the sauce. To make *caroenum*, reduce 500 ml wine to 200 ml. Add 2 tablespoons of honey, 100 ml *passum*, or dessert wine, and salt or *garum* to taste. Take the meat out of the oven and leave it to rest while you finish the sauce. Pour off the fat from the roasting tin, then deglaze it with the wine and honey mixture. Pour this into a saucepan, add the roasting juices and fat to taste.

Carve the boar into thin slices at the table, and serve the sweet sauce separately.

Boar from the Sea

*Aliter in apro: aqua marina cum ramulis lauri aprum elixas
quousque manescat. Corium ei tolles. Cum sale, sinapi, eceto inferes.*

Another way of cooking boar: boil the boar in seawater with sprigs
of bay until it is done. Remove the skin and serve with salt,
mustard and vinegar.   (Ap. 331)

This dish is so simple that it needs little interpretation. The boar
will take a few hours to cook, according to its size. There seems little
point in adding salt to a boar that has been cooked in seawater, but
the mustard and vinegar will sharpen the flavour.

Terentine Sea-Boar Ham

*Perna apruna ita impletur terentina: per articulum, pernae palum
mittes ita ut cutem a carne separes, ut posit condimentum acipere
per cornulum et iniversa impleatur. Teres piper, bacam lauri, rutam:
si volueris, laser adicies, liquamen optimum, caroenum et olei viridis
guttas. Cum impleta fuerit, constringitur illa pars, qua impleta est,
ex lino et mittitur in zenam. Elixatur in aqua marina cum lauri
turionibus et anetho.*

Wild boar ham in the Terentine style is stuffed as follows: poke a
stick into the joint side of the ham, so that the skin comes away
from the meat and the aromatics can be added through a pipe and
fill the entire ham. Grind pepper, bay berry, rue and, if you wish,
laser, as well as the best *liquamen, caroenum,* and a little green olive
oil. When the ham is stuffed with this, tightly sew the opening
through which it has been stuffed with a piece of string and place
the ham in the pot. Boil in brine with bay shoots and dill.

(Ap. 340)

1 fresh unsalted ham, with the skin
500 ml full-bodied red wine
1 tablespoon peppercorns

1 tablespoon bay berries
1 tablespoon rue seed
asafoetida or a few cloves garlic
garum or salt
sprigs of dill
100 ml olive oil
seawater or brine
sprig of bay with young shoots

Remove the bone from the ham, or ask the butcher to do it for you. Reduce the wine to 100 ml. Grind together the spices, dill and salt, and mix them to a paste with the reduced wine and the olive oil. Separate the skin from the ham with a boning knife or a skewer. Put the filling into a piping bag and pipe it under the skin and into the hollow left by the bone. Leave the ham to marinate for a few hours then tie it firmly together with string.

Bring the seawater or brine to the boil with a sprig of fresh, light-green bay leaves, and cook for 2 hours. Leave it to drain, and carve it in the dining room.

ROAST DEER – VENISON

Apicius mentioned the two varieties of Italian deer, the roe (*capreus*) and the red deer (*cervus*). He didn't refer to moose, antelopes or other related animals. Venison was boiled or roasted whole, and the sauces he noted are suited to either method. Wipe the meat and wrap it in a few layers of pork caul. Turn the oven to its highest setting. Put in the meat and let it brown for 15 minutes. Then reduce the oven temperature to 180°C/350°F/Gas 4 and continue to roast, allowing about 10 minutes for each 500g. Take it out and let it rest for half an hour before carving.

Herb Sauce for Roast Roe Deer

Ius in caprea assa: piper, condimentum, rutam, cepam, mel, liquamen, passum, oleum modice. Amulum iam buliit.

A sauce for [roast] deer: pepper, herbs, rue, onion, honey, *garum*, *passum*, a little oil. Thicken with *amulum* when it is boiling.

(Ap. 350)

1 onion, finely chopped
2 tablespoons olive oil
1 tablespoon flour or *amulum*
500 ml *passum*, or raisin or dessert wine
1 teaspoon honey
sprig of green rue, finely chopped
bunch of mixed herbs, to taste, finely chopped
pepper
salt or *garum*

Sauté the onion in the olive oil, then add flour, stir well and continue to cook for a minute. Reduce the heat and pour in the *passum*, or wine, stirring continuously until you have a smooth sauce. Add the honey, the rue and the other herbs, and continue to simmer. Season with pepper, and salt or *garum*.

Prune Sauce for Roast Red Deer

Aliter in cervum assum iura ferventina: piper, ligusticum, petroselinum, damascene macerate, vinum, mel, acetum, liquamen, oleum modice, agitabis porro et satureia.

A sauce for roast red deer: pepper, lovage, parsley, soaked Damascus prunes, wine, honey, vinegar, *garum*, a little oil; stir with a leek and savory.

(Ap. 248)

250 g prunes, pitted
500 ml red wine
200 ml *passum*
1 tablespoon honey
1 teaspoon crushed peppercorns
2 tablespoon fresh chopped lovage
1 bunch fresh parsley, chopped
1 tablespoon olive oil

garum or salt to taste
leek and savory, optional

Soak the pitted prunes for 2 days with the wine, *passum*, honey, pepper and the chopped lovage and parsley. Then put it all into a blender and whiz until smooth. Turn the mixture into a small saucepan and cook over a low heat, stirring continuously for a few minutes. Add the olive oil, stir well, then season with *garum* or salt. You can stir the sauce with leek or savory, as Apicius suggests. Pass the sauce through a sieve and serve.

RABBIT AND HARE

Although rabbits count as game, they were not native to northern Europe: they were introduced by the Romans as domesticated animals. All the rabbits (and pheasants) in northern Europe are descended from Roman breeding establishments.

Rabbits are good at escaping, and the Romans knew that rabbit runs had to be enclosed with fences or walls that went several metres into the ground. Even so, some managed to find a gap and hopped to freedom. Even in the wild, rabbits breed rapidly, which is fun for the huntsman but less so for the cook: domesticated rabbit is fatty and tender, while their wild cousins are stringy and tough.

Apicius says that you can only make meatballs with rabbit, but he gives several recipes for hare.

Pegasus Hare Stuffed with Chicken Liver

Leporem farsilem: leporm curas, ornas, quadratum imponis. Adicies in mortarium piper, ligusticum, origanum, suffundes liquamen, adicies iecenera gallinarum cocta, cerebella cocta, pulpam concisam, ova cruda tria, liquamine temperabis. Omento tetes et charta et surclas. Lento igni subassas. Adicies in mortarium piper, ligusticum, fricabis, suffundes liqaumen, vino et liquamine temperabis, facies ut ferveat. Cum ferbuerit, amulo obligas, et leporem subassatum perfundes. Piper asperges et inferes.

Stuffed hare: gut the hare, skin it and tie it and put it into a bowl.
In the mortar, grind pepper, lovage and oregano. Pour in some
garum. Add boiled chicken livers, chopped, boiled brains and
3 raw eggs mixed with *garum*.

Wrap in pork caul and in paper and seal. Roast over a low
flame. In the mortar, grind pepper and lovage. Mix and pour in
garum and wine. Bring to the boil. When boiling, thicken with
amulum and pour over the roast hare. Grind pepper over it and
serve.

In some recipes Apicius gave the instructions for boning hare,
but not here, although it would make it easier to carve. Hare and
rabbit are boned in much the same way as poultry (see page 312), the
only difference being that the hare is opened via the belly. You could
ask your butcher to do it. Otherwise, leave the gutted hare intact,
including the head.

1 hare
pork caul

for the stuffing
200g chicken livers
3 eggs
100g fat minced pork
100g boiled calf's brains
1 teaspoon crushed pepper
2 tablespoons ground anchovies
1 teaspoon chopped fresh lovage
1 teaspoon dried oregano

for the sauce
1 tablespoon olive oil
2 teaspoon flour
300ml sweet red wine
1 teaspoon ground pepper
1 teaspoon chopped lovage
2 teaspoons *garum*

Preheat the oven to 200°C/400°F/Gas 6.

First make the stuffing. Boil or fry the chicken livers until they are cooked, then whiz them in a blender with the rest of the stuffing ingredients. Put it into the hare's belly cavity, pin it together with cocktail sticks and keep these in place with string. Tie the feet to the body. Stick a thread through the skull via the eyes. Pull the head back and tie to the body, to bring the beast into a lively shape.

Wrap the hare in the pork caul (you can add a few rashers of bacon, too, if you like, to prevent it drying out, then in greaseproof paper or aluminium foil. Put it into the oven for 30 minutes. Then remove the foil and return the hare to the oven to brown the caul. Baste it regularly.

To prepare the sauce, heat the olive oil, stir in the flour and cook for a minute. Pour in the wine, and let it reduce until you have a thin, smooth sauce. Stir in the other ingredients, cook for a minute, then pour over the hare as soon as it is ready. In the *Satyricon* a hare cooked in this way is decorated with little wings so that it looks like Pegasus, the flying horse.

DORMOUSE (*glis*)

In northern Europe the dormouse lives in the wild. In most countries it is a protected species, which means that it cannot be caught and eaten. In ancient Rome, too, a sumptuary law (passed by Emilius Scaurus in 115 BC) forbade the eating of dormice, but no one paid any

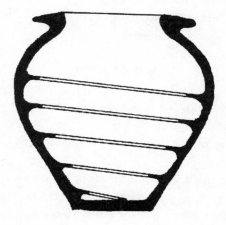

Figure 6.8 – Glirarium

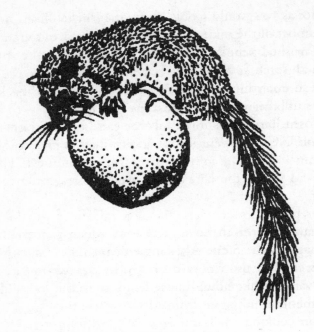

Figure 6.9 – The dormouse

attention, and the dormouse was often on the menu and, in fact, was bred for the table. The animals were allowed to live free in a fenced-off garden. When dormice hibernate, they become thinner, and the Romans wanted to prevent this. During the winter season, they put the fattened mice into a large jar equipped with an internal spiral rim, a *glirarium*. The dormouse, partly because of its size, remained an expensive delicacy. It was also to be found in Trimalchio's dinner.

Stuffed Mouse

Glires: isicio porcino, item pulpis ex omni membro glirum, trito cum pipere, nucleis, lasere, liquamine farcies glires, et sutos in tegula positos mittes in furnum aut farsos in clibano coques.

Mice: stuff the mice with minced pork, mouse meat from all parts of the mouse ground with pepper, pine kernels, laser and *garum*. Sew the mouse up and put on a tile on the stove. Or roast in a portable oven.   (Ap. 408)

Gut mice as you would rabbit, then wash them. Take a quarter of the total number of the mice and remove the meat from the bones. Pound it with crushed pepper, then add the same quantity of minced pork, along with some *asafoetida*, garlic and *garum* or salt.

Knead everything together well and put it into a piping bag. Use this to stuff the remaining mice. Apicius writes that they should be sewn closed, but this is not always necessary. Pour over some oil and roast at 180°C/350°F/Gas 4 for 15 minutes, then serve.

SNAILS

Snails have been eaten since prehistoric times, and excavations from as long ago as the Stone Age have revealed piles of their shells. The Romans enjoyed the vineyard snails that are still popular today and smaller varieties like house-snails. Land-snails the size of a human fist were sometimes imported from Africa, where they are still eaten.

Before cooking, snails must spend 3 days imprisoned to excrete any poisonous matter. During that time they may be fed on bran, flour, herbs and milk, which improves their flavour. Shortly before they are to be cooked, sprinkle them with salt, which causes them to foam, then wash off the slime.

Cocleas lacte pastas: accipies cocleas, spongizabis, membranam tolles, ut possint prodire. Adicies in vas lac et salem uno die, ceteris diebus lac per se et omni hora mundabis stercus. Cum pastae fuerint, ut non possint se retrahere, ex oleo frigis. Mittes oenogarum . . .

Milk-fed snails: take snails, sponge them clean. Remove the membrane so that they can come out. On the first day add milk with [a little] salt to the pot [where the snails are]. The following day only milk. Remove the dung every hour. When the snails are so fat they can't get back into their shells, fry them in oil. Serve with *oenogarum*. (Ap. 326)

Or:

Aliter cocleas: viventes in lac siligineum infundes: ubi pastae fuerint, coques.

Another way of cooking snails: marinate them alive in milk with flour. When they are fattened, boil them.   (Ap. 328)

Snails with Laser or Garlic

Cocleas: sale puro et oleo assabis cocleas: lasere, liquamine, pipere oleo suffundis.

Snails: fry the snails in oil with pure salt. Pour on *laser*, pepper, *liquamen* and oil.   (Ap. 327)

This recipe is remarkably similar to our Snails in Garlic Butter: in which the *laser* is merely replaced with the garlic, and the olive oil with butter.

VII

FROM THE AIR

Concerning Wild, Tame and Aviary Birds and Their Eggs

THE FARMYARD

Goose

The most important of the farmyard birds was the goose. It was appreciated not only for its liver, meat, fat, down, feathers and eggs, but also as an avian guard-dog.

In 390 BC the Gauls invaded Italy. No one could stop them, and they reached Rome. Most of the populace had fled the city with their provisions, but a number of senators and soldiers stayed on, having withdrawn to Rome's ancient fortress, the Capitol, where the temples of Juno and Jupiter stood. The Gauls discovered a route by which they could climb up to the Capitol, and decided to do so at night.

The Romans were asleep, but when the first of the Gauls arrived, the geese, which were dedicated to Juno, started to gaggle. The Romans woke up, defeated the Gauls and the city was saved. From then on, geese were honoured: the censors were given the task, in perpetuity, of supplying their food and the guard-dogs, which had neglected their duty, were punished: each year a living dog was nailed to a cross of elderwood between the temples of Iuventas and Summanus. The rotting corpses were left there in memory of the siege of Rome, and as a warning to their fellows.

Chicken

Less glorious, but of similar importance in the farmyard, was the chicken. Originally from Asia, this bird was familiar to the Romans from earliest times. They got up to the crow of the cockerel, and feeding the chickens was one of the first tasks of the day. It was a bad omen if the chickens weren't hungry. If they ate placidly but with gusto, an average day would follow. If they couldn't get the food down fast enough and grains fell out of their beaks, it would be a particularly auspicious day.

Chicken has never been excessively expensive. When C. Fannius, in 161 BC, drew up sumptuary laws against excessive luxury (see page 21–2), all poultry was forbidden except chicken. The chicken was important for egg production, so a farmer should not slaughter one before it was three years old when, according to Columella (Coll. R.R. V-24), egg-laying declined. In general, then, the Romans would have eaten old hens, rather than succulent young ones. Unfortunately for farmers the law was that cockerels had to be spared: only one was needed per hen-house and as an alarm clock. But cockerels could be sold for fighting, which was popular among schoolboys. In Greece, the cockerel was a traditional gift from an older man to a younger if he wanted to get him into bed. Clearly the Greek custom was borrowed by some Romans, like Eumolpus in the *Satyricon*:

> I had another chance the following night. I changed my voice and whispered, 'If I am allowed to touch this boy unashamedly with my hands without it troubling him, tomorrow I will give him two of the best fighting-cocks.'　　　　　　　　　　　　　　　(Petr. 86)

Perhaps Roman mothers were unhappy about this practice for eventually another use was found for superfluous cockerels:

> Of the three kinds of hens that there are, the correct name for the farmyard chicken is 'hen', the male is called 'cock', and the half-male sort, which has been castrated, is the 'capon'. Cocks are castrated by holding a red-hot iron between their legs until it bursts. The resulting wound is smeared with clay.　　　　(Varr. III-ix)

A capon was not a cockerel, so it was exempt from the law against eating them. Also capons became fat naturally and therefore had very tender flesh, which circumvented the law against fattening poultry.

Fattening

Chickens and geese are fattened as follows: lock up chickens that have just started laying. Make balls of white or wholewheat flour. Soak them in water and press them into the beaks of the birds, a little more each day. You must make what you can of their own hunger. Feed them twice a day. At twelve o'clock they must be watered, but the water should not be allowed to stand for more than an hour. A goose is fed in the same way, apart from the fact that twice a day it is first given something to drink and then something to eat.

Young wood pigeons are force-fed as follows: once the wood pigeon is caught, give it boiled and roasted broad beans by blowing them into its beak with your mouth. Give it water in the same way. Do this for seven days.   (Cat. R.R. LXXXIX and XC)

A fattened wood pigeon was a delicacy that was greatly in demand, and cost 200 HS per bundle in the first century AD. Other wild birds were fattened for the table, such as blackbirds, finches, titmice, quails, ortolans and larks.

The duck was a favourite subject in frescoes, but some found their flavour dull. Swan, too, was raised for the table, but the most impressive domesticated bird was the peacock.

Peacock: you admire him, often he spreads his jewel-encrusted tail. How can you, unfeeling man, hand this creature over to the cook?

(Mart. XIII-1xx)

Romans ate all birds, apart from the woodpecker. Plutarch asked why this was so.

Why do the Latins have such respect for the woodpecker that they don't eat it? Is it because Picus* was turned into a woodpecker by his wife, with a magic potion, and that he gives oracles and prophecies to anyone who seeks his advice?   (Plut. 268)

WILD BIRDS

It was not only woodpeckers that made prophecies. All birds were invested with this power because they were seen as messengers between heaven and earth. The woods echoed with their song, which the Romans interpreted as the voice of the gods. The cry of the owl, dedicated to Minerva, presaged death. The cooing of the dove, the bird of Venus, was interpreted as a message of love. The hammering of the woodpecker, however, which sounded like a form of Morse code, could be endlessly interpreted.

The Romans also read the flight and behaviour of birds. This was an art that had been developed by the Etruscans. Originally seers staked out an area of sky – the *templum* – by placing two sticks at a distance from each other in the ground. Then they sat down on a three-legged stool to study the sky. If, for example, an eagle flew into the *templum* from the right, the god Jupiter was looking down on them favourably. The croak of a crow – Apollo – did not bode well.

The messengers of the gods were shamelessly eaten. Crows, magpies, titmice, thrushes and pelicans all ended up on the dinner table. Large birds could be shot with a bow and arrow, smaller ones captured with nets or long, sticky, limed reeds. Trimalchio's dinner was the scene of one such event:

> Then servants came in and replaced the curtains with cloths showing nets and beaters with hunting rods and all kinds of other hunting equipment. We were just wondering what to expect when a loud cry came in from outside the dining room. And behold, Spartan dogs came in and ran around the table.

* The god Picus, king of Italy, father of Faunus, grandfather of Latinus, husband of Circe the sorceress.

A dish was brought in, bearing an enormous wild pig. It was wearing a cap of freedom,* and from its tusks hung two baskets made of palm twigs, one holding dried dates, the other containing fresh ones. Around it lay piglets made of *coptaplacenta*† with their mouths around the pig's nipples. This told us that we were looking at a sow. These piglets were our *apophoreta*. The man who came forward to hand around the pieces of pork was not the carver who had previously been carving the poultry, but a great bearded man with swathes around his legs and a hunter's cloak of ornamental silk. He took his hunting knife and hurled it violently into the flank of the boar. Out burst thrushes, which flew into the room.

As they fluttered through the dining room, the bird-catchers stood ready with their lime-sticks. They were able to catch the birds within a very short time. Trimalchio ordered that everyone should have his share.

(Petr. 40)

Some birds were valued for their spectacular appearance. Sometimes the peacock, the pheasant or the guinea fowl were roasted then had their plumage restored to them. This is not too difficult to achieve. To prepare a bird in this fashion, take off the feathers with the skin. Cure the skin with coarse sea salt, so that it dries out a little, and wash it off just before you dress the roast bird in it. Birds with impressive beaks, such as the ibis, flamingo, parrot and ostrich, look striking even without their feathers.

Thrush

Other birds fetched high prices because of their delicate flavour. Thrushes were considered even more delicious than flamingo tongues or parrot brains. In the market, dead thrushes were sold suspended from a ring. Martial writes:

---

* The *pileus*, a felt cap like the caps worn in the French revolution, also known as the Phrygian cap. Slaves wore them when they were freed. During the festivities of the Saturnalia everyone wore them.
† A kind of pastry.

You may have a wreath of woven roses or costly nard. Give me
rather a wreath of thrushes.   (Mart. XIII-51)

In another poem Martial declares that he considers thrushes the most
delicious of birds, and Horace agrees:

By Hercules, I can see nothing strange in people eating up their
fortunes, for nothing is more delicious than thrushes, or a fat
sow's womb.   (Hor. I-xv)

Figpecker

Another small bird vied for the title 'most desirable bird': the *ficedula*,
usually translated literally as 'figpecker'. It does not eat figs, but flies or
berries. Martial was aware that its name was inappropriate.

Figpecker: 'I am thought to live on figs, but I am fed sweet grapes
– so why not grape-pecker?'

The *ficedula* is more correctly known as the pied flycatcher. About
the size of a robin, it is a migrant bird present throughout most of
northern Europe in the summer. The Romans did not consider it
necessary to gut these tiny, tasty birds, and swallowed them in a single
mouthful.

The song of the figpecker, and the fact that it is distantly related
to the thrush family, gave rise to the story that the Romans regularly
sat down to a feast of nightingales. The figpecker is mentioned in
many recipes, but nightingales were highly esteemed for their song.
A single nightingale might cost more than a slave. The highest prize
ever commanded by a nightingale was 600,000 HS, the price of about
two hundred slaves, for an albino bird that the emperor Claudius gave
to his beloved Agrippina. It was perverse to eat them. However,

The most remarkable meal was a *patina* dish by the tragedy actor
Clodius Aesopus, which was worth 100,000 HS, in which he
served birds that sang a certain song, or which had been taught
to speak. He had bought the birds for 6000 HS each, his sole
purpose being to eat them, and thus to feed on something almost

Figure 7.1 – Ficedula

cannibalistic. He did not even have respect for the fact that he had made his own fortune with his voice.   (Plin. N.H. X-1xxii)

Aviaries

Pliny, who was perfectly at ease with such cruelties as the force-feeding of geese, hated aviaries:

> Aviaries in which all kinds of birds are caged up were begun by Marcus Laenius Strabo, a knight from Brindisi. He was the one who gave us the practice of locking up creatures whose natural place is the open sky.   (Plin. N.H. X-1xxii)

Some kinds of aviary were not so bad: they consisted of a flying space screened off by fine nets and surrounded by columns. There were sticks and branches, too, on which the birds could perch. Varro recommends that a stream should flow through the aviary, because stagnant water smelt unpleasant. In some cases the stream was large enough to build islands and keep ducks. It was pleasant not only for birds but for people:

> There are two kinds of aviary. One for decoration, like the one

built by our friend Varro, near Casium, to which admirers flock.
The other is for trade. In this latter kind of aviary poultry can be
bred for the market . . . Lucullus claimed that he had built an
aviary near Tusculum that combined both kinds. Under a single
roof he had installed both an aviary and a *triclinium*, where he was
able to serve elegant dinners. At the same time he could see one
bird cooked on his plate while the others were fluttering around,
imprisoned behind the windows.

It wasn't such a success, though, because the pleasure that
the birds gave the eye as they fluttered about was not as great
as the violence done to the nose by their stench. (Varr. R.R. III-iv 3)

The second kind of aviary, in which birds were kept to be fattened,
was far less agreeable. Varro recommends that it should be surrounded
by walls, with windows so small that the birds could only see where
their food and drink was, or how to get to their perches without an
accident. The Romans were convinced that birds fattened more quickly
in the dark, since they were less active. Varro has another explanation:

> The window must be small and placed in such a way that trees or
> birds cannot be seen outside, because such a view makes the birds
> homesick, and that makes them thin.   (Varr. R.R. III-v)

Poultry Pie

All birds, from quails and ibises to storks and ostriches, can be cooked
in pastry crust.

> *Avem sapidorem et atiliorem facies et ei pinguedinem servabis, si eam
> farina oleo subacta contextam in furnum miseris.*

Poultry can be made tastier and more nutritious, and more use
can be made of its fat, if you wrap it in a dough of oil and flour
and put it in the oven.   (Ap. 232)

Under a pastry crust poultry roasts in its own fat so does not need
to be basted. All birds, large and small, can be treated in this way, but
it is best suited to fat poultry. If the bird is lean, moisten it with fat –

suet, bacon fat, goose fat, olive oil or even butter. Take a plucked and guttered bird. Carefully separate the skin from the flesh of the breast and the leg by pushing your hand between the skin and the meat. Mix your chosen fat with salt, pepper and herbs, then push it under the skin and over the meat. Press the skin back into place, then sprinkle it with salt. Stuff other flavourings into the cavity. Preheat the oven to 200°C/400°F/Gas 6.

Make an oil pastry dough (see page 195) and roll it out. Wrap the bird in it and decorate it with any pastry trimming. Place it on a baking tray and put it into the oven for 10 minutes, then reduce the heat to 170°C/325°F/Gas 3. The cooking time depends on the size of the bird: a quail will be ready in 30 minutes, a chicken takes 1 hour, and a swan 3 hours. It might make sense (and be more Roman) to boil the swan before you put it into the pie crust.

Stewed Poultry with Olives

Aliver avem: in ventrum eius fractas olives novas mittis et consutam sic elixabis. Deinde coctas olives eximes.

A variant for poultry: stuff chopped fresh olives into its belly and sew it shut. Boil the bird like that. Remove the boiled olives at the end.

(Ap. 233)

For a chicken, take about a pound of black olives, pitted and not too salty. Coarsely chop the olives, mix with anchovy paste, if desired, and use it to stuff the cavity (a boned chicken is particularly good with this stuffing, see Chicken Galantine, page 311–3).

Close the cavity with cocktail sticks. Apicius does not suggest this but you could brown the chicken in a little olive oil before you stew it. Then put it into a pan with plenty of vegetable stock and simmer gently for at least an hour.

Goose Liver

Goose liver was just as popular among the ancient Romans as it is among contemporary French gourmets. It was dedicated to Isis. The goddess of the fashionable elite received a more sophisticated offering than most.

> The Capitol was unable to protect the goose from having to give up its liver as an offering to you, Isis, daughter of Inachus.
>
> (Ov. Fasti I-453)

Apicius did not give recipes for goose liver, but does give recipes under *ficatum*, fig-liver (see page 258). It could be roasted, or fried in a little oil, but it was also delicious cold or in pâté. Martial liked the liver to be served whole:

> When you see how the liver has swollen larger than the whole goose itself, you cry in surprise, 'Hello, where have you come from?'
>
> (Mart. XIII 58)

Boiled Goose with Herb Pesto

The rest of the goose was eaten as well. According to Pliny, the best geese came from Germania, but were also imported from Gaul and Belgia. He noted that the German word for this bird was *gans*, as it is today (Plin. N.H. X-xxvii).

Apicius gives only two sauces for boiled goose. One is a white sauce based on pine nuts, with caraway, cumin, thyme, onion and vinaigrette, and the other is a cold herb mixture.

> *Anserem elixeum calidum ex iure frigido apiciano: teres piper, ligustcum, coriandri semen, mentam, rutam, refundis liquamen et oleum modice, temperas. Anserem elixum ferventem sabano mundo exsiccabis, ius perfundis et inferes.*

> Hot boiled goose with a cold sauce à la Apicius: grind pepper, lovage, coriander seed, mint and rue, pour in some *garum* and a small amount of oil. Dry the boiled goose with a clean cloth, pour the sauce over it and serve.
>
> (Ap. 237)

Boil the gutted goose in a strong broth (for example, with white wine, or vinegar, herbs, leek, onion and plenty of salt) for about 2 hours.

Remove the skin before serving, and fry it to render the fat. Keep it in the fridge to use as required.

> *for the sauce*
> 1 teaspoon coriander seed
> 1 teaspoon pepper
> 3 teaspoons rue seed
> 1 teaspoon lovage seed or leaf
> 1 spring fresh green mint
> salt or *garum*
> extra virgin olive oil

Pound the herbs and spices in a mortar with 2 tablespoons of salt or a little more *garum*. Pour on a thin stream of oil until the herb mixture has the consistency of pesto.

Roast Duck Breast

Because it spends so much of its time swimming, the wild duck has powerful legs, which cook more slowly than the tender breast. Do not roast the duck breasts on their own: cut them off the carcass when they are done, and continue cooking the legs. Martial writes:

> Serve the duck whole, but only the breast and the neck are tasty.
> The rest must go back to the kitchen.   (Mart. XIII 52)

To roast a wild duck, wrap either bacon fat or pork caul around it, then roast on the barbecue, or in the oven at 200°C/400°F/Gas 6 for 30 minutes. Then pour off the fat, turn up the oven to its highest setting and allow the skin to brown. The breast meat can stay red. Serve with your own choice of sauce.

Duck (or Crane) with Turnips

> *Gruem vel anatem ex rapis: lavas, ornas, et in olla elixabis cum aqua, sale et anetho dimidia coctura. Rapas coque, ut expbromari possint. Levabis de olla, et iterum lavabis, et in caccabum mittis anatem cum*

Figure 7.2

oleo et liquamine et fasciculo porri et coriandri. Rapam lotam et
minutatim concisam desuper mittis, facies ut coquatur. Modica
coctura mittis defritum ut coloret. Ius tale parabus: piper, cuminum,
coriandrum, laseris radicem, suffundis acetum et ius de suo sibi,
reexinanies super anatem ut ferveat. Cum ferbuertit amulo obligas et
super rapas adicies. Piper aspargis et adponis.

Crane or duck with turnips: wash the bird, tie and boil until half
cooked in a pot of water with salt and dill. Also boil the turnips
so that they lose their sharpness. Remove the duck from the pot
and wash it again. Put the dock in a pot with oil, *garum* and a
bundle of leek with coriander. Add a washed and chopped turnip
and bring to the boil. Add *defrutum* to colour when it has boiled
a while.

   The sauce is made like this: pepper, cumin, coriander, laser
root, add vinegar to the duck broth. Pour this over the duck again
and boil. When it is boiling mix with the *amulum* and pour over
the turnips. Sprinkle with pepper and serve.   (Ap. 216)

Duck with turnips is well known in France, *canard aux navets*, but the
duck is not boiled beforehand, as it is in Apicius' recipe. This may have
been necessary to remove the fishy taste that wild duck sometimes have.

   1 wild duck
   1 bunch fresh dill or anis

1 bunch fresh coriander
5 teaspoons olive oil
1 kg turnips
3 cloves garlic
1 teaspoon cumin seeds
1 teaspoon peppercorns
1 teaspoon coriander seed
2 teaspoons flour or *amulum*
dash of vinegar
dash of *defrutum*
1 leek

Bring a large saucepan of salted water to the boil with the dill and fresh coriander. Put in the duck and let it simmer for a few minutes. Heat 3 teaspoons of the olive oil in another large saucepan or casserole. Put in the duck and cover it with water. Half cover the pan, then simmer for 1–2 hours, until the duck is cooked. Add the turnips about 20 minutes before the end. Meanwhile pound together the garlic and the spices.

Remove the duck from the stock and wrap it in a cloth moistened with the stock to keep warm. Pour the stock through a sieve into a shallow pan, bring to the boil and reduce it by half, stirring. In another pan, heat the remaining olive oil, then stir in the flour or *amulum*. Flavour with vinegar and colour with *defrutum*. Add the reduced stock gradually, and stir to a smooth sauce. Add the spices and the leek. Discard the dill and coriander. Let the sauce cook through while you remove the skin from the duck and carve off the breasts. Place the duck in the sauce and bring it to the boil again. Arrange the duck on a serving-dish surrounded with the turnips, then pour over the sauce.

Crane (or Stork)

Apicius gave six recipes 'for crane or duck'. This means that he thought of them as similar, although they are very different in size. However, both birds eat fish, as is sometimes evident from the flavour of their meat. Perhaps for the same reason, Pliny compared the crane with the stork:

Figure 7.3 – Poulterer

Cornelius Nepos, who died during the reign of Augustus, complained about the fattening of thrushes, which had begun not
long before. He added that storks are tastier than cranes. Nowadays the crane is one of the most desirable birds, and no one
touches the stork any more.'   (Plin. N.H. X-xxx)

Cranes and storks are rare in western Europe nowadays, but in Pliny's
date they were as common as herons and swans. Apicius advises:

When cooking crane, ensure that the head is not in the water.
When it is cooked, wrap the crane in a hot cloth and pull off the
head which removes the sinews as well, leaving only the meat and
the bones. The sinews are impossible to chew.   (Ap. 215)

As a sauce for boiled crane or duck, Apicius suggested the following:

*Aliter in gruem vel anatem elixam: piper, ligusticum, cuminum,
coriandrum siccum, mentam, origanum, nucleos, caryotam, liquamen, oleum, mel, sinape et vinum.*

Another sauce for boiled crane or duck: pepper, lovage, cumin,
dried coriander, mint, oregano, pine nuts, dates, *garum*, honey,
mustard and wine.   (Ap. 217)

A rather terse list of ingredients. It is hard to decide which is the dominant flavour. Dates and mint are overwhelming, but combine well with duck. The pine nuts were probably used only to bind the sauce. Pound together the ingredients in quantities to suit your taste.

Ostrich Ragoût

Until the 1980s the ostrich was considered as exotic as an elephant, but since then it has become available in supermarkets. Cooking a whole ostrich is an enormous task, but Apicius provides a recipe for ostrich:

In struthione elixo: piper, mentam, cuminum assume, apii semen, dactylos vel caryotas, mel, acetum, passum, liquamen, et oleum modice et in caccabo facies ut bulliat. Amulo obligas, et sic partes struthionis in lance perfundis, ete desuper piper aspargis. Si autem in condituram coquere volueris, alicam addis.

For boiled ostrich: pepper, mint, roast cumin, celery seed, dates or Jericho dates, honey, vinegar, *passum*, *garum*, a little oil. Put these in the pot and bring to the boil. Bind with *amulum*, pour over the pieces of ostrich in a serving dish and sprinkle with pepper. If you wish to cook the ostrich in the sauce, add *alica*.

(Ap. 212)

You may prefer to roast or fry your ostrich, rather than boil it. Whichever method you choose, this sauce goes with it well. For 500 g ostrich pieces, fried or boiled, you will need:

2 teaspoon flour
2 tablespoons olive oil
300 ml *passum* (dessert wine)
1 tablespoon roast cumin seeds
1 teaspoon celery seeds
3 pitted candied dates
3 tablespoons *garum* or a 50 g tin of anchovies
1 teaspoon peppercorns
2 tablespoons fresh chopped mint
1 teaspoon honey
3 tablespoons strong vinegar

Make a roux with the flour and 1 tablespoon of the olive oil, add the *passum,* and continue to stir until the sauce is smooth. Pound together in the following order: the cumin, celery seeds, dates, *garum* or anchovies, peppercorns, chopped mint, the remaining olive oil, the honey and vinegar. Add this to the thickened wine sauce. Then stir in the ostrich pieces and let them heat through in the sauce.

Vinaigrette for Ostrich

Aliter in struthione elixo: piper, lugusticum, thymum aut satureiam, mel, sinape, acetum, liquamen, et oleum.

Another recipe for boiled ostrich: pepper, lovage, thyme or savory, honey, mustard, vinegar, *garum* and oil. (Ap. 212)

100 ml light wine vinegar or white wine
100 ml *garum*
300 ml oil
1 teaspoon honey
1 teaspoon peppercorns, ground
1 teaspoon made mustard
1 teaspoon thyme leaves, stalks removed
1 teaspoon freshly chopped lovage

Mix all the ingredients together thoroughly and serve with boiled, roast or fried ostrich.

Flamingo (or Parrot)

It is curious that the recipe for flamingo should be suitable for parrot but maybe we should trust Apicius who had more experience of eating these birds than we do.

In phoenicoptero: phoenicopterum eliberas, lavas, ornas, includas in caccabum, adicies aquam, salem, anethum et aceti modicum. Dimidia coctura alligas fascibulum porri et coriandri, et coquatur. Prope cocturam defritum mittis, coloras. Adicies in mortarium piper, cuminum, coriandrum, laseris radicem, mentam, rutam, fricabis, suffundis acetum, adicies caryotam, ius de suo sibi perfundis. Reexinanies in eundem caccabum, amulo obligas, ius perfundis et inferes. Idem facies in psittaco.

For flamingo: pluck the flamingo, wash, tie and put it into the pot. Add water, dill and a little vinegar. When it is half cooked, add a bundle of leek with coriander and cook. When it is ready, add *defrutum* to colour.

In the mortar, pound pepper, cumin, coriander, *laser* root, mint, rue. Mix together. Add vinegar and a date, as well as some of the stock. Put this in the pot, bind with *amulum*, pour the sauce over the bird and serve. Prepare parrot in the same way.

(Ap. 234)

Chicken with Laser or Garlic

Pullum laseratum: pullum aperies a navi, lavabis, ornabis et in cumana ponis. Teres piper, ligustcum, laser vivum, suffundis liquamen, vino et liquamene temperabis et mittis pullo. Coctus si fuerit, pipere aspersum inferes.

Chicken with *laser*: carefully open the chicken, wash, decorate and put into a Cuman pot. Grind pepper, lovage, and fresh *laser*, moisten with *garum*, mix with wine and *garum*, pour this over the chicken. When cooked, sprinkle with pepper and serve.

(Ap. 243)

We cannot use this recipe because its main ingredient is *laser*, which is extinct. Here we cannot even replace it with *asafoetida*, because Apicius specifies fresh *laser*, the green leaf or moist root. The only logical substitute is garlic, and when you use it, the recipe suddenly becomes familiar: chicken casseroled with garlic and wine is eaten throughout Europe.

Take a large chicken (in Italy, a capon is traditionally used for this dish) and an unglazed clay casserole dish with a lid, slightly larger than the chicken. You can fry the chicken before you roast it to colour it, but that isn't really necessary. '*Ornabis*,' Apicius writes, meaning 'decorate', or 'dress' which might mean you should tie the legs together so that the chicken retains its plump, compact shape. For the sauce you will need:

> 1 teaspoon lovage seed
> ½ head garlic, peeled
> 2 tablespoons peppercorns
> 10 salted anchovies or 100 ml *garum*
> 500 ml white wine or light red wine

Preheat the oven to 180°C/350°F/Gas 4.

Grind the lovage to powder. Add the garlic and the peppercorns, and pound to a paste with the anchovies, or add the *garum*. Stuff part of this mixture between the skin and the flesh of the chicken. Put the rest into the belly cavity. Tie up the chicken and place it in the casserole. Pour over the wine, put the lid on the casserole and place it in the oven for 30–40 minutes, or until the chicken is cooked. Check occasionally to ensure that it is not drying out. If the skin has not coloured enough, place the chicken under a hot grill for a few minutes before serving.

Chicken Heliogabalus with White Sauce

Pullus Varianus: pullum coques iure hoc: liquamine oleo, vino, fasciculum porri, coriandri, saturelae. Cum coctus fuerit, teres piper, nucleos cyathos duos et ius de suo sibi suffundis et fasciculos proicies. Lacte temperas, et reexinanies mortarium supra pullum, ut ferveat. Obligas eundem albamentis ovorum tritis, ponis in lance et iure supra scripto perfundis. Hoc ius candidum appellatur.

Chicken Varius: boil a chicken in the following stock: *garum*, oil and wine, with a bundle of leek, coriander and savory.

When the chicken is cooked, grind pepper, pine nuts, 100 ml *garum* and the stock, with the bundle of herbs removed. Mix with milk and pour the contents of the mortar over the chicken. Bring to the boil and mix with chopped egg white to thicken. Place the chicken on a serving dish and pour the sauce over it. This is called white sauce.   (Ap. 249)

This recipe might have been named after the decadent emperor Varius Heliogabalus.

>   1 small leek
>   1 large bunch fresh coriander
>   a few stalks of savory
>   1 boiling chicken
>   *garum*, or salt to taste
>   olive oil
>   2 litres white wine, not too dry
>   200g pine nuts
>   1 teaspoon peppercorns, ground
>   500ml full-cream milk, sheep's if possible
>   3 cooked egg whites, pounded

Cut the leek lengthwise and wash. Tie it into a bundle with the savory and put it into a saucepan a little larger than the chicken.

Place the chicken on the herbs and pour in a dish of *garum* and a little olive oil. Cover the chicken with the wine then bring it slowly to the boil. Skim off the skum, then let the chicken simmer for 1½ hours.

Turn off the heat and pour off half the wine stock into another pan and reduce to half its original quantity over a high heat. The chicken stays in the remaining liquid to keep warm.

Grind the pine nuts to a paste, with the pepper and the *garum*. Add the paste to the reduced wine, milk, stir, then add the egg whites. Taste and add salt if necessary. Remove the chicken from its pot and cover, then pour over the sauce.

Galantine of Chicken, Capon or Suckling Pig

Pullus farsilis: pullum sicuti liquaminatum a cevice expedies. Teres piper, ligusticum, zingiber, pulpam caesam, alicam elixam, teres cerebellum ex iure coctum, ova confringis et commisces, ut unum corpus efficias. Liquamine temperas et oleum modice mittis, piper integrum, nucleos abundanter. Fac impensam et imples pullum vel porcellum, ita ut laxamentum habeat. Similiter in cap facies. Ossibus eiectis coques.

Stuffed chicken: bone the chicken from the neck. Grind pepper, lovage, ginger, mince, boiled pearled spelt. Pound brains boiled in stock. Separate the eggs and stir together the yolks until the mixture forms a solid mass. Add *garum* and a small amount of oil, whole peppercorns and a quantity of pine nuts. Stuff the chicken or suckling pig with this, so that there is a little room left over. Prepare a capon in the same way. Cook without the bones.

(Ap. 253)

A galantine delights guests, because the chicken retains its shape although it has been boned. It is easy to carve too. Nowadays galantine is normally eaten cold, but it is very juicy and delicious straight from the oven. Ask your butcher to bone the chicken and give you the carcass for stock.

1 large chicken, or capon, boned
white wine
1 pair small lamb's brains, cleaned, membrane and veins removed
1 teaspoon lovage seed
garum, anchovy paste or salt
1 teaspoon freshly gated ginger root
75 g pearled spelt
2 eggs
100 g pine nuts
2 teaspoons peppercorns
olive oil

Boning a chicken sounds more complicated than it actually is. All you need is a pair of kitchen shears, a sharp knife and two strong hands. Start by cutting and opening the chicken along the spine. Make a long incision from head to tail. Break off the legg and wing bones. Stick your fingers between the chicken breast and the breastbone and pull carefully away. Free the drumsticks from bone as well. Leave the leg-bones below the knee, and the wing-bones. Having boned the chicken, roast the bones in the oven. Deglaze the pan with a little white wine. Pour this into a large saucepan, put in the roasted carcass and make a stock. Use the stock to cook the brains, strain and reserve the stock.

In the mortar, grind together the lovage seed, *garum*, anchovy or salt with the ginger. Put this mixture into a blender with the boiled, pearled spelt, the brains and the eggs. Whiz then add the whole pine nuts, whole peppercorns, some *garum* to taste and the olive oil, and whiz again to blend.

Place the stuffing in the chicken and pin the skin together with cocktail sticks, then tie them together with a zigzagging piece of string. Push the bird into its natural shape and secure it with string. Place it in a saucepan with the strained stock. Bring it slowly to a simmer, keeping it just below boiling point, and cook 1½ hours. Serve warm, or leave it to cool in the stock. Remove the chicken from the stock and put it in the fridge. Replace the bones in the stock, and reduce it. Strain it and leave it to set to a tasty jelly. Use this to decorate the chicken.

Roast Pigeon with Herb Mayonnaise

In palumbis columbis. In assis: piper, ligusticum, coriandrum, careum, cepam siccam, mentam, ovi vitellum, caryotam, mel, acetum, liquamen, oleum et vinum.

For turtle-dove or wood pigeon: roast pepper, lovage, coriander, caraway, dried onion, mint, egg-yolk, date, honey, vinegar, *garum*, oil and wine.

(Ap. 223)

It's a good idea to snip open the pigeon along the spine. Then you can fold it out flat with a bony side and a fleshy side. This is a good way to roast all kinds of poultry on the barbecue. Brush with olive oil, pepper and salt, then lay the bird with the fleshy side down, for a few minutes to brown. Then turn it and cook on the other side until it is done.

2 egg yolks
2 tablespoons strong vinegar
1 teaspoon honey
olive oil
1 teaspoon lovage seeds
1 teaspoon caraway seeds
1 tablespoon dried onion
100g fresh mint
50g fresh coriander

1 date
4 anchovies
1 teaspoon peppercorns
50 ml strong white wine

Whisk together the egg yolks, the vinegar and the honey. Then beat in the olive oil until you have the consistency of mayonnaise.

Crush the lovage and caraway seeds to a powder in the mortar, one after the other, and sieve. Grind in the dried onion, fresh mint and fresh coriander, then the date, the anchovies and peppercorns. Thin the paste a little with white wine. Beat this mixture into the mayonnaise and serve with the roast pigeon.

EGGS

In ancient Rome elegant people sucked raw eggs. Cochlear spoons had a sharp point, which was used to pick snails out of their shells but which also handy for piercing a hole in an egg shell. They pricked holes at both ends of the egg, which prevented the shell breaking when the egg was sucked. However, the Romans thought the purpose of the second hole was to let the spirit of the egg escape. Martial refers to this in a poem about the spoon:

> *Spoons*
> I'm normally used for snails
> But I'm no less useful for eggs.
> Do you know why I'd rather be called a cochlear?
>
> (Mart. XIV-cxxi)

Figure 7.4 – Coclear

The spoon was afraid of ghosts.

Raw eggs involved no work for the cook – but some of the most luxurious and complex dishes from ancient Rome were made with eggs.

Fried Eggs

Ova frixa: oenogarata.

Fried eggs: serve with *oenogarum*.   (Ap. 329)

Fry eggs with a little olive oil then pour over some *oenogarum*, or anchovy paste thinned with white wine.

Boiled Eggs

Ova elixa: liquamine, oleo, mero vel ex liquamine, pipere, lasere.

Boiled eggs: *garum*, oil wine or *liquamen*, pepper and *laser*.
                                                        (Ap. 329)

Prick a hole in each egg to let out the air, which might break the egg during boiling. Put the eggs into cold water. Bring to the boil and cook for about 5 minutes, then leave to cool. Peel the eggs and cut them in half. For 5 eggs, finely crush 1 clove of garlic with some pepper and 5 anchovies. Add the egg yolks and pound smooth. Add a little olive oil and a little wine and stir well. Pile the mixture into the egg whites.

Boiled Eggs with Rue and Tuna or Anchovies

Mox vetus et tenui maior cordyla lacerto, sed quam cum rutae frondibus ova tegebant.

Then salted tunas, larger than a *cordyla**, were served, covering eggs with stalks of rue.   (Mart. XI-52)

---

* Untranslatable fish.

This isn't so much a recipe as a line of verse. But it is such a simple dish that it is not difficult to reproduce. The main problem is the translation of *lacerto*. Some dictionaries define it as 'tuna', others 'mackerel'. The two fish are related as, indeed, they are to the anchovy.

The word *tenui* suggests that the fish were small, and *vetus* (old) that they were salted, so the anchovy looks more likely, especially as it is a traditional accompaniment to eggs. However, tuna or mackerel is no less delicious. Leave a fillet of tuna in coarse salt for 6 hours, or mackerel for 3 hours. Then wipe the fish dry and brush it with a little olive oil. Hang tuna in the wind for 6 hours or mackerel for 3. Slice the fish thinly and lay a piece on half of a hard- or soft-boiled egg. Decorate with a stalk of rue and a few drops of oil.

Soft-Boiled Eggs in Pine-Nut Sauce

In ovis hapalis: piper, ligustcum, nucleos infusos. Suffundes mel, acetum; liquamine temperabis.

For soft-boiled eggs: pepper, soaked pine nuts. Add honey and vinegar and mix with *garum*.   (Ap. 329)

for 4 small eggs
200 g pine nuts
2 teaspoons ground pepper
1 teaspoon honey
4 tablespoons *garum* or anchovy paste

Soak the pine nuts overnight in water. Then drain and grind them finely in the blender or pound them in a large mortar. Add the pepper, honey and *garum*. Heat the sauce in a bain-marie. Meanwhile put the eggs into a pan of cold water and bring to the boil. Let them cook for 3½ minutes, then take them off the heat, plunge them into cold water and peel them carefully. The outer edge of the egg white must be firm, but it must be soft inside. Put the eggs, left whole, into a deep serving bowl and pour over the sauce. Serve.

This recipe can be adapted easily to other eggs, such as quail's eggs.

In that case keep an eye on the cooking-time: a quail's egg will be firm in 1 minute.

Soufflé Omelette of Milk and Honey

Ova spongia ex lacte: ova quattuor, lactis heminam, olei unicam in se dissolvis, ita ut unum corpus facias. In patellam subtilem adicies olei modicum, facies ut bulliat, et adicies impensam quam parasti. Una parte fuerit coctum, in disco vertes, melle perfundis, piper aspargis et inferes.

Soufflé omelette with milk: take 4 eggs, 273 ml milk with 27 g oil dissolved in it. Mix all together to form a whole. Put a little oil into a thin pan and heat. Pour in the mixture. Tip the omelette out on a round plate when one side is cooked. Pour on honey and pepper. Serve.   (Ap. 307)

Nowadays we fold omelettes, but Apicius clearly didn't. As soon as his omelette was cooked 'on one side' he put it on a round plate, so the top must have been rather squidgy. Honey was poured over it, then sprinkled with pepper.

Milk *Patina* (Extravagant Egg Tart)

Patina ex lacte: nucleos infundes et siccas. Echinos recentes inpreparatos habebis: accipies patinam, et in eam compones singula infra scripta; mediana malvarum et betarum et porros maturos, apios, holus molle et viridian elixa, pullum carptum ex iure coctum, cerebella elixa, lucanica, ova dura per medium incisa. Mittes longaones porcinos ex iure terentino farsos, coctos, concisos, iecinera pullorum, pulpas piscis aselli fricti, urticas marinas, pulpas ostreorum, caseos recentes. Alternis compones nucleos et piper integrum asperges. Ius tale perfundis: piper, ligusticum, apii semen, silfi, coques. At abi cocta fuerit, lacte colas, cui cruda ova commisces, ut unmu corpus fiat, et super illa omnia perfundes. Cum cocta fuerit, echinos recentioes, piper asperges et inferes.

Figure 7.5 – Egg shop

Milk *patina*: soak pine nuts and dry. Have fresh, gutted sea urchins to hand. Take a *patina* pan and in it place a layer of the following ingredients: mallow-heart and French bean, ripe leek, white celery, vegetable purée, boiled vegetables, pieces of chicken cooked in stock, boiled brains, Lucanian sausages, hard-boiled and halved eggs, sausages filled with pork and Terentine sauce, boiled and finely sliced, chicken livers, fried cod fillets, jellyfish, oysters without their shells and soft cheese. Put the pine nuts on top of this and sprinkle with whole peppercorns.

　　Make the sauce as follows: pepper, lovage, celery seed, *laser*. Boil it all up. When cooked, pour over the milk, beaten to a mass with the eggs. Pour this mixture over everything. When it is cooked, decorate with sea urchins. Sprinkle with pepper and serve.　　　　　　　　　　　　　　　　　　　　　　　(Ap. 133)

Apicius' name for this dish, *Milk Patina*, is euphemistic because it contains vegetables, liver, poultry, fish and shellfish too.

　　4 tablespoons peppercorns
　　1 tablespoon lovage seeds
　　2 tablespoons celery seeds
　　1 pinch *asafoetida*, or several cloves of garlic, crushed
　　300 g boiled pork sausages, peeled and finely chopped
　　100 ml Terentine sauce of pepper, bay berry, rue, *garum* and oil
　　　　(see page 284–5)
　　200 g chopped mallow and green bean sprouts
　　1 medium leek, with green part, very finely chopped

2 stems celery, boiled, strings removed and thinly sliced
200g purée of lettuce, alexanders or celery leaves (see page 229–30)
200g boiled vegetables, such as parsley, cabbage leaves, beetroot,
    artichoke or cardoon
400g chicken thighs, cooked
1 pair boiled calf's brains, membrane and veins removed, diced
3 Lucanian sausages (see page 261–2), peeled and thinly sliced
4 hard-boiled eggs
250g chicken livers, fried in oil, diced
250g fried cod fillets
200g dried pieces of jelly-fish, soaked
12 fresh oysters
200g pine nuts
300g fresh sheep's cheese, or crumbled soft cheese, or ricotta
18 raw eggs
400 ml sheep's milk
6 fresh sea urchins

Preheat the oven to 180°C/350°F/Gas 4.

Grease a large baking tin, or line a shallow round dish with grease-proof paper.

Grind together 2 tablespoons of the peppercorns, with the celery seeds, lovage seeds and the *asafoetida* or garlic. Stir the sausagemeat into the sauce. Then place all the ingredients in the baking tin, in the order given by Apicius. Cover it and put it into the oven for 15–20 minutes. Beat the raw eggs with the milk and add the herbs and spices, then season to taste with salt.

Take the tin out of the oven and pour off any juices. Pour over the egg mixture. Stir it in, then shake the tin to allow any air bubbles to escape. Put it back into the oven for about 2 hours. Serve either hot or cold, but if the tart is allowed to cool it is less likely to collapse. Turn it out on to a serving plate and remove the greaseproof paper. Crown it with a wreath of sea urchins. (To clean sea urchins, see page 336).

Pancake Tart à l'Apicius

Patina apiciana sic facies: frusta suminis cocti, pulpas piscium, pulpas pulli, ficedulas vel pectoral turdorum cocta et quaecumque optima fuerti sunt: haec omnia concides teres piper, ligusticum, suffundes liquamen, vinum, passum, et in caccabum mittis ut calefiat, et amulo obligas. Antea tamen pulpas concisas universas illuc mittes, et sic bulliat. At, ubi coctum fuerit, levabis cum piperis granis integris et in patellam alternis de trulla refundes cum piperis granis integris et nucleis pineis, ita ut per singular coria substernas diploidem, in laganum similiter: quotquot lagana posueris, tot trullas impensae desuper adiecies. Unum vero laganum fistula percuties et super impones. Piper asparges. Ante tamen illas pulpas ovis confractis obligas, et sic in caccabum mittes cum implesa. Patellam aeneam qualem debes habere infra ostenditur.

Patina Apiciana is made as follows: cooked sow's udders, fish fillets, chicken, figpecker or breast of turtle-dove, and whatever else takes your fancy. Chop it all finely, apart from the figpecker.* Beat a little oil into some raw eggs.

Grind pepper and lovage, pour in *garum*, wine, *passum* and heat up in a pot. Bind with *amulum*. Add the various chopped meats and cook.

When it has cooked, transfer the ragoût and its sauce to the *patella* pan and spread it out in layers, with whole peppercorns and pine nuts. Do it in such a way that there is a pancake under each layer. Each time you put down a pancake, pour the contents of the spoon over it. Prick a little hole in the last pancake with a reed, and leave the reed in it.†

Grind pepper. Before adding the meat to the pot, you should have mixed it with egg.‡   (Ap. 134)

This *patina* is clearly more refined than the previous one. There is no need to give another list of ingredients and quantities, since Apicius writes that you should include whatever you like.

Put in the best poultry and fish. Boil or fry this as you wish, and remove the bones. Apicius used *amulum* to bind everything together,

---

* All the ingredients of the *patina* are free of bone, spine, shell and peel, apart from the figpecker, which is used whole.
† The reed serves as a kind of little chimney from which steam can escape during cooking.
‡ Apicius has forgotten to put this instruction in its proper chronological place in the recipe.

Figure 7.6 – Travellers in *a caupona*

but béchamel sauce is just as good. Flavour it with *passum* (sweet dessert wine or Vin Santo) and dry white wine. Add a fair amount of pepper, both ground and whole, *garum* or anchovy paste and ground lovage seeds. Stir some beaten eggs through the pieces of meat and fish. Preheat the oven to 180°C/350°F/Gas 4.

Make some batter, fry pancakes with milk, flour and eggs, then fry the pancakes. Place a pancake in a circular baking dish of about the same diameter. Spoon the meat and fish filling over the pancake, cover it with another and repeat until the ingredients are used up, ending with a pancake. Make a little hole in it and insert a straw.

Put the *patina* into the oven for about 45 minutes, then serve.

The Shield of Minerva

This famous '*patina* of *patinae*' was created by the brother of Emperor Vitellius. The imperial family outdid Apicius in luxury.

The most famous meal was given by his brother, on the occasion of the arrival of the emperor in Rome. It is said that two thousand of the choicest fish were served, along with seven thousand birds. He himself outdid everyone* with a *patina* that he called 'The Shield of Minerva, Protectress of the City', because of its great size. In it he included parrot-fish livers, pheasant brains and peacock brains, flamingo tongues and the spleens of moray eels.

(Suet. Vitell. XIII)

This is not a recipe, but the description of a dish, although some quantities are given. We may assume that the dish was prepared after the fashion of one of the two *patinas* described above, as a pancake tart or an egg tart. Reproducing it presents a number of difficulties. Where would we find a large supply of flamingo tongues? Emperor Vitellius could get hold of whatever he wanted, but everything had its price:

By Hercules, Emperor Vitellius once assembled a *patina* that cost him 1,000,000 HS.　　　　　　　　　　　　　　(Plin N.H.)

---

* Emperor Vitellius himself had a hand in the cooking.

VIII

FROM THE WATER

Concerning Fish and Shellfish

For the British, who are accustomed to travelling the oceans and whose ancestors braved the icy Arctic waters in search of whales and herring, it may be difficult to imagine why the Romans were intimidated by the warm waters of the Mediterranean. They thought maritime travel dangerous, and until they went to war with Africans and Greeks saw no need for it. After that, they kept seagoing to a minimum. In the winter, the sea was closed (Mare Clausum). As a result, marine fish were expensive in Rome:

> And fish is costly. Cato hit the nail on the head when, in his battle against luxury and excess in Rome, he said that a fish costs more than a cow. And the asking price for a barrel of smoked fish in Rome would not buy a hundred sheep the meat of an ox.
>
> (Plut. IV 4. 668)

One suspects that Plutarch might have been exaggerating a little. Enough customers were willing to pay high prices. Athenaeus quotes Greek literature:

> When Plato criticized Aristippus for buying so much fish, Aristippus replied that he had paid only 2 obols. Plato replied that he would have bought it himself at that price, to which Aristippus answered, 'You see, Plato, I'm not that fond of fish, but you're too fond of money.'
>
> (Ath. VIII-343d)

In Rome, Cato criticized the expensive Greek mania for fish. Throughout the first century BC, people spent huge amounts of money

Figure 8.1 – Bowl

on oysters, sea urchins, crabs, octopus and morays, and the less spectacular red mullet, tuna, dolphin and mackerel. A few moneyed fish-lovers began to breed fish:

> Oyster ponds were first invented by Sergius Orata, in the Gulf of Baia, in the time of the orator Lucius Crassus, before the Marsian war. His motive was not greed, but avarice, because he had already become rich with the invention of showers that he installed in his villas before selling them on.
>
> He was the first to identify Lucrino oysters as the most flavoursome. The quality of fish always depends on where they come from. Wolf-fish from the Tiber, for example, is finest between the two bridges. Turbot from Ravenna is good, as is moray from Sicily, sturgeon from Rhodes and so on. I will not repeat the whole shopping list.
>
> The British coast was not yet used for oyster fishing when Orata praised the oysters of Lucrino. It was still worth taking the trouble to bring oysters from the tip of Italy, from Brindisi. To prevent squabbles occurring in the sea between the two delicacies, the oysters, hungry from their long journey from Brindisi, were fed in the Lago Lucrino.
>
> During the same period Licinius Murena was developing fish-ponds for all kinds of other fish. He was copied by Philippus

and Hortensius. They enjoyed a great deal of success with it. Lucullus had built a channel through a mountain, which cost more than the whole estate. For that reason Pompeius Magnus called him 'Xerxes in a toga'. After the death of Lucullus the fish from his pond were sold for 4 million HS.

(Plin. N.H. IX-LXXIX-XXX)

Lucullus and Julius Caesar were equals in wealth and fame, but their careers took different turns. Caesar moved mountains in the area of politics, Lucullus in the field of gastronomy.

Moray Eel (*murena*)

A '*piscina*' was a fishpond in Roman times, rather than the swimming pool of today. Roman children would not have jumped into a *piscina*, because some ponds contained the ferocious carnivorous morays. Romans had a passion for this menacing creature:

> The first to develop a special *piscina* for the moray was Gaius Hirrius, who supplied six thousand morays for Caesar's triumphal banquets. He gave them for free. He didn't want money or anything else in return.
> This was the beginning of our love for this unique fish. In Baculo [near Baia], the orator Hortensius had a pond containing a moray which he loved so much that he is said to have wept when the animal passed away. On the same farm, Antonia, the wife of Drusus, decorated her favourite moray with ear-rings. The creature was so famous that many people flocked to Baculo just to see it.
> (Plin. N.H. IX-1xxix)

Some morays have beautiful patterns on their backs, but the Mediterranean varieties are not as spectacular as their tropical cousins. It was the creature's ferocity that delighted the sensationalistic Romans. Pollo famously believed that moray was most delicious when fed on human flesh. When he had it prepared for him, he ate only the liver.

Roast Moray

Ius in murena assa: piper, ligusticum, satureiam, crocomagma, cepam, pruna damascena enucleata, vinum, mulsum, acetum, liquamen, defritum, oleum, et coques.

Sauce for roast moray: pepper, lovage, savory, saffron, onion, pitted Damascus prune, *mulsum, liquamen, defrutum,* oil. Cook.

(Ap. 460)

In cities such as Naples, live moray is still available. If you are shopping elsewhere, you may substitute the common eel, although it isn't the same. Clean it and remove the fins as you would with other fish, but leave on the head. Cut the skin behind the head and strip it off the body. Attach the moray to a spit in a zigzag, then brush with oil, sprinkle with salt and roast on the barbecue.

for the sauce
2 prunes
4 glasses of red wine
1 tablespoon *garum*
1 dash of *mulsum*
1 tablespoon *defrutum*
1 teaspoon peppercorns
1 onion

Soak the prunes for 24 hours in the wine, *garum, mulsum,* and *defrutum* with the ground lovage and pepper. Whiz the onion in a blender. Add the prunes with the soaking liquid and blend to a smooth sauce. Heat this in a pan and let it reduce over a low heat, without boiling, for 20 minutes. Brush the eel with some of this mixture while it is roasting, so that it becomes red in colour and caramelizes. Serve the rest of the sauce as an accompaniment.

Conger Eel (*conger*)

Fish was not generally offered to the gods, but eel was an exception:

> Agatharcides says, in book six of his European History, that the
> Boeotians sacrificed conger eels, which were extremely large. They
> decorated the animals with wreaths, uttered prayers over them,
> and sprinkled them with *mola* as with other sacrificial offerings.
> When a foreigner expressed his surprise at these curious rituals
> and asked the reason for them, a Boeotian explained that it was
> his duty to propagate the customs of his ancestors, and not to
> answer for them to anyone else. (Ath. VII-297C)

Athenaeus also noted that the Greeks wrapped conger eels in the
leaves of the beetroot before roasting or boiling them. The relationship
between the tasty content and the foliage wrapped around it made
Greek poets think of a virgin clad in her bridal dress.

Roast Conger Eel

*Ius in congro asso: piper, ligusticum, cuminum frictum, origanum,
cepam siccam, ovorum vitella cocta, vinum, mulsum, liquamen,
defritum, et coques.*

Sauce for roast conger eel: pepper, lovage, roast cumin, oregano,
dried onion, hard-boiled egg yolk, wine, *mulsum*, honey, vinegar,
liquamen and *defrutum*. Boil. (Ap. 453)

Clean and skin a conger eel and roast it on a spit as you would the
moray (see page 326), then prepare the sauce.

for the sauce
2 tablespoons roast cumin seeds
2 teaspoons lovage seeds
1 teaspoon peppercorns
1 teaspoon oregano
1 tablespoon dried onion

2 hard-boiled egg yolks
300 ml wine, reduced by half

The recipe does not say whether red or white wine should be used. Two other wine products are also added, *mulsum* and *defrutum*. The former is made from white wine, the latter from red. Rosé may be the best choice.

Grind the cumin and the lovage seeds to powder, in a mortar, then put in the peppercorns and crush them roughly. Add the oregano and the dried onion. Mash the egg yolks with some of the wine, then beat in the rest. Add the spices and reduce the sauce over a low heat to thicken it. Cover the conger with the sauce and serve.

Fried Electric Eel (*torpedo*)

The electric eel, which electrocutes its prey, was eaten because it was fascinating, not because everyone liked the taste:

> Hicesius says that the electric eel is neither tasty nor juicy, and a little grainy in texture, but it is healthy . . . And Archestratus says, 'An electric eel fried in oil, with wine, aromatic herbs and a little grated cheese.'* And Alexis writes in Galateia: 'The electric eel should be stuffed, it is said, and fried whole.'
>
> (Ath. VII-314a and d)

The electric eel can grow very large. It is probably easier to fillet it and cut it into smaller pieces before you fry it in olive oil, unless you have a pan big enough to cook the monster whole, as Alexis suggested.

When the fish has browned, deglaze the hot pan with white wine and dried aromatic herbs. Baste the fish with the roasting juices while the moisture evaporates.

Many Italians would be horrified, but if you wish to follow Archestratus, grate some Parmesan over it.

---

* It was not unusual to grate cheese over fish,

Herb Mayonnaise with Boiled (Electric) Eel

To boil electric eel or other eels you need a large fish kettle or a saucepan. If using a saucepan, coil up the eel. In a fish kettle it can be laid out in a zigzag: fix the eel in place with heatproof bowls filled with water. The fish will retain the shape in which it is cooked. After cooling, remove the skin. All cooked fish can be eaten either hot or cold. Apicius suggests a cold mayonnaise:

In torpedo elixa: piper, ligustcum, petroselinum, mentam, origanum, ovi medium, mel, liquamen, passum, vinum, oleum. Si voles, addes sinape, acetum. Si calidum volueris uvam passam addes.

For boiled electric eel: pepper, lovage, parsley, mint, oregano, egg yolks, honey, *garum*, *passum*, oil. If you wish you can add vinegar and mustard. If you want it warm, add raisins. (Ap. 416)

3 tablespoons vinegar
2 egg yolks
olive oil
1 tablespoon mustard
1 tablespoon anchovy paste
3 tablespoons *passum*
3 tablespoons white wine
1 teaspoon crushed pepper
1 teaspoon ground lovage seed
50g fresh parsley
50g fresh mint
1 teaspoon dried oregano

Beat the vinegar into the egg yolks then slowly drip in the olive oil, beating until it emulsifies. Then trickle in the remains of the oil until it is all combined. Stir in the mustard. Put the rest of the ingredients into the blender and whiz. Add the paste to the mayonnaise and serve with the eel.

Fried Shark

Eels were not the only carnivorous fish on the Roman menu. Some people also ate shark, although others clearly had their doubts:

> Archestratus advises: 'Buy fillets of dogfish cut from the soft, lower parts of the fish, in the town of Thorone. Sprinkle with caraway seed, a little salt, and fry. Then add nothing apart from virgin oil. When the fish is cooked, serve with the sauces that go with it, but whatever you put in the casserole, do not use sacred spring water or wine vinegar, just pour some oil over it, and dry caraway seed and a bundle of aromatic leaves. Cook the dish over hot coals, without flames, and stir continuously to prevent burning. Not many mortals know this divine dish, or are able to eat it themselves. Certainly not those stupid people who are shocked because they say the shark is a man-eater. Any fish will eat human flesh if it gets the chance.'   (Ath. VIII-310e)

Cut fillets from the belly of the shark into 2 cm slices. Dust both sides with salt and pepper and perhaps a little flour. Then fry quickly until golden brown in very hot olive oil. Sprinkle with ground caraway seed (and aromatic herbs, if you like) and serve.

Fried Anchovy

Anchovies are so small and delicate that they do not need to be gutted, but it isn't hard to remove the intestines with the flick of a knife. The bones and the head can also be left intact.

> *Patina de apua fricta: apuam lavas, ova confringes, et cum apua commisces. Adiecies liquamen, vinum, oleum, facies ut ferveat, et cum ferbuerit, mittes apuam. Cum duxerit, subtiliter versas. Facies ut coloret, oenogarum simplex perfundes. Piper asparges et inferes.*

> *Patina* of fried anchovy: wash the anchovy. Break some eggs and add the anchovies. Take *liquamen*, wine and oil and bring to the boil. When it is boiling put the anchovies [into the pan]. When

they are beginning to cook turn them over carefully. Fry until they colour, then simply pour over *oenogarum*. Sprinkle with pepper and serve. (Ap. 140)

Fried fish are still a popular starter in Italy. Nowadays they are usually dusted with flour, not coated with egg as Apicius suggested. The only curious thing about Apicius' recipe is that he adds liquid to the frying oil, in the form of wine and *liquamen*, which means that the fish cannot colour, although he clearly intends them to. Flavour the anchovies by marinating them for a few hours in wine and *garum*. Then dry them and coat them in beaten egg. Remove the fish from the egg yolk one by one and fry them in plenty of olive oil. Handle them carefully in the pan or they will break up. When they are golden brown and crisp, remove them from the oil with a slotted spoon and drain off the excess oil on kitchen paper.

Nowadays in Italy fried fish are sometimes put in vinegar and breadcrumbs. Apicius suggests a sauce of wine and *garum* to go with them. Use white wine, or white wine vinegar. The sauce can be eaten at table as a dip.

Sardines Stuffed with Nuts

In sardis: sardam farsilem sic facere oportet: sarda exossatur, et teritur puleium, cuminum, piperis grana, menta, nuces, mel. Impletur et consuitur. Involvitur in charta et sic supra vaporem ignis in operculo componitur. Conditur ex oleo, caroeno, allece.

About sardines: stuffed sardines should be prepared as follows. The spine is removed. Grind pennyroyal, cumin, peppercorns, mint, nuts and honey. [The fish is] stuffed, sewn up and wrapped in paper, then placed above the heat of the fire in a pan with a lid. As a sauce use oil, *caroenum* and *allec*. (Ap. 431)

The above recipe refers not to small sardines but to *sarda*, a larger version of the same fish – a pilchard. The fish are small so don't bother to sew them unless one of your kitchen slaves is at a loose end.

Gut as with small sardines. Pull the fins carefully out of the fish. Make a small incision in the belly. Cut the head from the spine, and if you want to get rid of the head you can pull it off with the guts. Otherwise leave the head on. Manoeuvre your fingers between the flesh and the spine and pull the flesh from the spine. Leave on the tail, which keeps the fillets together. Reshape the fish to its original form.

> 100 g nuts, almonds or pistachios
> 20 pennyroyal leaves
> 20 mint leaves
> 1 teaspoon cumin
> 1 teapsoon peppercorns
> 1 teaspoon honey
> few drops of vinegar, optional

Preheat the oven to 200°C/400°F/Gas 6.

Lightly salt the inside of the sardines. Pound together all of the ingredients for the stuffing, divide it between the fish, close them and wrap them in greaseproof paper. The Romans used *charta emporica*, a cheaper kind of papyrus.

Place the parcels in a baking tin and then in the oven for about 15 minutes. Serve immediately.

Red Mullet (*mullus*)

Red mullet is still expensive, but it was worse in Roman times:

> M. Apicius, with his innate talent for luxury, found that [the red mullet] could be most excellently drowned in *garum sociorum*,* whose name he considered most apposite. He also came up with a kind of *allec*† made from the livers [of the red mullet].
>
> During the reign of Caligula one of the consuls, Asinius Celer, challenged all the wasters to pay 8000 HS for a red mullet. I don't know who won.
>
> This makes me think of those people who, complaining about the luxury, made much of the fact that one single cook was bought for more money than a horse. While nowadays cooks

---

* See page 145.
† See page 145–6.

are bought for the price of three horses, and the price of three
cooks is spent on a fish . . .   (Plin. N.H. IX-xxx 67)

Grilled Red Mullet

Apicius gave two sauces for grilled red mullet. The first is a vinaigrette
with lovage, honey and pine nuts, the second a kind of pesto.

*Aliter ius in mullos assos: rutam, mentam, coriandrum, feniculum,
omnia viridia, piper, ligusticum, mel, liquamen et oleum modice.*

Another sauce for grilled red mullet: rue, mint, coriander, fennel,
all fresh, pepper, lovage, honey, *garum* and a little oil.   (Ap. 456)

Take large bunches of fresh mint, coriander and fennel, but only a few
sprigs of rue, or the sauce will be too bitter. Wash the herbs and pound
them, then continue to pound as you pour in a thin stream of olive oil
until you have a thick sauce. Stir in a dash of *garum*, or anchovy paste
to taste, and a teaspoon of honey. The herbs and the oil should form
a thick sauce.

Red mullet is delicious grilled on the barbecue, wrapped in vine-
leaves to protect it. It is not necessary to gut the fish before preparing
it but it must be scaled. If you remove the guts, keep the liver and
replace it in the belly cavity before cooking: it is as delicious today as
it was in ancient times. The Romans also thought highly of the eyes
and cheeks of the fish.

Fried Red Mullet

*Patina mullorum loco salsi: mullos rades, in patina munda compones,
adicies olei quod satis est et salsum interpones. Facies ut ferveat. Cum
ferbuerit mulsum mittes aut passum. Piper asperges et inferes.*

A *patina* of red mullet in place of salted fish:* scale the red mullet
and place in a clean *patina*. Add as much oil as necessary. Between

* As a starter.

[the red mullet] place salted fish. Fry. When it is cooking add *mulsum,* or *passum.* Sprinkle with pepper and serve.   (Ap. 142)

Heat a little olive oil in a frying pan, and fry 3 salted anchovy fillets per red mullet. Then put in the mullet, and fry on both sides for 8 minutes. Remove the fish from the pan and keep it warm in a low oven. Deglaze the pan with a few glasses of mead or *passum* (or use Muscat de Beaumes de Venise). Let it reduce, then replace the fish in the pan. Sprinkle with coarsely ground black pepper and serve.

Patina of Sole with Egg

Patinam solearum: soleas battues et curates compones in patina. Adicies oleum, liquamen, vinum. Dum coquitur, teres piper, ligusticum, origanum, fricabis suffundes ius, ova cruda et unum corpus facies. Super soleas refunes, lento igni coques. Cum duxerit, piper asperges et inferes.

Place the cleaned and beaten sole in the *patina* pan. Add oil, *liquamen* and wine. Grind peppercorns, lovage and oregano and rub into the fish. While the fish is cooking, pour some of the fish stock over it. Bind the sauce with raw eggs. Pour this over the sole and cook over a low flame. When it sets, sprinkle with pepper and serve.   (Ap. 148)

As J. D. Vehling remarks, this recipe bears an uncanny resemblance to Escoffier's *sole au vin blanc chez soi.* Only the herbs are different: lovage and oregano rather than onion and parsley. And Escoffier does not allow the egg yolk to set, as Apicius does.

300 g sole fillets, skinned
100 ml heavy white wine
3 teaspoons *garum*
1 teaspoon peppercorns
1 teaspoon chopped fresh lovage
1 teaspoon dried oregano
1 egg, separated

Preheat the oven to 180°C/350°F/Gas 4.

Fillet the sole and remove the skin. Cut the flesh into large pieces and flatten them with a hammer or a rolling-pin. Grease a *patina* and place the pieces of fish in it with the wine, oil and the *garum*. Put the *patina* in a tub with boiling water and place the whole thing in a pre-heated oven.

Pound the peppercorns, the lovage and the oregano into a powder and bind with egg-yolk. Mix this with the cooking liquid of the sole, into a smooth sauce. Beat the egg white gently, then mix this in with the other condiments. Grease the pan again and pour the sauce over the pieces of fish. Place the *patina* in the oven until the egg mixture is slightly set. Sprinkle with coarsely ground pepper and serve.

Patina of Bream, Grey Mullet and Oysters

This is a different kind of *patina* from the previous one. Here the fish is chopped finely and fried eggs are cooked with it.

> *Patina de piscibus dentice, aurata et mugile: accipies pisces, curatos subassabis, postea eos in pulpas carpes. Deinde ostrea curabis. Adicies in mortarium piperis scripulos vi suffundies liquamen, fricabis. Postea adidies liquaminis cyathum unum vini cyathum umum, mittes in caccabum et olei unc iii et ostea. Oenogarum facies fervere. Cum ferbuerit, patina perunges et in pulpam supra scriptam mittes et condituram de ostreis. Facies ut ferveat. Cum ferbuerit franges ova xi, infundis super ostrea. Cum strinxerint, piper insparges et inferes.*

Patina of toothfish, sea bream and mullet.* Take the fish, and, once they have been cleaned, roast them lightly. Then cut them into pieces. Prepare the oysters. In the mortar grind 6 grams of peppercorns, moisten with *liquamen* and grind. Add 50 ml *liquamen* and 50 ml wine and put into the pot. Add 26 grams of oil and the oysters.

Bring the *oenogarum* to the boil. When it is boiling grease a *patina* and add the above named fish and the spiced oysters. Put

---

* The Romans inserted sea mullets in the anuses of those caught in the act of adultery.

on a high flame. When it is hot, break 11 eggs over the oyster mixture. When it is firm, sprinkle with pepper and serve.

(Ap. 151)

Apicius specifies some individual quantities, but not enough. He mentions 11 eggs, but not how much fish or how many oysters. The quantities of egg and pepper imply that you will need a lot of fish and as many oysters as you can find.

Open the oysters, collect the liquid and shuck the flesh. Put the oysters briefly into a pan with 6g coarsely ground black pepper, 50ml *liquamen*, 50ml wine and 30ml oil (as '*liquamen*' in this case, you could use a combination of the oyster liquid and *garum*) and cook with the oysters are firm.

Clean and fillet the fish. Heat some olive oil in a large frying pan and flash-fry the pieces of fish then add the oysters. When the moisture has evaporated and the pan is hot, break in the 11 eggs. As soon as they are cooked, sprinkle with pepper and salt and serve.

Sea Urchin (*echino*)

Sea urchins are both delicious and decorative. You can eat them raw. There is a small opening on the underside of the animal: snip round this with a pair of scissors, remove the little cap, and discard everything except the red roe and the juices. Serve the sea urchin in its shell on ice with a little pepper.

Apicius mentions that sea urchins were also salted:

Add the best *garum* to salted sea urchins, and they should look as though they are fresh, so that they can be eaten after a visit to a bathhouse.   (Ap. 429)

A salty snack was the ideal restorative after sweating it out in the sauna.

Stuffed Sea Urchin

Aliter in echino: lotum mittes in aqua calida, coques, levas, in patella compones addes folium, piper, mel, liquamen, olei modice, ova, et sic obligas. In thermospodio coques, piper asperges et inferes.

Another recipe for sea urchins: place the cleaned sea urchins in hot water and boil. Then remove them and place in a frying pan. Add leaves, pepper, honey, *garum*, a little oil, egg and mix. Cook them in a bain-marie. Sprinkle with pepper and serve.   (Ap. 427)

Clean 12 sea urchins as in the previous recipe then steam them. Pour off their juices into a bowl and add 6 small eggs. Stir, then add a level teaspoon of honey, a level teaspoon of the best anchovy paste, some coarsely ground black pepper and 2 tablespoons of best olive oil. Pick 2–3 young pale green leaves from a bay tree, or other leaves, and pound them in the mortar. Add them to the egg mixture. Beat everything lightly, then pour the mixture into the sea urchin shells and steam for 15 minutes until cooked. Serve with more freshly ground black pepper.

Jellyfish (*urtica*)

Many Roman recipes mention jellyfish, which is nowadays eaten only in the Far East. It is available, dried and salted, in Chinese and Japanese shops. Before it can be eaten it must be soaked for a few days changing the water frequently, unless it is bought ready-to-eat. In Roman times, it was often served as a salad (Plin. N.H. IX-1xviii).

Fish Pâté with Jellyfish

Patina de apua sine apua: pulpa piscis assi vel elixir minutatim facies ita abundanter, ut patinam qualem voles implore possis. Teres piper et modicum rutae, suffundes liquamen quod satis erit, sic et ova cruda confracta et olei modicum, et commisces in patina cum pulpis ut unum corpus fiat. Desuper leniter compones urticas marinas, ut non cum ovis misceantur. Impones ad vaporem, ut cum ovis ire non possint, et, cum siccaverint, super aspergis piper tritum et inferes. Ad mensam nemo agnoscet quid manducet.

A *patina* of anchovies without anchovies: take fillets of roast or boiled fish and pound enough of these to fill the *patina* pan of your choice. Grind pepper and a little rue. Pour in a good quantity of *garum*. Break eggs and stir them with a little oil through the fish mixture in the pan to an even consistency. Place the jellyfish carefully on top of this, without mixing it with the eggs. Cook all of this in steam* to prevent the jellyfish mixing with the eggs. When it is dry, sprinkle with ground pepper and serve. No one at table will know what he is eating.   (Ap. 132)

100g salted jellyfish
400g filleted fish
1 teaspoon crushed pepper
1 teaspoon rue seed
3 eggs

Wash the jellyfish and leave it to soak for several days. Put the rest of the ingredients into a blender and whiz to a paste. Grease an oven dish and pour in the fish mixture. Place a layer of jellyfish on top. Put the dish into a steamer and steam for 1 hour. Eat either hot or cold.

Cuttlefish, Squid and Octopus (*loligo, sepia* and *polypus*)

The quality of cuttlefish, squid and octopus varies according to the size of the fish. Tiny ones can be cooked quickly then served whole in a little vinegar. When they are larger they must be gutted.

The head and the tentacles should be removed from cuttlefish weighing more than 100g. Cut the head from the tentacles, but leave the tentacles connected to each other. Remove and discard the hard beak from between the tentacles. Pull the intestines out of the body sac and discard. Rinse out the sac under running water, then peel off the membrane.

* Or smoke.

Figure 8.2 – A *triclinium* meal draws to a close

With cuttlefish, squid and octopus weighing more than 1 kg it may be a good idea to tenderize the body, either by beating it against rocks or with a kitchen mallet. Then cut it into rounds.

Stuffed Cuttlefish

Sic farcies eam sepiam coctam: cerebella elixa teres cum pipere, cui commisces ova cruda quod satis erit, piper integrum, isicia minuta et sic consues et in bullientem ollam mittes ita ut coire impensa possit.

This is how to stuff boiled cuttlefish: finely pound boiled brains, their membrane and veins removed, with pepper. Mix with a sufficiency of raw eggs, peppercorns and small meatballs. [Stuff the cuttlefish with this,] sew it shut and place it in a pot with boiling water so that the stuffing can set.   (Ap. 419)

Apicius stuffs his cuttlefish with brains and small meatballs, a luxurious variation on a recipe that was widespread in antiquity. Athenaeus describes cuttlefish stuffed with normal pork mince (Ath. VII-293c). If you don't wish to use brains, try herbed pre-cooked minced meat, and leave out the meatballs.

9 cuttlefish
2 lamb's brains
2 eggs
pork, lamb or fish meatballs
30 whole peppercorns
freshly ground black pepper
1 litre fish stock

Clean the cuttlefish as described above. Boil the brains, then remove the skin and membranes. Pound the brains finely with a little pepper, then beat in the eggs and the peppercorns. Work this into a stiff paste, then add the meatballs.

Stuff the body sacs of the cuttlefish loosely – they will shrink in cooking. Sew them shut, or pin them with cocktail sticks. Place them carefully in some stock, bring them to the boil and let them simmer for 7 minutes, or longer, depending on their size. Then remove from the stock. When they have cooled cut them in half or into rings and serve.

Sauce for Stuffed Cuttlefish

Apicius gives two sauces for stuffed cuttlefish. A herb pesto and the following:

> *In lolligine farcili: ligusticum, coriandrum, apii semen, ovi vitellum, mel, acetum, liquamen, vinum et oleum. Obligabis.*

> For stuffed cuttlefish: lovage, coriander, celery seeds, egg yolk, honey, vinegar, *liquamen*, wine and oil. Bind.   (Ap. 417)

Apicius gives no instructions for binding the sauce. This is not unusual: his reader was expected to know such things. The ingredients are suitable for a cold mayonnaise:

2 egg yolks
1 teaspoon vinegar
1 teaspoon *garum* or salt
1 tablespoon white wine

1 teaspoon honey
100 ml olive oil
1 teaspoon celery seeds
1 teaspoon lovage seeds
1 teaspoon coriander seeds

Beat the egg yolks with the vinegar, *garum*, wine and honey. Then drip the olive oil as you beat, increasing the quantity as it is absorbed into the eggs. Continue until it has all been incorporated. Flavour the mayonnaise with the ground spices.

Boiled Octopus

The dramatic shape of the octopus appears in many Roman mosaics. Pliny doubted the animal's intelligence:

> They eat shellfish, opening the shells with their tentacles. Their caves can thus be identified from the fact that there are so many shells lying about. But the octopus is considered to be a stupid animal, because it will swim right up to a human hand.
>
> (Plin. N.H. IX-86)

And it was reckless indeed of the octopus to swim up to the hand of a Roman gourmet. Served whole, an octopus gave the impression that the host had killed a dangerous sea monster. But Apicius gives only an extremely curt recipe for it:

> *In polypo: pipere, liquamine, lasere, inferes.*

> For octopus: pepper, *liquamen* and *laser*. Serve.   (Ap. 422)

Don't remove the skin or the beautiful colours will be lost. The cooking time depends on the texture required, which is subject to fashion. Octopus remains tender if it is boiled for up to 5 minutes, then left to cool slowly, some people do this three times, but many old recipes suggest cooking it for several hours, albeit over a low heat, in white wine, water and herbs. Nowadays garlic is added, but Apicius used *laser*. You could dissolve a little *asafoetida* in the stock.

Lobster (*locusta*)

Like the octopus, lobsters and crayfish were favourite subjects in Roman art. They are depicted in sea battles with other animals and in still-lifes with other foods. Pliny describes how to cook them.

> This is the only animal whose flesh does not become firm unless put live into boiling water.   (Plin. N.H. IX 95)

A lobster is cooked in about 7 minutes, according to size. When it is done, halve and serve with the following sauce.

Sauce for Lobster and Spiny Lobster

Ius in lucusta et cammaris: indura cepam pallachinam concisam. Eius piper, ligusticum, careum, cuminum, caryotam, mel, acetum, vinum, liquamen, oleum, defritum. Hoc ius adicito sinapi in elixuris.

Sauce for lobster and spiny lobster: fry finely chopped shallots golden brown. Grind pepper, lovage [seeds], caraway seeds, cumin seeds, a date, honey, vinegar, *garum*, oil and *defrutum*. Add mustard and serve with the boiled fish.   (Ap. 409)

Take 1 teaspoon of all the spices Apicius mentions and grind finely. Pound a small pitted fresh date with 4 tablespoons of vinegar, 2 tablespoons of *garum*, 1 tablespoon of *defrutum* and 50 ml oil. Add the spices and a tablespoon of mustard. Spread the sauce over slices of boiled lobster.

Roast Lobster with Coriander

Lucustas assas sic facies: aperiuntur locustae, ut absolet, cum testa sua et infunditur eis piperatum, coriandratum, et sic in craticula assantur. Cum siccaverint, adicies ius in craticula quotiens siccaverint quousque assantur bene, inferes.

Make grilled lobster as follows: split the lobster and leave it in its shell as usual. Moisten with pepper sauce and coriander sauce and grill. If it is drying out, pour extra sauce into the shell until the meat is cooked. Serve. (Ap. 410)

Kill the lobster with a kitchen knife and split it lengthwise. Prepare a pepper and coriander sauce with equal proportions of vinegar, *garum* and oil. Add finely chopped pepper and coriander seed. Brush the lobster with a little of the vinaigrette and place on the grill of the barbecue, meat side down. Scorch the flesh and then turn. Now pour more of the vinaigrette over the shell and grill until the lobster is cooked. Serve in the shell.

Sausages of Lobster or Other Fish

Isicia fiunt marina de cammaris, de lolligine, de sepia, de lucusta. Isicium condies pipere, liquamine, cumino, laseris radice.

Sausages can be made from prawns, cuttlefish, squid and lobster. Flavour with pepper, *liquamen*, cumin and *laser*. (Ap. 37)

Figure 8.3

You can make sausages not only from the above fish, but also from crab, mussels, oysters and other shellfish, as listed by Opilius Macrinus. Nowadays most fish pâtés are prepared in baking tins.

1 teaspoon cumin seeds
1 teaspoon peppercorns
1kg lobster (cleaned), or other fish
1 teaspoon lovage seeds
1 pinch *asafoetida*
2 teaspoons *garum*

Grind the cumin, the lovage and the pepper to a powder. Cut the fish into pieces and whiz it in the blender. Add the other ingredients and whiz again.

Put the mixture into sausage skins (see page 257–8), then simmer the fish sausages for 15 minutes. Allow to cool, then slice and serve.

Lobster Balls

Aliter lucustam: isicia de cauda eius sic facies: folium noci uvam prius demes et elixas deinde pulpam, concides, cum liquamine, pipere et ovis isicia formabis.

Another lobster recipe: pâté of lobster tail is made as follows. First remove the roe and finely crush the boiled flesh. Season with pepper and *garum* and shape into little balls with egg.   (Ap. 412)

First boil the lobster for a few minutes. Remove the shell and chop the meat, season with pepper and *garum* (or salt), bind with egg yolk and shape into balls. Don't cool, but serve immediately.

Mayonnaise for Oysters

In ostreis: piper, ligusticum, ovi vitellum, acetum, liquamen oleum et vinum. Si volueris mel addes.

For oysters: pepper, lovage, egg-yolk, vinegar, *garum*, oil and wine. If you wish, add honey.   (Ap. 423)

Apicius does not state whether this is a sauce for raw, boiled or fried oysters. The mayonnaise is probably best suited to mussels steamed open in the smoke from the barbecue. Prepare the mayonnaise in the usual way (see page 329).

Mussels

In mitulis: liquamen, porrum concisum, cuminum, passum, satureiam, vinum, mixtum facies aquatius et tibi mitulos coques.

For mussels: *liquamen*, chopped leek, cumin, *passum*, savory, wine. Mix this with water and boil the mussels in it.   (Ap. 418)

2 kg mussels
2 small leeks
1 bunch fresh savory
1 teaspoon cumin
50 ml good *garum*, made from anchovies
100 ml *passum* (dessert wine)
100 ml white wine
100 ml water

Clean the mussels under cold running water and remove the beards. Wash the leeks and chop them into rings. Put everything into a large pan, seal with the lid and bring it to the boil. Put in the mussels and seal the pan again. Boil for a few minutes, then take the pan off the heat and stir. Cook for a few more minutes until all the mussels have opened. Serve immediately.

Mussel Balls

Isicia ex sphondylis: * *elixatos sphondylos conteres et nervos eorum eximes, diende cum eis alicam elixatam et ova conteres, piper, liquamen. Isicia ex his facies cum nucleis et pipere. In omento assabis, oenogara perfundes, et pro isiciis inferes.*

---

* According to Bertrand Guégan this refers to a kind of mussel.

Mussel balls: grind the boiled mussels and remove the sinews. Then grind them with spelt, egg, peppercorns and *garum*. Shape them into balls with pine nuts. Roast in pork caul. Pour over *oenogarum* and serve as meatballs.   (Ap. 42)

2 kg fresh mussels
garum to taste
100 g spelt grits
2 eggs
100 g pine nuts
1 teaspoon peppercorns
pork caul

Steam the mussels until they open and remove them from their shells. Pound them to a paste. Reduce the cooking liquid to a third of its volume, add some *garum* and use this as *liquamen*.

Soak the spelt grits overnight, then cook and pound them. Beat the eggs with a little *liquamen* (or *garum*) to salt them. Then knead together all of the ingredients. Add the whole pine nuts and peppercorns unbroken. Shape the mussel mixture into balls and wrap them in pork caul to prevent them falling apart. Roast them on the hot ashes of the barbecue and serve with a sauce *oenogarum*, or *garum* with vinegar.

Roast Tuna

Ius in cordula assa: piper, ligustcum, mentam, cepam, aceti modicum et oleum.

Sauce for roast tuna: pepper, lovage, mint, onion, a little vinegar, and oil.   (Ap. 435)

for the vinaigrette
3 tablespoons strong vinegar
2 tablespoons *garum,* or vinegar with anchovy paste
9 tablespoons olive oil
4 finely chopped shallots
1 teaspoon pepper
1 teaspoon lovage seeds
25 g fresh mint

Put all of the vinaigrette ingredients into a jar and shake well to blend them together.

Brush your tuna fillets with oil, pepper and salt, then grill them on one side over a hot barbecue. Turn them and brush the roasted side with the vinaigrette. Repeat. The tuna flesh should be pink inside so don't let it overcook. Serve with the remains of the vinaigrette.

Dolphin Balls

Since the dolphin is a mammal, its flesh is somewhere between tuna and beef. Apicius rolled it into balls.

Isicia de thursione: enevabis, concides minutatim. Teres piper, ligusticum, origanum, petroselinum, coriandrum, cuminum, rutae bacam, mentam siccam, ipsum thursionem. Isicia deformabis. Vinum, liquamen, oleum, coques, coctum in patellam collocabis. Ius in ea facies: piper, ligusticum, satureiam, cepam, vinum, liquamen, oleum. Patellam pone sut coquatur. Ovis obligabis, piper asperges et inferes.

Dolphin balls: remove the skin and cut into small pieces. Grind pepper, lovage, oregano, parsley, coriander, cumin, rue berries, dried mint and the dolphin flesh. Shape into little balls. Cook in wine, *garum* and oil. When the balls are cooked, put them in a patella pan. Make the sauce like this: pepper, lovage, savory, onion, wine, *garum*, oil. Put this in the patella and heat. Mix with eggs, sprinkle with pepper and serve.   (Ap. 138)

700g minced dolphin
pork caul
1 teaspoon pepper
1 teaspoon lovage seed
1 teaspoon cumin
1 teaspoon rue berries
1 teaspoon dried oregano
1 tablespoon dried mint
25g fresh parsley
25g fresh coriander

for the sauce
1 teaspoon pepper
1 teaspoon lovage seed
1 tablespoon freshly chopped savory
1 onion
3 egg yolks
pepper
300 ml white wine
3 tablespoons oil
100 ml *garum*

Grind the spices for the mince mixture in the mortar, and chop the fresh herbs. Mix all the seasonings through the mince and roll into balls. Wrap these balls in pork caul and fry in the oil until golden brown. Then add the wine and the *garum* and simmer to reduce the liquid.

Meanwhile grind the spices for the sauce in the mortar, and mash in the onion. Then take the balls out of the liquid and place in an oven dish. Add the onion and the spices to the cooking liquid and reduce this further. Take the sauce off the flame and allow to cool a little. Beat the egg yolks and warm up the sauce, stirring constantly until it thickens. Pour over the dolphin balls, sprinkle with coarse pepper and serve.

Appendix

WEIGHTS AND MEASURES

	Metric		Imperial
scrupulus	1.13	g	
drachma	3.40		
semunica	13.63		half ounce
unica	27.27		ounce
sextans	54.54		2 ounces
quadrans	81.75		quarter pound
semis	163.72		half pound
libra	327.45		pound
cocleare	11	ml	teaspoon
ligula	rough		tablespoon
calix	rough		wineglass
ciatus	45		
acetabum	68		
quartarius	136		
hemina	273		half pint
sextarius	547		pint
congius	3.2	litres	
semimodius	4.3		
modius	8.7		
urna	13.1		
amphora	26.2		
culleus	525.2		

MONEY

Roman (in the time of Nero)

quadrans × 4   =   1 *as*
as × 4   =   1 *sestertius*
sestertius × 4   =   1 *denarius*
denarius × 25   =   1 *aureus*
aureus × 45   =   1 pound of gold
denarius × 96   =   1 pound of silver

Greek

obol × 6   =   1 drachma
drachma (=denarius) × 100   =   1 mina
mina × 60   =   1 talent

Prices

*In the time of Nero (AD 70)**

Prices in *sestertius* (HS)

3	6.5 kg wheat
0.75	6.5 kg lupin seeds
1	400 ml oil
0.25	a glass of house wine
1	a glass of Falernian wine
0.25	a pot of porridge
0.25	a plate
0.50	a beaker
0.25	a lamp

* Robert Étienne: *La vie quotidienne à Pompeii.*

0.06	entry to the bathhouse (Juv. VI-446)
2	services of a prostitute
15	a *tunica*
360	a silver sieve
2525	a cheap slave
100,000	a very expensive slave (Mart. II-62)

In the time of Diocletian (AD 301)*

Prices in *sestertius* (HS)

400	6.5 kg wheat
240	6.5 kg barley
1.60	a head of lettuce
1.60	a cabbage
4	an egg
160	a rabbit
600	a hare
80	a duck
30	a chicken
48	327 g pork
48	327 g mutton
48	327 g beef
64	327 g ham
96	327 g expensive fish
64	327 g cheap fish
160	560 ml virgin oil
96	560 ml second-pressing oil
48	560 ml cheap oil
120	560 ml good wine
96	560 ml ordinary wine
32	560 ml cheap wine
160	560 ml good honey
80	560 ml ordinary honey
32	750 g salt

* Nico Valerio: *La tavola degli Antichi*; Simon Goodenough: *Citizens of Rome*.

Glossary

Wine Products

defrutum	must syrup
sapa	must reduced to ⅓
caroenum	must reduced to ⅔
conditum	herbed wine
passum	raisin wine (dessert wine)
mulsum	spiced wine
lora	slaves' wine
posca	cold drink

Garum Products

garum	clear fish sauce
liquamen	clear fish sauce
allec	thick fish sauce, anchovy sauce
hydrogarum	fish sauce with water
oenogarum	fish sauce with wine
oxygarum	fish sauce with vinegar

Grain Products

amulum	thickener
tractum	kind of biscuit
mola	sacrificial flour of spelt with salt
alica	spelt grits

Dishes

patina	egg dish
placenta	traditional pastry
libum	sacrificial cake
puls	grain porridge
mola salsa	salt with spelt flour
epithyrum	tapenade
hypotrimma	Roman 'pashka'
polenta	grain dish
melca	yoghurt
moretum	mortar dish
conchicla	pulse dish

Other Terms

focus	hearth
furnus	oven
triclinium	reclining bench or dining room
lares	domestic gods
penates	gods of the store-room
rudix	stick
coclear	snail spoon
salutatio	morning visit
symposium	carousal
comissatio	carousal
symposiarch	toast-master
cottabus	wine-game
popina	pub
taberna	restaurant
promulsis	starter
gustatio	starter
prandium	lunch
cena	dinner
vesperna	supper
pultarius	porridge pot
repositorium	buffet

phiale	sacrificial bowl
pistor	mortar slave or baker
lemures	ghosts
lustratio	hand washing
mensa	table or course
lararium	house altar

Bibliography

Benko, Stephen, *Pagan Rome and the Early Christians*, Batsford, London, 1985

Collectore, Cassiano Basso, *Geoponica*, Pet. Needham, London, 1704

Courtine, Robert, *Larousse Gastronomique*, Librairie Larousse, Paris, 1984

Dictionnaire des Antiquités Romaines, Librairie de Firmin Frères, Fils et Cie, Paris, 1873

Dosi, A., and F. Schnell, *Le Abitudini Alimentari dei Romeni*, Edizioni Quasar, Rome, 1986

Pasti e Vasellame da Tavola, Edizioni Quasar, Rome, 1986

I Romeni in Cucina, Edizioni Quasar, Rome, 1986

Le Feste di Roma Antica, Edizioni Quasar, Rome, 1986

Flower, B., and E. Rosenbaum, *Apicius, The Roman Cookery Book*, Harrap, London, 1980 (from which we have also taken the numbering of the recipes)

Guégan, Bertrand, *Les Dix Livres de Cuisine d'Apicius*, René Bonnel, Editeur, Paris, 1933

Giacosa, Ilaria Gozzini, *A cena da Lucullo*, Edizioni Piemme, Casale Monferrato, 1986

Istituto Poligrafico e Zecca dello Stato, *L'Alimentazione nel Mondo Antico*, Rome, 1987

Newton, Tascabili Economici, *Apicio: La Cucina dell'antica Roma*, Rome, 1990

Ogilvie, R. M., *The Romans and their Gods*, The Hogarth Press, London, 1986

Ricotti, Eugenia Salza Pina, *L'Arte del Convito nella Roma Antica*, l'Erma di Bretschneider, Rome, 1983

Vehling, J. D., *Apicius, Cookery and Dining in Imperial Rome*, Dover Publications Inc, New York, 1977

Valerio, Nico, *La Tavola degli Antichi*, Mondadori, Milan, 1989

De Waardt, J., Voedsel voorschriften in boeteboeken, motieven voor het handhaven van voedsel voorschriften *in vroeg middeleeuwse Ierse boeteboeken*, 500–1100, Erasmus Publishing, Rotterdam, 1996

We have also referred to the following books published by Loeb Classical Library, Harvard University Press, London (UK), and Cambridge, Massachusetts (USA):

Apul.:	L. Apuleius, *Madaurensis Metamorphoseion*
Ath.:	Athenaeus, *Deipnosophistae*
Cat.:	M. Porcius Cato, *De Re Rustica*
Cels.:	A. C. Celsus, *De Medicina*
Col.:	L. I. M. Columella, *Re Rustica*
Hor.:	Horatius Flaccus, *Sermonum*
Iuv.:	D. I. Iuvenalis, *Saturae*
Mart.:	M.V. Martialis, *Epigrammaton*
Min. Fel.:	Minucius Felix, *Octavianus*
Ov.:	P. Ovidius Naso, *Fasti*
Petr.:	C. Petronius Arbiter, *Satyricon*
Plin.:	C. Plinius Secundus (Maior), *Naturis Historia*
Plut.:	Plutarchus, *Moralia*
Suet.:	G. S. T. Suetonius, *Vitae Caesarum*
Tac.:	P. Cornelius Tacitus, *Germania*
Tert.:	Q. S. F. Tertullianus, *Apologeticus & De Spectaculis*
Varr.:	M. T. Varro, *Rerum Rusticarum & Lingua Latina*
Vitr.:	M. V. P. Vitruvius, *De Architectura*

Additional thanks to: the brothers Oscar and Johan van Dijk, Stefan Helleman, Paul Sebes, Jaela van Tijn, Marcello de Simone, Pierre Bouvier, David Rijser, Noortje Tan, Jennie Scobie, Miek Faas, Marlein Overakker, Ruud Boxma.

Illustration Sources

Illustrations are by Marcello de Simone from items in the following museums:

Museo Nazionale, Naples – 0.1, 1.2, 1.3, 2.8, 2.12, 2.14, 2.15, 2.16, 2.21, 3.4, 5.3, 6.7, 7.2, 7.6, 8.2, 8.3

Museo della Civiltà Romana, Rome – 1.5, 2.10, 2.17, 4.1, 5.1, 5.6, 7.5

The British Museum, London – 2.18, 4.3a, 4.3c, 4.3d, 7.4

Museo di Villa Giulia, Rome – 2.9, 2.19b, 2.20, 5.4

National Museum, Tripoli – 6.6

Louvre, Paris – 2.3, 6.1

Museo Archeologico, Florence – 1.1., 3.1

Museo Lateranese, Romel – 3.3

Römisch-Germanisches Museum, Keulen – 2.19e

Rijksmuseum van Oudheden, Leiden – 2.19c, 2.19d

National Museum, Athens – 3.2

Palazzo Barberini, Athens – 2.6

Museo Sigismundo Castromediano, Lecce: – 2.19A, 8.1

Villa dei Misterii, Pompeii – 4.2

Casa de Vetii, Pompeii – 4.3B

Musei Vaticani, Vatican City – 5.2

Museo Civico, Piacenza – 6.2

Archaeological Museum, Heraklion – 6.5

Museo Archeologico, Verona – 6.4

Casa della Testa di Maiale, Pompeii – 6.3

Museo di Villa Torlonia, Rome – 7.3

Basilica di S. Apollinare Nuovo, Ravenna – 1.4
National Museum, Copenhagen – 2.13
Museo Ostiense, Ostia – 5.5

Reconstructions: Patrick Faas – 2.8, 6.7, 6.8, 7.1

Conversion Tables

Tables show approximate equivalent measurements.

Liquid Measure

Imperial fluid ounces	US spoons	Imperial spoons	Metric millilitres
	1 teaspoon	1 teaspoon	5
¼	2 teaspoons	1 dessertspoon	10
½	1 tablespoon	1 tablespoon	15
1	2 tablespoons	2 tablespoons	30
2	¼ cup	4 tablespoons	60
4	½ cup		125
5		¼ pint or 1 gill	150
6	¾ cup		175
8	1 cup		250
9			275
10	1¼ cups	½ pint	300
12	1½ cups		375
15		¾ pint	450
16	2 cups		500
18	2¼ cups		550
20	2½ cups	1 pint	600
24	3 cups		750

Solid Measure

US and Imperial		Metric	
Ounces	Pounds	Grams	Kilos
1		30	
2		60	
3½		105	
4	¼	125	
5		150	
6		180	
8	½	250	¼
9		280	
12	¾	360	
16	1	500	½
18		560	
20	1¼	610	
24½	1½	720	

Oven Temperatures

Fahrenheit	Celsius	Gas Mark	Description
225	110	¼	Cool
250	130	½	
275	140	1	Very Slow
300	150	2	
325	160	3	Slow
350	175	4	Moderate
375	190	5	
400	200	6	Moderately Hot
425	220	7	Fairly Hot
450	230	8	Hot
475	240	9	Very Hot
500	250	10	Extremely Hot

INDEX